D1062640

RETHINKING CURRICULUM STUDIES

Rethinking Curriculum Studies

A Radical Approach

Edited by
MARTIN LAWN and LEN BARTON

CROOM HELM LONDON

A HALSTED PRESS BOOK
JOHN WILEY & SONS
New York

Croom Helm Ltd, 2-10 St John's Road, London SW11

British Library Cataloguing in Publication Data
Rethinking curriculum studies.
1. Education – Great Britain – Curricula
I. Lawn, Martin
II. Barton, Len
375'.00941 LB1564.G7

ISBN 0-7099-0438-X
ISBN 0-7099-1602-7 Pbk

Published in the U.S.A.
by Halsted Press, a Division of
John Wiley & Sons, Inc., New York
ISBN: 0-470-27097-7

Printed and bound in Great Britain by
Biddles Ltd, Guildford and King's Lynn

CONTENTS

List of Abbreviations

Part One: Introduction

Introduction 11

1. Theory and Practice and the Reconceptualisation of Curriculum Studies
   William Pinar and Madeleine Grumet 20

Part Two: Critical Reappraisal

Introduction 45

2. Curriculum Studies: A Critique of Some Recent British Orthodoxies
   Geoff Whitty 48

3. Radical Education: The Pedagogical Subtext
   Maureen Clark and David Davies 71

Part Three: New Directions

Introduction 113

4. Restitution and Reconstruction of Educational Experience: An Autobiographical Method for Curriculum Theory
   Madeleine Grumet 115

5. Social Structure, Ideology and Curriculum
   Michael Apple 131

6. The Deliberative Approach to the Study of the Curriculum and Its Relation to Critical Pluralism
   William Reid 160

Part Four: Curriculum Practice

Introduction 191

7. Getting Involved in Curriculum Research: A Personal History
   Rob Walker 193

8. Practice and Theory
   Mike Golby 214

9. Curriculum Politics and Emancipation
Martin Lawn and Len Barton 237

Notes on Contributors 248

Author Index 249

Subject Index 251

ABBREVIATIONS

(The following lists only those abbreviations not extended in the text.)

AERA	American Educational Research Association
APU	Assessment of Performance Unit
BERA	British Educational Research Association
CSE	Certificate of Secondary Education
DES	Department of Education and Science
GNP	Gross National Product
HMSO	Her Majesty's Stationery Office
INSET	In Service Education for Teachers
NFER	National Foundation for Educational Research
RSLA	Raising of the School Leaving Age
SSRC	Social Science Research Council
TES	*Times Educational Supplement*
TUC	Trades Union Congress

Part One

INTRODUCTION

INTRODUCTION

This book has been written during a period in which teachers and schools are being criticised for many different reasons, by people both within and without the educational system.[1] Varying degrees of depression, frustration and conflict are being experienced by teachers, pupils and local administrators. One type of response is voiced in the words of a science teacher who maintains: 'I think too much is expected of us. For most people it is impossible to do the job even adequately' (Pick and Walker, 1976, p. 15).

Some participants, themselves unsure about their role, or the type of education that is important, are also critical of the system, as can be seen from the following examples of teachers' comments:

> I am increasingly unclear as to what schools are for. I've got the feeling that many, perhaps most, embody values which I find alien or perverse. I'm obsessed with the way they depersonalise kids. (Grace, 1978, p. 203)

or:

> Teachers are not encouraged to take seriously their actual classroom work as opposed to their organisational and disciplinary responsibilities, so that any kind of optimism that one would feel is, I think, killed by the system, killed by what is required of a person. I think you have to have tremendous resilience in this Authority to stick by your desire to teach. (Pick and Walker, 1976, p. 18)

While the teaching profession is experiencing this sense of uncertainty and pressure, the state itself is re-examining its commitment to education, a field in which it has always had a number of interests. First, the educational system is one of the main vehicles for a society's social and economic reproduction. Secondly, it provides a means of increasing capital assets – by, for example, the expansion of the economy through investment in trained manpower. Lastly, the state has acted as a promotor of such social and educational ideologies as the concepts of equal opportunity and education as an avenue to social mobility. The present crisis in education has come about because these aims of the state, in themselves consistent, are not being effectively met by the system.

This situation has arisen partly as a result of the relative weakness of those mediatory mechanisms of the state which are responsible for controlling education and partly through certain conflicts within the system, including expressions and actions of resistance by pupils and teachers.

There is an urgent need to adjust the content, operation and control of the school curriculum and the state is acting forcefully in a number of ways. Significant developments include a remodelled Schools Council, with reduced teacher involvement and an interventionist position on curriculum change, a reorganised national inspectorate (now to include an educational task force producing 'suggestions' for the curriculum and increasing supervision over it), and the establishment of an Assessment of Performance Unit – a Department of Education and Science Unit operating nationwide testing around 'suggested' curriculum areas. All these central administrative initiatives have taken place within a major public relations exercise on the school curriculum, starting with a speech by James Callaghan (then Prime Minister) at Ruskin College in 1976, and followed by the Green Paper on Education (DES, 1977a) and the Department of Education and Science questionnaire (DES, 1977b) to Local Education Authorities on their curriculum administration. In a discussion about issues relating to the Great Debate, Adam Hopkins argues:

> Most of the anxiety before, during and after the Great Debate has revolved around two questions: how to raise standards and how to bring school and the 'world of work' a little closer. But underlying the public discussion, there has been one other major unresolved theme: the question of who should hold the power. (Hopkins, 1978, p. 172)

Certainly the national reorganisation of curriculum control has been effectively reinforced by school changes which have been due to cutbacks in educational finance and falling pupil numbers; other effects, in addition to the rationalisation of the school curriculum, include teacher redeployment and the closure of teacher centres and resource services.

Why do we choose to introduce a book on curriculum studies by alluding to these particular events? One reason is that other books in this area tend to neglect prevailing contemporary circumstances and events, seeming to exist in a world that is far removed from the social and economic realities currently influencing education. For us, these realities must be part of the consideration of curriculum research and practice. We believe that, mainly on account of the relative status of theory and practice and of the tension between them in this area, the applied field of curriculum study is largely incapable of coping with such extra-curricular factors. Certainly, with few exceptions,[2] it has not produced the adequate political and structural analyses of the relationship of the state and the curriculum that are so urgently needed; furthermore, it seems largely unable to connect with the day-to-day events, thoughts, actions and struggles of the school teachers.

From our analysis so far we hope the reader will appreciate that we totally support the view that education cannot be viewed in a vacuum, or as a value-free process. Commentators from both left and right of the political spectrum have acknowledged that the educational provisions of a society, including the curriculum, serve particular social and political goals. Liberal thinkers such as Mary Warnock maintain that

> if the state is to supply education, what sort of education is it going to supply? To whom? And for how long? These and other related questions are quite manifestly *political* . . . Thus the notion that politics might be kept out of education is *absurd*. (our emphasis) (Warnock, 1979)

While there is a fundamental agreement amongst such commentators, important points of contention are the nature, extent and consequences of 'politics', their inter-relationship with wider ideological and socio-economic concerns and how people both receive and respond to these in their daily living.

We are not suggesting that *all* teachers perceive *each* of these issues as a personal, pressing problem. What we are maintaining is that for many teachers and other participants in the educational scene, one or a combination of these – or other factors we have not identified like head-teachers or an irrelevant curriculum – are creating tensions and stress that influence teacher-pupil, teacher-teacher, teacher-parent, teacher-Local Authority and teacher-state relationships. Now all too often, as Grace succinctly reminds us:

> Teachers . . . have provided easy targets for critical attack, without sufficient effort having been made to locate them, historically,

> within their work situations or within the wider contradictions of society or to appreciate their attempts to deal with these contradictions. (Grace, 1978, p. 5)

What is valuable about analysing these points is that, since they seek to portray teachers as actively engaged in mediating contradictory expectations at the ideological and practical level, we need to take cognisance of the ways in which such individuals interact in their working situations. The difficulties involved in teaching are numerous and must not be underestimated.[3] Writing on this topic, Chessum points out:

> There are, for instance, obvious potential conflicts between the expectation that schools will maximise their pupils' examination success whilst creating a supportive learning environment for the many children who, for various reasons, are unlikely to obtain any qualifications. Equally, there is considerable potential difficulty reconciling idealistic notions of child-centred, individually tailored education with the expectation that schools will teach children discipline and conformity to external rules. (Chessum, 1980)

In order to understand and explain such questions, we need to delineate the historical, structural and contextual factors involved as well as the interpretations and strategies that teachers use to cope with the realities of their job and how each of these inter-relate in a dynamic process. This includes appreciating the complexity of individuals, their thoughts, feelings and needs and the degree to which they can reflect upon and emancipate themselves from the circumstances in which they are in.

A vital concern for curriculum studies, particularly in the contemporary context, is the dynamic relationship between the individual and the collective, the self and its material circumstances, the teacher and the state. It is in the curriculum that this dynamic is to be found. Within curriculum studies analysis of self and structure *and* the dynamic between the two, has been seriously under-researched. Why should this be so?

Curriculum studies[4] developed in Britain from the middle 1960s. It took as its organisational 'grammar' a number of disparate areas, derived from the movement for curriculum innovation in the United States. These discrete areas, which we may call input, design, testing and consumption, were in turn influenced by industrial management. Writing about schools in the 1970s in the United States, Giroux says:

> Moreover, in the seventies, as financial aid to education has decreased and radical critics have dwindled in number, the positivist orientation to schooling appears to be stronger than ever. Calls for accountability in education, coupled with back-to-basics and systems management approaches to education have strengthened rather than weakened the traditional positivist paradigm in the curriculum field. (Giroux, 1980a)

In Britain, curriculum studies developed with the expansion of teacher education, the curriculum project movement and the publication of an Open University course, *Curriculum: Context, Design and Development* (1971). While it still contained some of the essential ideas derived from earlier influences, new areas were added: ideologies of education, management of schools, policy analysis and evaluation research. It is sometimes felt that the influence of management theory has been resisted in Britain and that a much more pragmatic approach has been developed. Often it is argued that the field of curriculum studies is distinguished by its concern with practicalities and may be eclectic in its search for theoretical support.

We think that there are contradictions in this account of the development of curriculum studies. Pragmatism and eclecticism seem oddly matched with the prevailing technical determinism of rational curriculum planning, received knowledge, research development and dissemination models. This problem does not seem to arise in the United States where there appears to be a clear relationship between industrial change and educational reorganisation. It is our contention that this pragmatic approach hides the very same relationship between industry and education in Britain. The ideology of teacher autonomy, now diminishing, has always masked a fairly direct relationship, which in recent times has become more overt. The contradiction between an official explanation, based on autonomy and professionalism, and a determining practice based on managerial needs and interests has been intensified by the growth of a centralised curriculum initiative by the state and teacher resistance to curriculum change. There has always been a gap between curriculum studies based on or dominated by managerial influence and a curriculum practice controlled by teachers, and it is now widening.

We do not see the problems in curriculum studies resulting from its relative youthfulness. Saying that 'in a developing area there is no consensus as to its boundaries, its internal structure, even in its problems and procedures' (Richards, 1978) avoids the issues that we have raised: whose purposes does curriculum studies serve and what is the relationship between theory and practice within it?

How can this particular book contribute to the advancement of curriculum studies? First, this book is concerned with examining issues relating to theory and practice. By including new theoretical perspectives the intention is to widen the frames of analyses, and therefore the concepts, methods, understandings and explanations that are significant and can be used by those engaged in this area of study. We hope it will open up some debate about the connection between the theoretical choices we make in the selection of topics for study and our aims. Secondly, the substantive area chosen for this book, the 'self' and 'structure', is explored and discussed in a manner that highlights some of the contradictions and tensions between them. Thirdly, many of the contributors provide the reader with a personal commentary on many of their previous writings and ideas. This is extremely helpful in developing an understanding of a wider series of arguments in terms of how the writer perceives them. By giving attention to the availability and possible usefulness of different perspectives we hope that a dialogue will be established in which a cross-fertilisation of ideas and practices will emerge from research and analyses going on in the field.

The task is demanding and an indication of the requirements is provided by Apple in his discussion of understanding structural and everyday phenomena. He contends:

> Not only does it need to be structural – that is, it must, at the level of theory, be general enough to provide fruitful explanations of how the social order is both organised and controlled so that the differential benefits are largely accounted for – but, at the same time, it should not be so general as to be unable to account for the everyday actions, struggles, and experiences of the real actors in their day to day lives in and out of schools. (Apple, 1980)

This task demands sensitivity, imagination and an ability to make connections. We believe that these issues are relevant wherever the curriculum is a topic of research and discussion and that, by its inclusion of writers from the United States, the book will be of great value in the comparative field.

What is needed in curriculum studies is a critical appraisal of the way the area is described, an assessment of purposes or intentions, and a critique of superficial analysis and easy solutions. Hidden assumptions must be revealed and evaluated. This book is intended to be a lively and creative contribution to a field not noted for these qualities. Our own approach owes something to the attitude and procedure of Dashiell Hammett's detective, the 'Continental Op':

> The Op is called in or sent out on a case. Something has been stolen, someone has been murdered – it doesn't matter. The Op interviews the person or persons most immediately accessible. They may be innocent or guilty – it doesn't matter; it is an indifferent circumstance. Guilty or innocent, they provide the Op with an account of what they really know, of what they assert really happened. The Op begins to investigate, he compares these accounts with others that he gathers; he snoops about; he does research; he shadows people, arranges confrontations between those who want to avoid one another, and so on. What he soon discovers is that the 'reality' that anyone involved will swear to is in fact a construction, a fabrication, a fiction, a faked and alternate reality – and that it has been gotten together before he ever arrived on the scene. And the Op's work therefore is to deconstruct, decompose, deplot and defictionalize that 'reality' and to construct or reconstruct out of it a true 'fiction' i.e. an account of what 'really' happened. (Hammett, 1975, pp. xix-xx)

It maybe that a coherent attempt to make sense of what is learned is in fact another 'fiction' but it is open to question. Is there room for excitement and uncertainty in curriculum studies?

Martin Lawn
Len Barton

Notes

1. Criticisms may be found in the *Black Papers on Education*, first issued in 1969 by the Critical Quarterly Society and later in a collected edition (Cox and Boyson, 1975; Cox and Dyson, 1971), or in *Teaching Styles and Pupil Processes* (Bennett, 1976). The latter work received massive exposure, bringing with it a condemnation of 'progressive' as opposed to 'traditional' methods of teaching.

The William Tyndale affair brought into the open a great deal of criticism of the educational system and the role of the school in contemporary society, for an account of which see Robin Auld's report of the official enquiry (Auld, 1976).

2. One example of work contributing to this form of analysis is that of Michael Apple in the United States, much of which he refers to in this book. Another important American writer in this field, less well-known in this country, is Henry Giroux (Giroux, 1980b, pp. 20-46).

Work of a related nature in this country is largely being written or encouraged by sociologists of education who have an interest in the curriculum (Whitty and Young, 1976; Cohen and Miller, 1980, pp. 45-50).

3. An example of the current pressing problems is to be seen in the sacking of the Nottingham nursery school teacher 'who refused to teach a class she considered unsafe and educationally untenable' (*TES*, 1980) after losing a helper through staffing cuts by the Local Authority. See, also, *A Social Danger? A Study of Organised Teachers* (Ozga and Lawn, 1981).

4. Our treatment of this field is, by its very nature, brief and at times may appear to be over-simplified. Several contributors to this book offer further analyses of the area. We would refer the reader to *An Introduction to Curriculum Studies* (Taylor and Richards, 1979) or to 'Curriculum Studies: Reconceptualism or Reconstruction' (Lawn and Barton, 1980, pp. 47-56).

Bibliography

Apple, M. (1980) 'Analyzing Determinations: Understanding and Evaluating the Production of Social Outcomes in School', *Curriculum Inquiry*, 10, spring

Auld, R. (1976) *The William Tyndale Junior and Infants Schools: Report of the Public Inquiry . . . into the Teaching Organisation and Management . . .* , ILEA, London

Bennett, N. (1976) *Teaching Styles and Pupil Processes*, Open Books, London

Chessum, R. (1980) 'Teacher Ideologies and Pupil Disaffection' in L. Barton, R. Meighan and S. Walker (eds.), *Schooling Ideology and the Curriculum*, Falmer Press

Cohen, H. and Miller, A. (1980) 'Curriculum Theory and Practice: Some Guidelines for Discussion', *Curriculum*, vol. 1, no. 1

Cox, C.B. and Boyson, R. (eds.) (1975) *Black Paper 1975: the Fight for Education*, Dent, London

Cox, C.B. and Dyson, A. (eds.) (1971) *The Black Papers on Education*, Davis-Poynter, London

Department of Education and Science (1977a) *Education in Schools: a Consultative Document*, Cmnd 6889, HMSO

Department of Education and Science (1977b) *Local Education Authority Arrangements for the School Curriculum*, Circular 14, HMSO

Giroux, H. (1980a) 'Schooling and the Culture of Positivism: Notes on the Death of History', *Educational Theory*

Giroux, H. (1980b) 'Beyond the Limits of Radical Educational Reform: Toward a Critical Theory of Education', *Journal of Curriculum Theorizing*, Graduate School of Education, Univ. of

Rochester, New York, vol. 2, no. 1
Grace, G. (1978) *Teachers, Ideology and Control*, Routledge and Kegan Paul, London
Hammett, Dashiell (1975) *The Continental Op*, Stephen Marcus (ed.), Macmillan, London
Hopkins, A. (1978) *The School Debate*, Penguin Books, Harmondsworth
Lawn, M. and Barton, L. (1980) 'Curriculum Studies: Reconceptualism or Reconstruction, *Journal of Curriculum Theorizing*, vol. 2, no. 1
Open University (1972) *Curriculum: Context, Design and Development*, Course E 283, Open Univ. Press, Milton Keynes
Ozga, J.T. and Lawn, M.(1981) *A Social Danger? A Study of Organised Teachers*, The Falmer Press, Lewes
Pick, C. and Walker, R. (eds.) (1976) *Other Rooms, Other Voices*, , Centre for Applied Research in Education, Univ. of East Anglia
Richards, Colin (1978) *Curriculum Studies: an Introductory, Annotated Bibliography*, Nafferton Books, Driffield
Taylor, P. and Richards, C. (1979) *An Introduction to Curriculum Studies*, NFER, Slough
Times Educational Supplement (1980) 25 April
Warnock, M. (1979) *Education: a Way Ahead*, Basil Blackwell, Oxford
Whitty, G. and Young, M. (eds.) (1976) *Explorations in the Politics of School Knowledge*, Nafferton Books: Studies in Education Ltd, Driffield

1 THEORY AND PRACTICE AND THE RECONCEPTUALISATION OF CURRICULUM STUDIES

William Pinar and Madeleine Grumet

Origins of the Field

The curriculum field did not begin as a field at all. Unlike educational psychology, philosophy of education and sociology of education, the field of curriculum did not originate as an extension or application of an extant discipline. Rather, the field is usually said to have begun in Denver in the 1920s as a result of administrative 'need'. Evidently Denver Superintendent Jesse Newlon decided that someone in the central office ought to be attending to the curriculum, in specific subjects, in specific schools, and through the district overall (Cremin, 1975). So he hired a classroom teacher, perhaps one who had indicated interest in curriculum matters, as the first curriculum director or co-ordinator. This origin is very important in understanding why the American curriculum field developed as it did, and why it is undergoing what it is now undergoing. In the next few pages, we will sketch this development, concluding with a description and analysis of the contemporary situation in the United States.

Because the field did not begin as an extension or application of an extant field, it had no method of working, nor a consensually determined set of problems to be solved, no formulated relationship to philosophy and psychology of education, nor to the traditional disciplines such as history or chemistry. Rather, 'curriculum' began as an administrative designation – that is, as an area for which an administrator had responsibility. This is crucial to understanding the historical course of the field, and the particular relationship between theory and practice which has obtained in it. A curriculum co-ordinator is responsible to several constituencies. First, he is responsible to the students, although this responsibility is primarily rhetorical, given that he or she has little direct contact with students. Secondly, he is responsible to the teachers, a constituency which has become more powerful in the past two decades than in the previous four, a development due to increased union strength among teachers and increased interest among teachers in major items such as curriculum. Third, he is responsible to parents and residents in the local school district, who can bring considerable pressure to bear upon administrative officials. A notorious illustration of public pressure is drawn when conservative groups want specific books removed from the curriculum or even the library. Finally, he is responsible to his 'superior' – usually the superintendent in school district administrative hierarchies. In this case, the superintendent's interest tends to be foremost the maintenance of harmony. By maintaining harmony the superintendent manages to depoliticise his constituency. The absence of explicit conflicts, the obfuscation of particular concerns prevent those interest groups from forming who might demand that they be allowed to influence curriculum decisions. Instead it is the superintendent and his administrators who interpret his constituents' needs. Rather than becoming the medium through which an entire community negotiates the selection and transmission of the signs that signify its world, the curriculum has become the medium through which a professional elite ministers to its dependent clientele. The patient receiving these acts of mercy is the nation's youth, its pathology confirmed by its vulnerability, its neighbourhood or its resistance to schooling.

Thus while the curriculum co-ordinator (or in many US districts an 'Assistant Superintendent for Curriculum') may aspire to keep the curriculum as congruent as possible with relevant advances in the disciplines, and with the latest curriculum designs and evaluative schemes, he must aspire as well to keep teachers', parents', and superintendents' attention away from the curriculum. He works to avoid their complaints that it is too facile, too difficult, too backward, too forward, too liberal, too conservative. He may go beyond this essentially 'trouble-shooting' function by instituting new curriculum designs, such as the elective system (in which students can elect quarterly a course in twentieth-century British literature, or the ecology movement, instead of a year-long historical survey of English literature, or a year-long course in general science). In these cases he attempts to implement the new design; he attempts to convert theory into practice. More concretely, he tries to persuade teachers, students and others to accept new terms and new organisations of what they do already. It is a matter of management and employees, not really a matter of theory and practice, although contemporary understanding of these notions make possible, even easy, his appropriation of them.

At this point, however, we want to emphasise that the American curricular field began in administrative convenience, not in intellectual necessity. It began, and has remained until this past decade, a field interested in 'solving practical problems' rather than in intellectually understanding, in coherent, systematised ways, the multi-dimensional functions of curriculum, and specifically its function in the phenomenon of human learning. The earliest curriculum texts reflected this interest, as evidenced by *The Curriculum* and *How to Make a Curriculum* (Bobbitt, 1918, 1924), *Curriculum Development* (Caswell, 1935) and *Curriculum Construction* (Charters, 1923). Curriculum was accepted as a legitimate subfield of education by the 1930s, the first programmes being housed in departments of educational administration and secondary education. In 1938 the nation's first department of curriculum and teaching was established at Teachers College, Columbia University. The traditional curriculum text that is most remembered today was published by the University of Chicago Press in 1949; it was the syllabus for Education 360 at the University of Chicago, *Basic Principles of Curriculum and Instruction* (Tyler, 1949).[1]

Tyler's questions – (1) What educational purposes should the school seek to attain? (2) How can learning experiences be selected which are likely to be useful in attaining these objectives? (3) How can learning experiences be organized for effective instruction? (4) How can the effectiveness of learning experiences be evaluated? – emphasise the problem-solving nature of the curriculum venture during its infancy. These questions are not designed to generate theories of the curriculum, to collect data concerning its complex presence in schools nor to contribute to a discipline increasingly conscious of its problems and assumptions. The major texts which followed Tyler's all accepted this administrative or managerial function of the curriculum field. Professors of curriculum were primarily in the 'business' of preparing school personnel, and such preparation needed to emphasise those 'practical' problems members of an administrative hierarchy might face in working to placate an increasing number of conflicting interest groups: students, teachers, parents, and fellow administrators. While the rhetoric of professors, students and texts continued to indicate a fundamental concern for education, this concern was, and often continues to be, so abstractly expressed that it amounts to little else but platitude. The not-so-hidden curriculum of curriculum courses is a 'prep' course for survival as a more-or-less (depending upon the size and character of the district) visible member of an administrative 'tèam'. School administrators have always tended to be a sensitive, vulnerable lot, and worry in advance over unsettling problems which cause disharmony – worrying that such conflicts disrupt, in their words, 'the educational process', but disrupt as well the smoothness of daily life in a principal's or superintendent's office.

Classic texts in the traditional mode are: *Fundamentals of Curriculum Development* (Smith, Stanley and Shores, 1957), *Curriculum Development* (Tabä, 1962) and *Curriculum Planning for Modern Schools* (Saylor and Alexander, 1966). They all exhibit this conventional view of curriculum training. Tyler's once thin, economical little book had, by the early 1960s, grown thick with items which a future school administrator responsible for the curriculum might conceivably want to know in advance. The managerial concern with smooth operations, with placating competing involvement groups, remains the consuming interest; it is an interest in knowledge Habermas terms 'technical.' That is, we want to know possible problems and their solutions in advance in order to control their outcomes. We want knowledge in order to apply it to situations still in the future. Thus curriculum theory is information future curriculum co-ordinators learn in order to apply to practical situations later. This is a view of the relationship between theory and practice which has obtained since the seventeenth century in the West. It will be useful to us to situate the view of theory and practice which prevailed in the curriculum field during its first forty years (and exists still to a reduced extent), a view so common to science and social science that it tends to be taken as inevitable.

The value of theory was not aways construed to be its practical utility. In ancient times, specifically in pre-Roman Greece, theory corresponded to what Aristotle called the 'contemplative life'. What we now term 'practice' corresponded to what Aristotle termed 'political life'. Nicholas Lobkowicz credits Aristotle with being the first Western theoretician and philosopher to contrast theory and practice (Lobkowicz, 1967, p. 4). Both were regarded by the Greeks as two dimensions of the same life, although distinct dimensions (Lobkowicz, 1967, p. 25). Each citizen was to cultivate his contemplative life, his life separate from the bustle and controversy of political life, a life finally aimed at the cultivation of spirit and wisdom:

> Certainly we find in Plato the idea that philosophy aims at God. Contemplative wisdom is even described as a sort of rapture, as when Socrates suddenly stops in the middle of the marketplace and, thinking about something he cannot resolve, remains standing for a full twenty-four hours, surrounded by his puzzled fellow citizens. (Lobkowicz, 1967, p. 49)

In contemplation one developed one's views of human life, specifically one's own life, including views of ethics and politics. But missing is the sense that such theory could be 'applied' to practical life, that the laws of ethics and politics developed in contemplation could possibly cover the gamut of possibilities of human action in social life. Nor was there any reason to. Human perfection, such that was attainable, occurred in contemplation, not in social life. The duties of the citizen, while serious, were generally regarded as inferior to the obligations of contemplation. Theory was infinitely more important than practice.

This relationship changes profoundly with Christianity. Lobkowicz comments:

> Gone is the unambiguous superiority of contemplative over active life; gone is the notion that all necessary activities are beneath the freedom and dignity of a perfect life; gone, finally, is the notion that all human doing is either an activity thoroughly meaningful in itself or else only a 'purification'. For Christian deeds of charity serve a world which is not the Christian's homestead, and yet they have to be carried out almost as if they were the only thing which really counted. (Lobkowicz, 1967, p. 66)

A certain 'other-worldliness' remains; after all, the Christian's acts of charity demonstrate his faith and his salvation. But, importantly, the latter occurs through creation of the former. By believing that Jesus was the Christ, one achieves everlasting life and avoids the punishment of hell. One need not 'earn' one's salvation through good works. Nor does it accrue from years of contemplation. One's salvation comes in a moment, in the moment in which one accepts Jesus as the Christ. This reliance upon faith undercuts the tradition of contemplation. Further, 'the Christian emphasis upon charity and love as opposed to mere knowledge has resulted, and from now on evermore radically will result, in an emphasis upon practice as opposed to theory until eventually practice will become the sole source of meaning and salvation' (Lobkowicz, 1967, p. 74).

It is in science that the inversion becomes complete. Before we sketch in what manner, let us note that during Europe's medieval period, a time when Christianity without science flourished, the origin of action remained in faith. Theory was demonstrated in practice in the sense that faith was demonstrated by acts of charity. Theory, i.e. faith in Christ, became something immutable, a truth of human life that remained outside human life, which was a reflection of it. What could be examined and acted upon was the mutable, the arena of human practice. Faith did not guide life in any linear way, although general rules such as the ten commandments were to be observed. But note that these rules are pre-Christian in origin and in attitude; it is faith – not rules – which undergirds Christian life. The ground has been laid for a 'situation ethics', a realisation that the modes of charitable expression alter with circumstances and persons. Ethics, for instance, 'is not a master plan according to which man acts, just as logic is not a master plan according to which man thinks; both are reflections upon what in most instances man does almost instinctively' (Lobkowicz, 1967, p. 77). Aquinas, perhaps the master Christian scholar, saw ethics, and by extension, theory, as depictions of what occurred, of what we do, not as stipulative rules or guides to what we ought to do. Faith in Christ, indeed, Christ himself, would guide each individual according to circumstances – theory as depiction of practice.

Theory as guide to practice receives its sharpest formulation in scientific thinking, illustrated pointedly in the thought of Francis Bacon. The basic outlines of the scientific attitude are evident in Bacon's thought, outlines which have changed little in the centuries following his work. Lobkowicz usefully delineates the distinctions between Greek, Christian, and scientific notions of theory and practice:

> But what neither the ancients nor the scholastics would have agreed with is Bacon's claim that *theoretical knowledge* has to prove itself by 'fruits and works'; moreover, they probably would not even have understood Bacon's assertion that theoretical knowledge ought to be striven for *because* it has some fruits. In other words, even though thinkers of earlier ages occasionally may have realized that theoretical knowledge may in some vague sense be useful and even bear some palpable fruits, they hardly would have been able to appreciate Bacon's emphatic claim that scientific knowledge should be judged in terms of, and pursued for the sake of, its practical usefulness. (Lobkowicz, 1967, p. 90)

Nietzsche speculated that Christianity gave birth to science in the Christian's obsession never to lie. In the compulsion to tell the truth came the systematic search for secular truth: science. And as Nietzsche noted, Christianity thus contained within itself the seeds of its own destruction. In its compulsive truthfulness it gave rise to a systematic search for truth which extended its attitude to all domains of human life, including a challenge to the faith in Christ which had initially sustained the interest in truth-telling. Truth was placed outside human history, and became located somewhere, sometime in the future, to be discovered by the judicious, persistant application of scientific method. Similarly, the scholastic's view that theory depicted practice gave way to theory as hypothesis to be tested, as guide to the manipulation of practice. One's practice was no longer an instinctive outgrowth of one's faith; rather it followed from one's predictive notions of efficacious action.

We are back in the introductory curriculum class in an American university. Gone is the Greek insight that theory is the cultivation of point of view, of transcendence of practical affairs, and that practical knowledge is knowledge in its own right (Lobkowicz, 1967, p. 118), imperfect but necessarily so. Gone is the notion that contemplation is essential to the cultivation of wisdom; gone is the Christian view that good works follow from faith. Present is the demand for knowledge of circumstances not yet present, theory which controls the future as it anticipates it. Theory is no longer achieved through distance from human affairs; it has become a mere appendage to it, judged and justified solely according to its ability to predict and control those affairs. It is little wonder that elementary curriculum students demand such knowledge; they merely reflect the view of theory and practice which prevails in a scientific age.

Two recent historical events have functioned to force a change in this traditional view of theory and practice in the curriculum field in the United States. That view had reached its zenith in the five or so years on either side of 1960. Curriculum specialists were being hired in record numbers as the rapidly increasing pool of public school students stimulated vast expansion of existing school districts and the creation of new ones. This period of rapid growth reinforced the view that the curriculum specialist was to manage the curriculum. Funding opportunities for curriculum development and implementation were many. But the Soviet launching of its satellite in 1957 was to signal the beginning of the end of the traditional curriculum field. That event fuelled the passion of the political right wing in the US, which had all along opposed progressive education by criticising it as soft, as undercutting academic excellence. These critics, such as US Navy Admiral Rickover, now had a concrete event as evidence that America was falling behind the Soviets and the flabby condition of the public school system was in large part to blame. In particular the curriculum was argued to be too responsive to issues of 'life adjustment' and 'social development' and insufficiently attentive to the latest breakthroughs in the sciences, primarily the natural sciences. With the change of administrations in Washington in 1960, a national curriculum reform movement was launched under the leadership, not of curriculum specialists, but of disciplinary specialists such as psychologist Jerome Bruner and physicist Jerrold Zacharias. This reform movement ignored the 'conventional wisdom' of curriculum field, and as Lawrence Cremin (1975) has pointed out, repeated many of its early mistakes. But that is another story; the one we are telling now leads us to note the consequence of the reform movement for the curriculum field. Because those whose academic specialisation and peculiar competence were largely ignored by federal funding agencies, a kind of 'death blow' was dealt to the status of the field. If the federal government did not respect the expertise of curriculum specialists why should anyone else? This question was not publicly asked. Nor was any immediate and noticeable drop in the status of curricularists evident. But over the years of the 1960s the attitude developed, especially among philosophers and psychologists of education, that the curriculum field was intellectually shabby, without conceptual substance.

Before we move to the second event which set the 'reconceptualisation' in motion, let us examine this attitude. Philosophers and psychologists of education during this period were allying themselves more closely with their colleagues in departments of philosophy and psychology. This occurrence was partly due to these colleagues' criticism of educational philosophers and psychologists as not 'doing' philosophy and psychology. The criticism can be viewed as part of the academic reaction and general conservatism following the shock of the Soviet space accomplishment of the late 1950s. Of course this conservatism would be muted as universities themselves became subjects of attack during the anti-war protests of the late 1960s and early 1970s, as the remainder of the 1970s saw a return to conservative views of schooling and disciplinary affiliation. Now, in fact, the more prestigious schools of education, such as Stanford, Chicago and Harvard, regularly hire, not PhDs in education for faculty posts, but PhDs in psychology and sociology 'with an interest' in curriculum or evaluation or another subfield of education. Under these conditions, it is easy to see how vulnerable the curriculum field would be. It never had a disciplinary affiliation; the conditions of its origin did not permit one, nor did its traditional function ask for one. Curriculum texts throughout the 1960s were, in genre, more reminiscent of journalism than serious theoretical or 'empirical' research. While this atheoretical and journalistic character of curriculum work had made it more accessible to school people and hence one of the more popular specialisations for graduate students in education, now it made the field helpless in the face of criticisms of 'academic excellence' and 'research' from formerly more friendly colleagues in other subfields of education. Initially, curricularists could ignore these criticisms, safe in the protection of large enrolments and still plentiful funding opportunities for in-service training (i.e. working with teachers and administrators on site, in their respective districts). But the second historical event changed that.

That event was the deterioration of the American economy. Whatever the causes – the cost of energy, the dissolution of the 1944 Bretton Woods agreement concerning international currency exchange relationships, the Nixon administration's decision to take the US dollar off the gold standard – the effect upon the curriculum field was marked. Now funding opportunities to develop curriculum, to work in school districts, relatively speaking, dried up. There came about an oversupply of teachers, and most schools of education in the US had more faculty members than the number of students would warrant. Part of this economic stress was temporarily relieved by increases in federal support for educational research, but this development was of little help to traditional curriculum specialists. They had no discipline in the conventional sense, and they conducted no research. Now their constituency was shrinking rapidly, and the criticism of intellectual shallowness from their colleagues could not be met with reports of plentiful FTEs ('full time equivalent', a common expression in the US to define students). The remaining foundation of the traditional curriculum field crumbled.

There had been a serious attempt to establish a discipline of curriculum in the 1960s. The US association of curriculum specialists, the Association for Supervision and Curriculum Development (ASCD), had convened a Commission on Curriculum Theory in the mid-1960s. But the commission failed to come to agreement on the contours of a discipline of curriculum, unlike the Commission on Instruction formed by the same organsiation at the same time. That commission established instruction as a variant of sociological and psychological research. But instruction had always been more closely allied with these disciplines than had curriculum. John Steven Mann had written of a 'discipline of curriculum' (Mann 1975). A number of individuals working in the tradition of social science attempted to specify the major conceptual elements and methodologies of research for the field. In this latter vein *Curriculum Theory* (Beauchamp, 1975) is perhaps the best example, although important and visible efforts were made by Mauritz Johnson (1970). Although Professor Beauchamp is currently completing work on a fourth edition, it must be concluded that this effort to establish a scientific field of curriculum stalled, as did the traditional field. In 1970

Joseph Schwab, a philosopher observing the state of affairs in the curriculum field, pronounced it 'moribund', a characterisation repeated through the decade (Huebner, 1976). It seemed, at that date, possible that the field would slowly disappear.

During the 1920s two men dominated the field of philosophy of education. For a short while, it was unclear which man's contribution would be remembered longer, whose would be regarded as the more significant. By the mid-1930s, however, John Dewey's reputation had surpassed Boyd Bode's, and today Bode's name is relatively forgotten. But during the zenith of his career, Bode observed the shape the developing curriculum field was taking, influenced by principles of 'scientific management', and asked one of his finest students, Harold Alberty, to leave philosophy of education and turn to the curriculum field in order to reconceive it along more humanistic lines. This Alberty did, with modest success, but it was his students – perhaps most prominently Paul R. Klohr – who laboured during the heyday of the 'managers' in the 1950s and 1960s to establish curriculum as a discipline which eschewed pseudo-practicality and scientism in favour of a self-critical and transformative vision. Along with Klohr were James B. Macdonald and Dwayne Huebner who had worked with Vergil Herrick at Wisconsin. Herrick, like Alberty, was working to move the curriculum field toward a more serious view of itself and its problems than the 'developers' seemed to exhibit. During these years, these individuals laboured alone, estranged from the mainstream of the field, and essentially unattended to. In May 1973 Huebner, Macdonald and others, with Klohr in attendance, would speak at a conference which was to initiate a series of yearly conferences which have functioned to reconceptualise the field. The nature of this reconceptualisation we will turn to momentarily, but let us first briefly review the historical conditions which made possible this movement in the field.

The curriculum field, as it was traditionally constituted as an atheoretical, journalistic field, focused upon practical problems of school personnel who were responsible for the curriculum in some fashion, had been dealt an irreparable blow by the selection of disciplinary specialists – such as the physicist, Zacharias – to lead the national curriculum reform movement. The Association for Supervision and Curriculum Development, which continued to grow in membership during this period by enlarging the area of its concern and appealing explicitly to school people, had organised a commission to attempt to put the field on a firmer footing, a commission which failed to come to agreement. As a field it was coming under increasing attack as primitive.

(In 1970, the prominent and widely respected Professor Schwab of the University of Chicago pronounced it 'moribund'.) By 1973 the American economy was set for its most serious recession since the world depression of the 1930s. And the surplus of certified school teachers was becoming large enough that clearly schools of education were soon to be considered too 'fat'. The weakest subfield of education was of course the most vulnerable. Given precipitous drops in its enrolment and given its non-disciplinary character, curriculum became the target for what should have been a mortal attack.

Independent of such criticism, working in the tradition of Herrick, Alberty, Huebner, Klohr and Macdonald, curricularists of the present writers' generation (loosely speaking, those who earned their doctoral degree during the period 1968 onward) attacked the narrowly practical function of the field, its atheoretical character, its unsystematic method of working, its more recent mirroring of scientific (mainstream social) method and ambition and its apolitical and ideological function. Quickly, two major currents of thought began to develop. One was closely tied to the Wisconsin and Columbia Universities tradition, one that was progressive in a Deweyan sense (and not in its popularised vulgarisation) and in the leftist political sense. While Huebner was still working in a hermeneutical mode by the time of the 1973 Rochester conference, he soon abandoned this work, and became preoccupied with questions of politics, attempting in a 1976 paper to integrate Piaget and Marx. In 1973 Macdonald called for a transcendental-developmental mode of education, and during that decade maintained a kind of 'middle ground' between the Marxists and critical theorists – like Apple (1979), Beyer (1979), Anyon (work forthcoming, 1980), Giroux (1980), Franklin (1979), Rosario (1979) and Wexler (1980) – and the hermeneutical and humanistic tradition associated with the present writers and more closely associated with the Ohio State tradition.[2] In a collection of essays, written by many of these curricularists, which Pinar edited (1975), the name of 'reconceptualists' became popularised.

Reconceptualisation

It is important to note that reconceptualisation was never prescriptive. It was not a code name for a twenty-year programme designed to revolutionise the schools. The sketch of reconceptualist work that follows is also descriptive rather than prescriptive, drawn from diverse writings which have appeared to share a coherent approach to the study of curriculum. In 1975 the term expressed an intuition. The papers, conferences and books of the last five years have provided evidence which we can identify as an early layer of reconceptualist thought, and the ground of this retrospective account.

Those who claimed the designation of reconceptualist did so in order to repudiate the limiting instrumentality that they saw dominating curriculum theory and research. Their repudiation of instrumentality did not, however, force reconceptualist theory into an acontextual field of ideal forms. On the contrary, acknowledging the rootedness of all curriculum theory in context, reconceptualists did not ignore situation, but seriously took up the term and challenged the boundaries and horizons that had previously delimited the field of curriculum theory. Reconceptualist notions of theory and practice are hinged on deliberate attempts to challenge the prevailing relationships of both the practitioner and the theorist to the world of educational activity that constitutes their situation.

Eschewing the demand that educational theory produce generalisations formed and fitted to permit neat packaging and dissemination as curriculum materials and programmes, reconceptualist theory sought to drive a wedge between theory and practice by suspending the instrumentalist intention. The assumption supporting this abstention was hardly a repudiation of that portion of responsibility that curricularists might assume for what goes on in schools. The suspension served to interrupt the very familiar responses that we as actors have to the situations in which we, ourselves, were raised. The school is a setting as familiar to all of us as our own apartments. We move through its halls, its rooms, with the habitual ease and body knowledge we use to rinse off the breakfast dishes or drive our cars to work. Our bodies as well as our minds know school time, school space, school words, school snickers, school power, school fear. The dullest actor among us could improvise the gestures and responses of the school child. We were all there, are still there. We even send our children there.

For none of us was school ever an 'educational environment'. It was our situation and our situation is never identical with our environment. *Environment* denotes a field before it is transfigured by human intention into a field for action. It is the field that is described by those, so-called, 'detached observers'. *Situation*, on the other hand, places the human actor at its centre. Its horizon is lodged within his perception and its meaning spans the distance between his history and his imagination. The remarkable sameness of school life, the familiar rituals that repeat themselves, year after year, in town after town, hardly accommodating to history or geography, all suggest that school is a situation so pervasive and persistent that it is easy for use to forget our contribution to its forms and to mistake it for a thing of nature rather than culture. Our understanding of nature is mediated by culture. From the instant that we receive biological life, we receive social life as well and all of our perceptions of the natural world are mediated by our intersubjective experience of it and of each other. Conversely, our intellectual activity, the free play of our imagination, the capacity for negation and transcendence, are held fast to moorings seemingly distant from spirit, tied to genetics, geography, economics, history. Conception as nature and conception as culture stand in dialectical relation to each other, simultaneously opposing and constituting each other. Reconceptualisation is the effort to name the tension between nature and culture, to discover those parts of culture that are not compelled by the laws of nature, and those parts of nature that are not necessary constraints but are the products of our own doing, and potentially our undoing. Reconceptualisation is the effort to study and name those relations and through that naming to transform the natural and social conditions that distort and constrain human freedom and community. Because education is such a complex expression of human history and aspiration, it is understandable that those appointed to study and design the curriculum often refuse to acknowledge the implications of their choices. We fall back upon naturalistic and environmental portrayals of school life in order to excuse ourselves from having to confront the contradictions and concerns that compel our attention once we acknowledge that schools are complex human situations in which we are deeply engaged.

It is the naturalistic fallacy that persists when we take schooling for granted, locked within our commonsense notions of it. It is within the naturalistic fallacy that we devise elaborate curriculum strategies to repeat and extend what is already there, cloaking the ancient reductionisms in homey, earthy terms like 'back to basics' and 'open classrooms'.

It is the environmental fallacy that pretends that the school is the situation where *they* rather than *we* live. This displacement of our own interest on to others permits the development of the scientific altruism that allows *us* to cater to *their* needs, once we have made our study and decided what they are. This version of instrumentality denies that the school is a human situation circumscribed by what Merleau-Ponty calls, 'an intentional arc', that radiates from the existential reality of a particular human being. It is this intentional arc that 'projects around us our future, our human setting, our physical and ideological and moral situation,or rather which results in our being situated in all these respects' (Merleau-Ponty, 1962). The quantitative research methods that psychologists and sociologists brought to the schools stripped them of both actors and situations, condemning curriculum research to the manipulation of variables in controlled environments.

Reconceptualist theory challenges the natural fallacy by asserting that issues of practice require a suspension of the taken-for-granted world of schooling. The hermeneutic theme in reconceptualist theory directs us back to the school situation. Using autobiographical and phenomenological analyses, it encourages us to attend to the experience we share of this lived world. These methods are employed to draw those oppressions and constraints that seem natural because they are so familiar out of consensual silence and into discourse.

Reconceptualist theory challenges the environmental fallacy by insisting that theoretical description of the school address a human situation. It requires, then, that we acknowledge that there is no psychological theory that is not simultaneously political, economic, historical, aesthetic and moral. By bringing a novelist's specificity to bear on the life world of school practice, on the one hand, and by drawing theory about school life into a complex metatheoretical matrix, on the other, reconceptualisation has intensified both the particularity that we associate with practice and the abstraction that we associate with theory, preferring the ancient polarities to contemporary positivism.

While we may reject the dualism of Greek thought that disassociated practical from contemplative experience, we must acknowledge that the polarity at least signified the capacity of that society to think in terms of what is and also of what might be. Although Greek idealism located 'what might be' in an eternally distant and ultimately separate world of eternal forms, it recognised signs and moments that would erupt in the course of everyday practical life and would point beyond themselves to meanings that undermined the practical sense in which they were embedded. It matters that Socrates interrupts the life and bustle of the marketplace for contemplation. It matters that it is in the midst of the marketplace that the contemplative moment erupts, that the abstention from the practical activity of the marketplace takes place as Socrates 'remains standing for a full twenty-four hours, surrounded by his puzzled fellow citizens'. Theory and practice, though seen as routes to two separate worlds, are allowed to intersect, creating junctions at which we hesitate, suspend our journey, ask directions. Socrates even violates the customary activity of the marketplace, as vendors and customers are forced to walk around his group which stays engaged in thought and discussion even as the vendors pack up their wares, close down their stalls and retire to their homes. He contradicts the activity of the marketplace by his stillness, its economy by his asceticism, its opening and closing by his staying. The distinctions that Greek thought maintained between the theoretical and the practical provided support for Socrates' ability to challenge the taken-for-granted limits that bounded the world he shared with the citizens of Athens, violating those boundaries by noticing markings that bore witness to alternative routes and frontiers. Stephen Strasser provides a distinction between the terms horizon and limits that we may apply to both Socratic and reconceptualist approaches to situation:

> A horizon is not a limit because a limit or a boundary is 'drawn', it is the result of a determination, an act of 'setting' a real or ideal determination. The limits on boundaries of a piece of land, for example, are fixed within the framework of the intersubjective economic activities of men. Similarly the limits or boundaries of a country depend on the political vicissitudes of its inhabitants and neighboring peoples. The two examples have this in common that, when the boundary line is being drawn, that which lies on the other side of the boundary is at least implicitly taken into account. The owner knows that someone else's property begins on the other side of the stone marking the boundary; the inhabitants of a country know that on the other side of a particular line there are people who belong to a different nation. In short, the concept of boundary or limit can serve as an exemplar for dialectical thinking. By positing the boundary or limit, consciousness, at the same time removes it. (Strasser, 1969, p. 31)

The horizon encompasses the land that lies on either side of the boundary. Ironically, the Greek world with its sharply demarcated boundaries between theory and practice, contemplation and politics, offered Greek citizens a world whose horizons contained within its limits both actuality and the possibility just beyond them. The Christian version of theory and practice, faith and good works blurs this boundary in two ways. First, faith is received. It is the acceptance of what is given, whereas contemplation must constantly pursue and discover its own rewards. So the first distinction between the boundary defining the Greek and Christian conceptions of theory and practice is the passivity that characterises the Christian access to the domain of faith as contrasted with the relentless questioning that characterised contemplation for the Greeks. Furthermore, by making the word flesh, Christianity provides Christ as the figure who crosses the boundary, reconciling the radical distinctions that separate spirit and body, faith and ethics, reason and politics. As the polarities are reduced the boundaries blur and the horizons shrink.

The scientific era succeeds in erasing the boundary between the actual and the possible completely by only acknowledging the possible in its existing and predictable manifestations in the practical world. In this era practical rationality draws both the poles of freedom and facticity, spirit and sensuality toward it, like a black hole absorbing and silencing all that surrounds it. Such was the situation that curriculum theorists received as their field.

The Lobkowicz analysis provides a developmental history of our situation, a genetic epistemology of bad faith.[3] The instrumental rationalism that dominated curriculum theory failed to honour either free will or facticity in its human action. Excessively abstract and rational, theorists had rarely grappled with life in schools, substituting printouts of the GNP for the commerce of Socrates' marketplace. Disclaiming responsibility for a point of view, theorists attributed their analyses to the needs of society or to the exigencies of schooling.

The project of reconceptualisation, it now appears, has been to restore those boundaries and polarities to the curriculum field that had collapsed into the relentless pursuit of progress understood as the extension and proliferation of the marketplace, what Freire called banking education (1973) and what Doyle called the process/product paradigm (1978). Since the 1920s and 1930s when progressivism had nurtured the debates between advocates of the child-centred curriculum and supporters of the society-centred curriculum, serious curriculum discourse had collapsed into the cheerful optimism of life adjustment movements, and of the curricular reform movement that reduced curriculum theory to a field experience for the social sciences, notably psychology and sociology.

The so-called romantic critics of the 1960s rediscovered the children who were trapped in the standardisation, racism and boredom of the nation's schools. Holt (1964), Kozol (1967), Herndon (1968) and Kohl (1967) gave these children names and voices and, for a while, free schools and open classrooms promised to provide space, time and communities that could receive their songs. Although the romantic critiques of practice as well as the practical innovations that they spawned were ephemeral, these attempts to attack and transform practice had cracked the complacency of curriculum theory, revealing an underlife that was barely present in Tyler's questions and Zacharias' schemes. The horizon of curriculum theory began to expand as reconceptualist students of curriculum began to recover the polarities and contradictions that had been muted in the three decades of technical rationality that followed World War II.

Reconceptualist theory picked up the practical with a vengeance. If the practical was to be the domain we dwell in and curriculum theory would address, we would populate it with real people, living, working, loving, dying in real places. The 1975 *ASCD Yearbook* (Macdonald and Zaret, 1975) brought such life to these places.[4] Huebner interrupted our chatter about schools with analyses of the language of curriculum theory (1975a). He contradicted the facile, rationalised jargon about 'purpose' and 'the learner' by evoking the complexity of language that is the expression of our response to a world saturated with surprise, concern and mystery. He challenged curriculum's conception of human temporality that revealed itself in behavioural objectives, in activity broken down into discrete units isolated from human community, from history, from past and future (1975b). He took curriculum talk as a text to be questioned and, along with others, encouraged a reflexive scrutiny of curriculum, that abstained from the production of programmes, units, even learning environments, to turn back upon these objects of our endeavours for information about the possibilities, compromises and betrayals contained within them. The activity was called hermeneutic, a term transferred from traditions of textual criticism that had, following the development of psychoanalysis and existential phenomenology, learned to study the signs that expressed personality and culture as an index to what was hidden as well as what was present, to see all signs as both simultaneously expressing and repressing meaning. Reconceptualists saw curriculum as a collection of signs subject to such interpretation, as evidence of the boundary that divided manifest from latent content and so they extended the horizon of curriculum theory to encompass the hidden curriculum as well as the obvious one.

No longer content to take up the documents of state or district curricula, or the kits, programmed materials and test scores as texts of curriculum, reconceptualist theory placed these rational designs on one side of the fence and placed the experience of these forms on the other. Maxine Greene's work had pointed to philosophy and literature as forms of discourse that would permit the expression of what was human about educational experience, hope and dread, doubt, love, anxiety and courage. We chose autobiography as a net to catch educational experience that was owned by particular people, curriculum that was drenched in their histories, poured through their bodies as well as their brains, connected to the places where they played and fought and ate and slept[5] (Grumet 1978a, Pinar 1978b).

In Wisconsin students of Apple and Kleibard, such as Franklin, Rosario and Beyer, also revealed the contradictions that resided in educational experience. They dislodged curriculum theory from its comfortable posture of objectivity bolstered with pretensions of political neutrality. Attacking the curriculum that ignored and thus delegitimatised students' and teachers' perceptions of the conflicts and inequities that pervaded their domestic, economic, environmental and political relations, they drew upon the work of the Frankfurt School, particularly the work of Jurgen Habermas, to reveal the structural relationships that bind consciousness, epistemology, social institutions, class structure and the means of production together into a totality. Neo-Marxist in approach, these writers eschewed the focus on the individual's experience that had served as a pathway to the practical for those pursuing a hermeneutic method, preferring to expose the structural relations that linked class interests to curriculum. Reconceptualist theory began to develop its own polarities. Neo-Marxist accused hermeneutic theorists of obscuring the social ground and contingency of individual experience. They challenged the idealism of its phenomenological orientation and the elitism of its psychoanalytic style of analysis, resting on verbal reports, introspection and imagination. The latter accused the neo-Marxists of reducing human experience to class structure, stripping human consciousness of its specificity, inventiveness and capacity for resistance as well as transcendence.

The dispute, drawing a line across the visage of reconceptualist theory, hardly defaced that project. By challenging each other's representations of our situation we have constantly reminded each other of the inevitably incomplete nature of our attempts to grasp and signify our practice. We have been reminded that theory and practice are each other's negation, that they exist constantly struggling to coincide and succeed only when they fail to meet in a perfect fit.

Contradictions between theory and practice compel us to acknowledge the tension in the relation of these two terms. Too often has educational theory been reduced to a form of idealism that must be instantly transformed into activity. Although the field situation provides a context where our theory and our practice confront one another, our goal is not to resolve their differences, nor to reduce one to the dimensions of the other. Rather, we play one against the other so as to disclose their limitations, and in so doing enlarge the capacity and intensify the focus of each. Just as what we think and know about our work is contradicted daily by the events in which we participate, the actual experience of teaching and the certainties that activity offers may be undermined by the questions and alternatives that theory cultivates.

Reconceptualist theory, then, is a critical exercise, descriptive rather than prescriptive, studying signs of educational practice to discover what might have been, what still may be. It presses back the categories of learner and curriculum to the relations that bind a person to his or her particular cultural, historical and political situation and then dissolves that person and that setting into the ineffable possibilities of the psychobiological individual making a home in the natural world. The categories of psychobiological individual and natural world are necessarily lodged in imagination, always on the other side of our practical knowledge. The positing of their existence, however, reminds us that what we take for nature is second nature, that situation and actor, even when stripped of all the assumptions that serve to camouflage their artifice, are always historical, social, mediated constructs. The limits and contradictions at each level point to the broader horizon beyond them, the distant edge of human experience which, while far removed from the perimeter of our daily practice, is still accessible to our theory.

It is not surprising that it is the field of curriculum theory that takes such a reconceptualisation for its project. The defensiveness that marked the style and the vagueness that marked the content of the field in the days of its incipience may have been an indication of the complexity of the task that the administrators merely glimpsed when they appointed a subordinate to look after the curriculum. Charged with the task of devising pedagogical structures that would house essential forms, competing epistemologies, ethics, aesthetics, and technology, curricularists are also expected to adapt these schemes to particular people in particular places. The demand that curricularists promote the practical and the ideal, the actual and the possible has led many of us to question these very categories, their mutuality as well as their polarity. Rather than finding these oppositions and contradictions an embarrassment, as we would if our only goal were instrumental efficiency made immediately transparent and accessible to a political constituency, reconceptual curriculum theory celebrates them, for their presence in curriculum theory permits the problem of 'what do I do on Monday?' to assume the depth and complexity that is proper to our human condition.

Notes

1. Tyler, today in his late seventies, still lectures widely. Professor Gail McCutcheon of Ohio State University is now working on what promises to be the definitive collection of his papers and her commentary on them.
2. In a 1980 paper by William H. Schubert of the University of Illinois at Chicago Circle and Professor George J. Posner of Cornell University, this lineage is traced and diagrammed in considerable detail.
3. The goal of 'bad faith', Sartre tells us, 'is to put oneself out of reach; it is an escape' (1966, p. 110). The objectification of actors and situations that pervades the scientific era and its instrumental approach to curriculum theory deserves, we suspect, this status of self-deception.
4. See, in particular, Macdonald's piece, 'The Quality of Everyday Life in Schools' (Macdonald, 1975a).
5. Approaches to curriculum research that draw their methods from aesthetics rather than social science are being developed in the United States under the rubrics ethnographic research and qualitative evaluation. George Willis's text (1978) is illustrative. The work of Roger Simon and Donald Dippo (1979) investigating the use of dramatic portrayals as a form for curriculum analysis suggests rich applications of this art. See also Grumet's (1978b, 1980) use of theatre as a metaphor for the experience of curriculum.

Bibliography

Anyon, Jean (work forthcoming) 'Schools as Agencies of Social Legitimation: An Analysis of US Classrooms and Curriculum Content', *Journal of Curriculum Theorizing*.

Apple, Michael (1979) 'On Analyzing Hegemony', *Journal of Curriculum Theorizing*, vol. 1, no. 1, winter, pp. 10-27

Beauchamp, George A. (1975) *Curriculum Theory*, 3rd edn, Kagg, Wilmette, Illinois

Beyer, Landon (1979) 'Cultural Forms as Therapeutic Encounters', *Curriculum Inquiry*, vol. 9, no. 4, pp. 349-60

Bobbitt, Franklin (1918) *How to Make a Curriculum*, Houghton Mifflin, Boston

Caswell, Hollis (1935) *Curriculum Development*, American Book Co., New York

Charters, W.W. (1923) *Curriculum Construction*, Macmillan, New York

Cremin, Lawrence (1975) 'Curriculum Making in the United States' in Pinar (1975, pp. 19-35)

Doyle, Walter (1978) 'Paradigms for Research on Teacher Effectiveness' in Shulman, L. (ed.), *Review of Research in Education*, vol. 5, F.E. Peacock, Itasca, Illinois

Duncan, James K. and Frymier, Jack R. (1967) 'Explorations in the Systematic Study of Curriculum', *Theory into Practice*, vol. 6, no. 4, pp. 180-99. (See also, in this issue, articles by Elsie Alberty, Dwayne Huebner, Paul R. Klohr, James B. Macdonald and Ross L. Mooney.)

Franklin, Barry M. (1979) 'Self-control and the Psychology of School Discipline', *Journal of Curriculum Theorizing*, vol. 1, no. 2, summer, pp. 238-54

Freire, Paulo (1973) *Pedagogy of the Oppressed*, Myra Bergman Ramos (trans.), Seabury Press, New York

Giroux, Henry A. (1980) 'Beyond the Limits of Radical Educational Reform: Toward a Critical Theory of Education', *Journal of Curriculum Theorizing*, vol. 2, no. 1, winter, pp. 47-56

Greene, Maxine (1973) *Teacher as Stranger*, Wadsworth Publishing Co. Belmont, California

Grumet, Madeleine R. (1978a) 'Songs and Situations: The Figure Ground Relation in a Case Study of *Currere*', in Willis (1978)

Grumet, Madeleine R. (1978b) 'Curriculum as Theatre: Merely Players', *Curriculum Inquiry*, vol. 8, no. 1, pp. 37-64

Grumet, Madeleine R. (1980) 'In Search of Theatre: Ritual Confrontation and the Suspense of Form' *Journal of Education*, 162:1, winter, pp. 93-110

Herndon, James (1968) *The Way it Spozed to Be*, Simon and Schuster, New York

Holt, John (1964) *How Children Fail*, Pitman, London

Huebner, Dwayne (1975a) 'Curricular Language and Classroom Meanings' in Pinar (1975)

Huebner, Dwayne (1975b) 'Curriculum as Concern for Man's Temporality' in Pinar (1975)

Huebner, Dwayne (1976) 'The Moribund Curriculum Field: its Wake and our Work', AERA

Johnson, Mauritz (1970) 'Appropriate Research Directions in Curriculum and Instruction', *Curriculum Theory Network*, 6, winter, 1970/1, pp. 24-37

Kohl, Herbert (1967) *36 Children*, New American Library, New York

Kozol, Jonathan (1967) *Death at an Early Age*, Houghton Mifflin, Boston

Lobkowicz, Nicholas (1967) *Theory and Practice*, Univ. of Notre Dame Press, Notre Dame
Macdonald, James (1975a) 'The Quality of Everyday Life in Schools' in Macdonald and Zaret (1975)
Macdonald, James (1975b) 'Curriculum and Human Interests' in Pinar (1975, pp. 283-94)
Macdonald, J. and Zaret, E. (eds.) (1975) *Schools in Search of Meaning: ASCD Yearbook.* Association for Supervision and Curriculum Development, Washington, DC
Mann, John Steven (1975) 'A Discipline of Curriculum Theory' in Pinar (1975, pp. 149-64)
Merleau-Ponty, Maurice (1962) *The Phenomenology of Perception*, Colin Wilson (trans.), Humanities Press, New York
Pinar, William F. (ed.) (1974) *Heightened Consciousness, Cultural Revolution and Curriculum Theory: Proceedings of the 1973 Rochester Conference*, McCutchan, Berkeley
Pinar, William F. (ed.) (1975) *Curriculum Theorizing: the Reconceptualists*, McCutchan, Berkeley
Pinar, William F. (1978a) 'Notes on the Curriculum Field 1978', *Educational Researcher*, vol. 7, no. 8, pp. 8-12.
Pinar, William F. (1978b) '*Currere:* a Case Study' in Willis (1978, pp. 318-42)
Rosario, José (1979) 'Aesthetics and the Curriculum: Persistency, Traditional Modes and a Different Perspective', *Journal of Curriculum Theorizing*, vol. 1, no. 1, winter, pp. 136-54
Sartre, Jean Paul (1966) *Being and Nothingness*, Hazel Barnes (trans.), Washington Square Press, New York
Saylor, J. Galen, and Alexander, William M. (1966) *Curriculum Planning for Modern Schools*. Holt, Rinehart, Winston, New York
Schubert, William H. and Posner, George G. (1980) 'Origins of the Curriculum Field Based on Mentor Student Relationships', *Journal of Curriculum Theorizing*, vol. 2, no. 2, summer, pp. 37-67
Schwab, Joseph (1970) *The Practical: a Language for Curriculum*, National Education Association, Washington
Seguel, Mary Louise (1966) *The Curriculum Field: its Formative Years*, Teachers' College Press, New York
Simon, Roger and Dippo, Donald (1980) 'Dramatic Analysis: Interpretive Inquiry for the Transformation of Social Settings', *Journal of Curriculum Theorizing*, vol. 2, no. 1, winter, pp. 109-34
Smith, Othanel, Stanley, William O. and Shores, J. Harlan (1975) *Fundamentals of Curriculum Development*, rev. edn., Harcourt,

Brace, New York
Strasser, Stephan (1969) *The Idea of Dialogal Phenomenology*, Duquesne Univ. Press, Pittsburgh
Taba, Hilda (1962) *Curriculum Development*, Harcourt, Brace, New York
Tyler, Ralph (1949) *Basic Principles of Curriculum and Instruction*, Univ. of Chicago Press, Chicago
Wexler, Philip (work forthcoming) 'Structure, Text and Subject: a Critical Sociology of School Knowledge' in Apple, Michael W. (ed.), *Cultural and Economic Reproduction in Education*, Routledge and Kegan Paul, London
Willis, George (ed.) (1978) *Qualitative Evaluation*, McCutchan, Berkeley

PART TWO

CRITICAL REAPPRAISAL

INTRODUCTION

To the extent that strongly deterministic, technocratic or managerial ideologies in curriculum studies have been resisted in Britain, it is the home-grown pragmatic tradition which has provided the forms of resistance. This tradition, which is referred to by curriculum writers but neither analysed nor situated historically or politically, is the subject of the first paper, by Geoff Whitty. Although it is usually described as pragmatic or eclectic, it may also be seen as rooted in notions of teacher autonomy and partnership with the state. Pragmatism, by its nature, defies clear definition but it is represented in the Whitty article by references to the work of Denis Lawton. This writer had an increasing influence in the 1970s with his attempt to revive an approach to curriculum study based on consensus politics and incremental change. Both papers in this section, while they refer to this British tradition, do make some attempt to explain its political and historical development. Taking their lead from Finn, Grant and Johnson (1977), they refer to this tradition as 'social-democratic'; included in this description is a relationship between the post-war state, the Labour Party and the educational system that has reduced socialism to considerations of educational opportunity and access to higher education. Lawton's work and, to some extent, that of other writers for the influential Open University course on curriculum design and development (referred to on p. 48), relate closely to the attempts of this social democratic tradition – working within curriculum studies – to view the curriculum as an agent of incremental change, a distributor of relevant knowledge and a site for national cultural and political reconciliation.

The social democratic tradition is the starting point for our two articles. It is not, however, fully explored here and much more work, of the kind already taking place in the sociology of education, needs to be done in the area of curriculum studies. But, for all its lack of distinctiveness, it is the key to a curriculum approach whose analyses have had hidden assumptions and whose proposals have had selected targets. A consensus tradition in curriculum research which has been, during recent years, gradually eroded by the mandates of a Labour government, concerning control of the curriculum and its content, has now been more rapidly demolished by the radical attitudes of a Conservative administration. Conflict, not consensus; purpose, not provision; these are the order of the day. Teachers are seen clearly as employees, not partners. Yet even radicals are unwilling to discard a useful ideology (as, for example, when teachers striking for better educational provisions are described as losing their professionalism) and so a valuable beginning is made by Whitty and Clark and Davies to raise, within curriculum studies, the assumptions and proposals of a social democratic tradition.

For Whitty, the important factor in Lawton's work is the way in which it delicately avoids structural arguments and spreads the conflict of ideas and class-based political and cultural analyses diffusely throughout curriculum studies. Lawton has written a number of books which are wide-ranging in their approach to curriculum problems and have been influential amongst student teachers because of their simplified arguments and optimistic tone. But his admirable solutions to complex problems are, as Whitty notes, based on spurious reasoning. What is interesting is the complete lack of critical analysis of his ideas and solutions in the field of curriculum studies.

Teachers are often treated, in British curriculum writing, either as inefficient operatives or as automatons. The chapter by Clark and Davies reveals to the wider public how many teachers see themselves. All the teachers' journals studied in their article are united by their concern for the crisis in the relationship between education and the state and to develop a socialist theory and practice of education. Sometimes, by inferences drawn from other arguments (the pedagogical subtext) rather than from those relating directly to the curriculum, the writers show that, unlike many of the curriculum pundits, these teachers feel bound by a concern for theoretical explanation *and* a need to alter or change practice. Each of the journals takes a different approach – ranging from producing elements of a radical curriculum to developing critcisms of progressive education and analysing the elements of control within and over a teacher's work. Unlike the managerial-technocratic perspective, in which teachers are seen as agents of a superior power, or the British social-democratic ideology, in which teachers are often described as partners and professionals, or even a neo-Marxist perspective, in which teachers are viewed as the witting or unwitting agents of capitalism, these teachers are active, reactive and radical on the curriculum. They seem to see themselves as having a space in which to operate, between the demands of capitalism and the state, the way these demands are mediated and their contradictory nature. The work of teachers like these has not previously been incorporated within the work of curriculum studies. Their analyses and practices have a particular value in response to a pessimism in education in crisis and a body of curriculum studies unable effectively to respond to a rapidly changing situation.

One aspect makes a significant contrast between the contents of these two papers and is of particular importance for our argument: that is, on the one hand, a pragmatic tradition, with its bland solutions, disguising the nature of problems and avoiding structural analyses; on the other, the radical, invigorating search for change by teachers, both in practice and in the generation of theory. There could be no greater illustration of the paucity of curriculum studies as a 'theoretical' area than to compare the analyses, processes and solutions of the Lawton-Skilbeck-Open University 'soft-sell' social democratic movement of the 1970s and the emergence of the radical teacher-debates of the same period.

2 CURRICULUM STUDIES: A CRITIQUE OF SOME RECENT BRITISH ORTHODOXIES

Geoff Whitty

Curriculum studies, as a distinctive field of educational theory and practice, is a relatively new arrival on the British scene, with its major journal, *The Journal of Curriculum Studies*, having only recently celebrated its tenth anniversary. Surprisingly absent, however, from the celebratory volume (Taylor, 1979) were any major representatives[1] of those approaches to curriculum studies which might be thought of as distinctively British in inspiration – that is, the work of Denis Lawton and his colleagues in the Curriculum Studies Department at the Institue of Education in London[2] and the activities of the group which has formed around Lawrence Stenhouse at the University of East Anglia.[3] Both these groups have self-consciously distanced themselves from the banalities of the sort of technicist approaches to the planning, development and evaluation of the curriculum which they saw as dominating the American scene and which seemed in danger of determining the nature of the field in Britain in the 1960s and early 1970s. They have both also had a powerful influence on the character of curriculum studies way beyond the confines of their own institutions, particularly through their involvement in the Open University curriculum course, E203, *Curriculum Design and Development.*[4] They have thus helped (even today when many American curriculum writers are themselves beginning to reject the earlier approaches and British officialdom has started to flirt with something not unlike them) to give curriculum studies in Britain a more liberal and humanistic flavour than its transatlantic counterpart. Their work may well appeal therefore to those on both sides of the Atlantic who are increasingly coming to question and reject the traditional paradigm in curriculum studies and, in particular, to those who see their own work in education as contributing to a quest for greater democracy and social justice in society. This paper will suggest that, even though these approaches have distinct advantages over the more conventional ones which they critically assess, they should themselves now be subjected to critical appraisal. Although the paper will focus on the work of Denis Lawton, it will also argue that, despite important differences of emphasis between the various writers involved, they all share something of an ambiguity about the purposes of the enterprise in which they are engaged and a collective refusal to address certain crucial structural issues raised, for instance, in contemporary work in the sociology of education. This detracts not only from their understanding of many of the phenomena which they discuss, but also from the viability and significance of their proposed or implied strategies of change.

Firstly, I want to make some general comments about the nature and importance of the field of curriculum studies in Britain today. For much of the post-war period the curriculum was sadly neglected as an area of concern by educational theorists and educational policy-makers alike, its nature having been either taken for granted or treated as a matter for teachers' professional judgement. Educational studies and social-democratic education policy were both organised along lines which made it difficult to discuss curriculum issues in a meaningful way and this was to have serious implications for their capacity to influence the reality of schooling. It is therefore very much to the credit of those writers whose work is considered in this paper that they have helped to bring curriculum issues into sharper focus even if, as I will argue, they have allowed our vision of the broader context of those issues to become blurred in the process. Yet it must also be said that the reluctance, until very recently, of theorists and politicians to involve themselves in the curriculum field has contributed to its relative under-development and thus to the disproportionate influence of the work discussed here.[5] In one of his most recent pronouncements about the state of the field which he helped to found in Britain, Denis Lawton claims that 'curriculum studies is not a field of educational enquiry to specialize in for those who want a quiet life in an ivory tower'. He suggests that it is a 'rather aggressive world' in which 'even jokes about the curriculum tend to have a cruel edge' (Lawton, 1979). But, to many people, the field of curriculum studies gives little impression of being intellectually alive, let alone 'aggressive' or 'cruel'. In many ways it has been largely parasitic upon the work of philosophers and sociologists of education who have themselves often been at pains to eschew the field and, indeed, sometimes any direct concern with pedagogical and policy issues at all. This has meant that curriculum theorists have often drawn upon outdated and simplistic versions of their work, with the unfortunate consequence that it has often been only via the emasculated versions used in departments of curriculum studies that philosophical and sociological perspectives have entered the consciousness of serving teachers and the ideological discourse of policy-making contexts. It also means that, in a period when the curriculum has suddenly, for the first time since the war, emerged as a live issue in the British political arena, the curriculum studies 'specialists' are those most likely to be called upon to contribute to the debate. Although, as I suggested earlier, the DES initially responded to political demands for accountability with some rather crude and outmoded models of curriculum-planning and control, there are already signs (Lawton, 1980; Sockett, 1980) that the advocates of the more liberal approaches are seeking to influence the direction of policy.

The nature of curriculum studies is thus likely to be of more than purely academic or even professional significance. I therefore now want to explore the work of Denis Lawton in some depth, since not only is he one of the most prolific writers in this field, he is also probably the one nearest to the major arenas of educational debate and policy-formation.[6] One of the strengths of Lawton's approach is that he certainly does not regard curriculum planning as a purely, or even largely, technical exercise and he recognises that curricular decision-making involves crucial cultural and political choices. Indeed, he was one of the first occupants of the middle ground of British politics to face up to this and to try to explore the implications of the work of those theorists to his right and left (Bantock 1968; Williams 1961; Young 1971) who had been arguing that case for some time. More than most writers in the curriculum field, at least until very recently, he has attempted to address theoretical issues about the nature of culture and to link his discussion of the curriculum to broader political concepts like social justice. He has made some specific proposals for the reform of the curriculum and has also proposed a new model of curricular decision-making around which a consensus about the curriculum might be achieved. I want, however, to suggest that both the style and the content of his argument often serve to obscure rather than to clarify the nature of the issues which he seeks to address and that, by emphasising the construction of consensus, he fails to consider in sufficient depth how such consensual curricular arrangements would, even if they were to be achieved, articulate with the broader structural features of society. Indeed, I would argue that his proposals derive from a mis-recognition of the social formation in which they have arisen and that they may effectively contribute to the construction of the sort of new hegemonic discourse about education which could help bolster a society hostile in nature to one in which his concept of social justice could have any real substance.

Let me therefore illustrate the way in which Lawton's basic approach seems almost to be designed to avoid confronting such issues and to mask them in the construction of a spurious consensual position to which it is assumed all rational persons will assent. Lawton adopts a tone of informed commonsense and, in his writing for teachers and administrators, as much as in his writing for school pupils, his tendency is always to establish 'what most sociologists would accept' (Lawton, 1975a) rather than to engage seriously with the very basic issues about which they differ. Yet, significantly, he seems able to justify his own position only by a distortion of some of the more interesting arguments which he hopes thereby to de-fuse, and the institutional separation of curriculum studies from other areas of educational theory ensures that only a minority of his readership will have had direct access to the arguments which he claims to have disposed of. It is interesting to notice how, like Entwistle (Entwistle, 1978, 1979), whose work has a certain affinity to his own, Lawton always chooses to discuss, and hence dismiss, the extreme version of any argument which differs from his own – often merely a caricature of such an argument. Thus, for instance, his target is '*Naïve* Progressivism' (Lawton, 1977) rather than those forms of progressivism which are actually influential, while elsewhere (Lawton, 1975b) he attacks a '*naïve and simplistic* interpretation of the Marxian assumptions about the *direct* relationship of the economic substructure and the cultural superstructure'. In the same book he opposes the view that '*everything* that the school offers is middle-class culture and, therefore, of *no* value' and the suggestion that '*all* science, history, art, philosophy, and morals' can be labelled as 'bourgeois' (my emphases).

Even where his strictures have a more genuine target, as in parts of his critique of the work of Michael F.D. Young and his associates (Young, 1971), one scans his work in vain for any mention of the way in which these writers have themselves taken criticism on board and attempted to refine their arguments.[7] In this way, Lawton can appear to dispose of positions which might call his own into question without ever seriously addressing them in their more sophisticated forms, which actually stress the complex and contradictory nature of schooling and seek to explore the nature of the relationship between economy and culture rather than assuming it to be a 'direct' one.[8] Even if we accept that, because of the institutional divisions between sociology of education and curriculum studies, Lawton would not have been aware of such work in the mid-1970s, it is clear from the following passage from his latest volume (Lawton, 1980) that he is aware of some of the vocabulary used in this work even though he again employs it in typically caricatured fashion:

> Some recent sociologists specializing in the sociology of the curriculum would have us believe that control of the curriculum is *simply* a question of bourgeois hegemony. They assume that in a capitalist society the *whole* of the cultural superstructure, including education, is a *reflection* of the values of the dominant group – the bourgeoisie or the capitalist ruling class. For this group of writers education is assumed to be a *totally* socialising influence. But I am suggesting that the question of the control of education is much more complicated than that. (my emphases) (Lawton, 1980, pp. 6-7)

Even if such a crude view of the curriculum was ever propagated (and it is interesting that no direct reference is given for it),[9] it is to the exploration of the very complexity to which Lawton points that sociologists have been committed over the past decade.

I have spent some time showing how Lawton's method of argument involves exaggeration and caricature because I believe it helps to explain the apparent plausibility of his position and also serves to make us wary of being seduced by his prescriptions. In fact, because he chooses to mount his argument via a series of supposed refutations of the work of other theorists, Lawton is able to avoid mounting a carefully constructed positive argument. Thus, in the context of caricatured alternatives, but possibly not in the context of some of the more real alternatives, an ill-defined pluralism can easily appear the most plausible social theory on offer and a consensual approach to curricular decision-making the strategy most likely to contribute towards social justice. His claims to have uncovered flaws in other theories and strategies create the space into which his own conception of a common-culture curriculum or a democratic model of curriculum planning can be slotted, with predictable regularity, at the end of virtually every volume he produces. While some of the flaws which he identifies in other theories do undoubtedly exist and while some of his policy prescriptions may have much to commend them, we would be better able to judge them in the light of a firm foundation of positive argument and a more genuine exploration of other views of the society and educational system in which they are intended to operate. It is, I am suggesting, as much his style of writing as the substantive content of Lawton's argument which makes it appear highly plausible and something to which all but a 'few extremists' (Lawton, 1977) could easily agree.

Let us turn, then, to his substantive proposals for a common-culture curriculum and co-operative model of curricular decision-making and control. These proposals have been developed over the past eight years or so in a series of complementary and overlapping publications, the most significant of which have been *Social Change, Educational Theory and Curriculum Planning* (1973), *Class, Culture and the Curriculum* (1975b), *Education and Social Justice* (1977) and *The Politics of the School Curriculum* (1980).[10] The earlier volumes outlined his conception of the curriculum as a 'selection from culture' and suggested that, in the interests of social justice, all pupils should be exposed to a selection from our 'common culture'. This produced his prescription of a curriculum centred around five core areas of knowledge – mathematics, the physical and biological sciences, the humanities and social studies, the expressive arts and moral education. He recognises, however, that the selection of these and, to an even greater extent, other elements of the curriculum is never likely to be an entirely uncontentious matter and, in the light of recent disputes between politicians and professionals over curricular issues, the later volumes focus upon the idea of a new model of curricular decision-making. He proposes a multi-level scheme of co-operative control in which all the relevant parties can reach broad agreement on the nature of the curriculum, with its detailed implementation and assessment being assigned to different groups at different levels of decision-making, from the context of national policy through to the individual teacher planning his or her lesson. He suggests that such a scheme should be implemented in the near future 'if we are to avoid further confusion and unnecessary conflict' (Lawton, 1980). While there might appear at first sight to be a certain tension between his own conviction that the curriculum should take a particular form and his proposals for a co-operative mechanism through which decisions about the curriculum should be made, it is clear that he regards the two proposals as essentially complementary and both as suggestions on which it ought to be possible to reach agreement with all rational and fairminded people.

What is disturbing is that Lawton almost seduces us into believing that his prescriptions are manifestly 'a good thing' on the basis of very little careful sociological analysis of the context in which they are intended to operate and without even giving us a very clear idea of what precisely his common-culture curriculum and his co-operative decision-making model are for – other, of course, than a basis for agreement. It is only when we pause to reflect upon such questions that we recognise the dangers of accepting his stunningly simple solutions to our current educational problems. The immediate appeal of a *common-culture* curriculum or a *co-operative* approach to curriculum planning is perhaps hardly surprising in the context of a prevailing ideology which tends to mask fundamental conflicts and inequalities in contemporary society. Yet in the context of the underlying power relations of that society, which he does not analyse in any depth, such proposals may well have effects very different from those which Lawton himself envisages. It is even quite conceivable that his rhetoric will merely be used to provide a legitimating gloss for the implementation of the sort of core curriculum which will actually contribute little to the realisation of social justice. In other words, the achievement of social justice in the context with which we are actually faced may necessitate not so much the avoidance of 'unnecessary conflict' as the bringing into sharper focus of some *necessary* conflicts over, amongst other things, the nature of the school curriculum.

The instant appeal of Lawton's demand for a consensus about his proposals in not necessarily a useful measure of their efficacy as instruments for the extension of democratic rights and the pursuance of social justice. There may, in fact, be a certain irony in a statement in *Education and Social Justice* where Lawton points to the way in which dangerous psychological half-truths about 'three types of children' entered the public consciousness and helped to legitimate that earlier supposed instrument of social justice, the tripartite system of secondary education. Of that episode, he said:

> In this, as in many other respects, it was not the scientific evidence or the opinions of experts which really mattered, but the over-simplified view which had been created in the minds of the population as a whole, and of teachers and educational administrators in particular. (Lawton, 1977, p. 46)

This should serve to remind us that the patent 'reasonableness' of a view is not enough to ensure its accuracy nor, indeed, is an appearance of egalitarianism sufficient to ensure that a policy is egalitarian in its effects. Thus the role of Lawton's own work in the reconstruction of hegemony out of the current crisis in education and in the legitimation of the forms of elitism and injustice which he claims to attack must itself be subject to careful scrutiny and any temptation to accept uncritically his notion of a common-culture curriculum should be resisted by those committed to an extension of social justice. This is not, however, to suggest that his work should be dismissed by such people but rather that it should be subjected to a serious critical analysis.

Interestingly, in the light of my foregoing comments, Lawton's work has, as yet, come in for very little critical appraisal in this country. In what follows, I shall therefore be drawing quite heavily upon a critique of his work produced recently by Uldis Ozolins of the University of Melbourne in Australia, where the work of the socio-ogy research group in cultural and educational studies seems to span the gulf between sociology of education and curriculum studies which has bedevilled the British scene. This paper (Ozolins, 1979) is particularly concerned with Lawton's *Class, Culture and the Curriculum* and concentrates upon his supposed refutation of the idea of a 'working-class curriculum' and claims that his own 'common-culture curriculum' would be to the benefit of the working class.

Before looking at Ozolins' criticisms, I want to suggest that the nature of Lawton's work is partially to be understood in terms of its relationship to conventional social democratic education policy in Britain, a relationship which becomes clearer in his later book, *Education and Social Justice*. Certainly there can be little doubt that Lawton's work represents something of an advance on the conventional social-democratic notion that educational and social justice are to be attained by improving access to an education whose content remains largely unproblematic. His sympathetic critique of Labour Party educational policy (Lawton, 1977, ch. 7) follows similar lines to other recent commentaries on this point. However, his recognition of the significance of curricular arrangements for the perpetuation and legitimation of social inequality and his subsequent argument that social justice would best be served by the introduction of his common culture curriculum should not necessarily be seen to stand or fall together. The suggestion that a differentiated curriculum is as divisive as a differentiated school system does not necessarily lead one to the conclusion that the addition of a common curriculum to a formal policy of comprehensive schooling will be any more successful than the latter alone, in achieving social justice. But, given Lawton's somewhat reified conception of the curriculum as something to be transmitted, his argument does often appear to be merely an extension of the formal equality of access position which has dominated Labour Party policy. Yet it was surely not just because the knowledge dimension of educational provision was neglected in traditional social democratic thinking, nor even because professional administrators with a vested interest in the preservation of the status quo outsmarted the politicians, that Labour Party education policies failed to realise their promise. Rather it was because (as some of the architects of those policies have now recognised) the nature of society, the state and education and the articulations between them were far more complex than such policies assumed. Again, it is noticeable that Lawton almost entirely neglects, even in his most recent work, to mention any of the literature which attempts, however unsuccessfully, to come to grips with such issues.

It seems to me that it is also this continuity with traditional social democratic approaches to education which helps to explain why 'Lawton tells us surprisingly little about what he expects the consequences of [his common-culture] curriculum to be' (Ozolins, 1979). While, in places, Lawton seems to recognise some of the tensions involved in what Finn, Grant and Johnson (1977) term the 'dual repertoire' of Labour Party policy, his own position retains many of the ambiguities which this entails. Thus, Ozolins is able to quote from *Class, Culture and the Curriculum* to suggest that Lawton's main purpose is to 'produce a few more good sixth-formers' and thus he is able to locate him in the Fabian 'capacity-catching' tradition. In *Education and Social Justice*, however, he shows a more 'egalitarian' concern with education as a 'right' and his common-core curriculum is thus seen as recognising the right of all children to 'real education'. Elsewhere in both these books he stresses the importance of transmitting a common culture as a way of reducing social division and antagonisms. There is, then, not only something of an ambiguity about what his proposals are designed for, but also the usual reluctance to explore rather than gloss over the relationship between arguments about social justice *in* education and those about social justice *through* education or even to tell us what precisely social justice might mean in either context. The difficulty of knowing what the consequences of Lawton's curricular proposals are expected to be is, then, a feature of the continuity between his work and prevailing social-democratic traditions, even though he himself suggests that the Labour Party needs 'to clarify fundamental principles . . . about society and education' as a prelude to doing 'their homework more carefully on important questions of detail in education' (Lawton, 1977). It is, however, the very congruity between his lack of clarity and a more general one within the Labour movement as a whole which contributes to the ease with which we can be lulled into accepting his policy prescriptions as self-evidently a good thing without really analysing their purposes or implications or their relationship to other aspects of social policy.

None of these issues can really be adequately dealt with in the absence of an analysis of the social formation and the role of education within it. This is not to say that Lawton entirely fails to recognise that schools are located in society or even that he is unaware of the dangers of seeming to suggest that schools can remedy all of society's ills. Indeed, he explicitly tell us at one point that 'the question of social justice in education cannot be separated from social justice in society at large, particularly the question of access to certain kinds of occupation' and that it 'is difficult to promote social justice in education without going some way towards eliminating social injustice in the wider community' (Lawton, 1977). Equally, he admits that 'schools cannot compensate for society, and schools should not be blamed for all the imperfections of society as a whole', although education can, he tells us, 'equip people to understand . . . society better and improve it' (Lawton, 1977). But, for the most part, such issues are bracketed and it is significant that all these quotations are, once again, comments made during critiques of other writers rather than as part of an explicit theory of society upon which Lawton's position is based. Even when he is discussing the essential bases of a prescriptive educational theory, he does not include amongst its components a theory of the nature of society,[11] even though the last of his comments quoted above implies that practical interventions in the social world are most likely to be effective if they are based on a proper understanding of society. Yet it is only in terms of a theory of society and a clearer conception of how struggles for social justice in education relate to similar struggles elsewhere that we can judge whether his prescriptions for a common-culture curriculum and a consensus model of curriculum planning are likely to be efficacious in achieving even the somewhat ambiguous social objectives to which Lawton adheres. In some contexts, as part of a clearer, broader strategy designed to further the interests of those currently disadvantaged in society, they might well have some merit. But on their own they might equally well contribute towards the construction of a new hegemonic settlement which effectively sustains the status quo. Only a more adequate analysis of the structural and conjunctural features of contemporary society could put us in a position to make an informed judgement about their merits.

If *Education and Social Justice* thus helps us to locate the ambiguities of Lawton's work within the ambiguities of a broader political tradition, it does little to remedy the essential weaknesses which Ozolins identifies in *Class, Culture and the Curriculum*, and it is to a fuller consideration of those weaknesses that we now turn. In a careful analysis of the case set out in that book, Ozolins demonstrates quite convincingly that Lawton avoids some of those crucial questions about the nature of contemporary society to which I have pointed above. He concludes that Lawton is 'politically ingenuous: he presents his idea of a common curriculum with very much the feeling that it is a philosophy whose time has come, but it is only arrived at by systematically ignoring class and culture conflict on a massive scale' (Ozolins, 1979, p. 62).

The paper shows Lawton's conceptions of class and culture to be crude in the extreme and indicates that he is highly ambivalent, if not somewhat inconsistent, about the admittedly highly complex relationship between culture and the social and economic environment. His case about the existence and nature of a common culture is seen to be developed via the mode of argument which I outlined earlier and 'without any substantial analysis of the working class in the contemporary class structure'. Yet, ultimately, Ozolins suggests, Lawton's curricular proposals emerge not so much from his somewhat confused discussion of class and culture but rather from a strategic retreat into the Hirstian 'forms of knowledge' (Hirst and Peters, 1970). The core areas of his curriculum are therefore derived from a 'structure and organisation of knowledge [which] is universal rather than culturally based'. But, even if such 'universal' forms can be distinguished analytically, the real problem facing those committed to social justice is not thereby removed. While Lawton does make brief mention of the problem of changing teacher and pupil attitudes, he seems to assume that the essential work has been done, once the abstract analysis has been carried out, and certainly does not face up to the complexities of translating it into a curriculum which can be taught meaningfully to all pupils in the real world. These complexities can, of course, be grasped adequately only via an understanding of the broader context in which the cultural transactions of schooling take place. It is not, therefore, simply a matter of distinguishing basic knowledge forms which should be made available to all pupils from 'middle-class manners, etiquette and lower-level middle-class values' (Lawton, 1975b), even if that were indeed a simple matter in itself.

The most telling part of Ozolins' critique is where he pursues this point and considers the likely effects of Lawton's 'common-culture curriculum' as a curriculum-in-use rather than as a reified abstraction. He points out the way in which Lawton conveniently ignores the work of the French sociologist Pierre Bourdieu (Bourdieu, 1971, 1976) which would raise major questions about the likely articulation between Lawton's curriculum-in-use and aspects of the broader social structure. It is therefore worth quoting Ozolins at some length on this point:

> Bourdieu . . . is concerned to show how it is that the academic curriculum itself serves as an instrument of differentiation and exclusion: it is not that pupils are taught vastly different sorts of curriculum, nor that teachers have prejudicial outlooks on their pupils; rather it is that a common curriculum, 'effectively' taught, will itself be a biased form of education. In *Knowledge and Control* (Young 1971), Bourdieu discusses the education of elites, and the way in which education of certain forms encourages cultural homogeneity among elites by emphasis on an academic curriculum. This curriculum serves to distinguish the elite and (because they fail to master it) severely restricts and rationalizes the life-chances of the working-class pupils. Elsewhere (Dale *et al.* 1976), Bourdieu has amplified these views in two directions: first that the school works in a biased manner by demanding of *every* child what only some children can give – a certain orientation to the culture of the school and the academic curriculum, a certain 'cultural capital' that reflects the cultural level of the home and provides the children of *some* families with the essential skills and attitudes ('cultural ethos') that lead to success in school. It is these children who are rewarded in school when their social gifts are interpreted as natural ability and interest. Secondly the curriculum of the school cannot be treated as a neutral object: some elements, particularly the letters, humanities and social sciences, are peculiarly dependent on the child's cultural capital. They are taught by a pedagogy which makes continual, *implicit* demands on a child's own social and cultural skills – the skills of subtlety, nuance, taste and manner which some children acquire 'naturally' from their own cultural milieu *and which are not capable of an explicit pedagogy*.
>
> Bourdieu's critique seriously questions the 'fairness' of a common curriculum, and also questions another of Lawton's alleged supports for his common curriculum – the work of Rawls (which incidentally and quite amazingly is introduced out of the blue in the *last* paragraph of the book): 'According to ideas about distributive justice which have been discussed by Rawls (1972) and others, it would seem to follow that pupils should have access to the same kind of curriculum unless good reasons can be shown for providing different curricula' (Lawton 1975b, p. 116).
>
> Bourdieu's work, by pointing to the profoundly inegalitarian consequences of a common curriculum, negates Lawton's . . . main thesis; argumentation on this point is not forthcoming from Lawton. (Ozolins, 1979, p. 46)

It is true that Lawton does recognise that we cannot assume that a curriculum which is common in conception will necessarily be enacted and received in an undifferentiated way, nor indeed would he consider it desirable that all pupils should have a *uniform* curriculum (Lawton 1973, 1975b). Yet, as Ozolins points out, these seem to be essentially side issues for Lawton and he clearly believes that, if we can persuade teachers to reflect upon and change inappropriate attitudes, it will be quite feasible to provide all children with the basic core understandings which he has identified. But Bourdieu suggests that the problem is an altogether deeper one and one much less capable of simple solution, certainly within the school. It is not that Lawton's proposals are without their strengths, but there are also strong grounds for taking seriously Bourdieu's argument that the elevation of the cultural arbitraries of particular social groups to the status of universals can contribute to a self-legitimating system of cultural and social reproduction. He tells us that there is *no* pedagogic action 'which does not inculcate some meanings not deducible from a universal principle' and that the work of schooling can always be carried out 'without either those who exercise it or those who undergo it ever ceasing to misrecognize its dependence on the power relations making up the social formation in which it is carried on' (Bourdieu and Passeron, 1977). While this argument clearly creates problems of its own, those who see current proposals for a common curriculum as a major route towards social justice ignore it at their peril. It is therefore little short of astonishing that Lawton – whose familiarity with at least one of the volumes in which Bourdieu's work appears is established via his other citations of it – should choose to do so.

While Bourdieu shows the issues surrounding a common curriculum to be much more complex than Lawton admits, Ozolins himself does not take refuge in these complexities to preach a counsel of despair. He is not to be counted amongst those who argue that there is no form of curriculum strategy which can usefully be employed in schools by those seeking social justice in society and he demonstrates that Lawton tries to justify his own consensus curriculum via a refutation of a caricature of other supposedly left approaches. Lawton is shown to base his critique of 'left' theorists on the attribution to them of the notion that a curriculum in the interests of the working class means a curriculum rooted in and *restricted to a celebration* of working-class life as it is – a view which Ozolins suggests it may be appropriate to attribute to Bantock on the right but is hardly attributable to any serious theorist on the left. Ozolins admits that 'we are only at the beginning of being able to define and elaborate a viable working-class curriculum', but says that 'it is neither philosophically nor educationally an incoherent concept of curricular development' and argues that attempted 'refutations' such as Lawton's should not be a serious deterrent to those who wish to pursue the idea of a curriculum which would *really* be in the interests of the working class. Thus, in place of Lawton's concern to establish a consensus around the concept of 'worthwhile' knowledge, Ozolins himself makes some tentative proposals for a curriculum which discriminates positively[12] in favour of knowledge which would be really useful to working-class pupils. This might well overlap with much of the content of Lawton's own curriculum, but the criteria of selection would be different.[13] This idea resonates with the educational programmes of the nineteenth-century radicals described by Richard Johnson (Johnson, 1979) who saw '*really* useful knowledge' as including knowledge 'concerning our conditions in life . . . [and] how to get out of our present troubles'. While fully democratic access to all forms of knowledge was seen as a future ideal, the immediate priority was a sort of 'spearhead knowledge' committed to the emancipation of the working class and the creation of a form of society in which all would have the right of access to knowledge and justice. Though the modern equivalent of such a curriculum would clearly relate to the realities of working-class life and presumably seek to develop a critique of prevailing society via the sorts of cultural penetrations already present within working-class culture, it would hardly be a mere celebration of it, given the role which writers such as Willis (1977) have suggested it plays in social reproduction. As Ozolins says:

> rather than just a study of working-class culture and working-class life [such a curriculum] must be a study of the relations of the working class to the rest of society: the forces by which this relationship is created and maintained, and the ways in which this relationship can be investigated, questioned and eventually transformed. (Ozolins 1979, p. 50)

In such a curriculum, 'situation-centred learning' is neither inherently limiting nor, as in Lawton's work, merely a way of catching pupils' interest in the disciplines.

While Ozolins' own brief curricular proposals are clearly only in an embryonic stage of development, and indeed are not entirely free from the sorts of weaknesses which he attributes to Lawton's, they do at least make clear that Lawton's is not the only approach to curriculum planning to be considered by those pursuing social justice. It also seems likely that such an approach would be less susceptible to hegemonic incorporation in that it has a much clearer and more consistent view of its purpose than is evident in Lawton's work; furthermore, in a section of the paper on the institutional form of schooling, Ozolins also demonstrates an awareness of the realities and difficulties of pursuing that purpose within such an institutional form. The paper is rather less clear about how its curriculum strategy articulates with other strategies of social change, but its author is quite clear that its purpose is to contribute to the struggle against the hegemonic forces in contemporary society rather than to risk the sort of accommodation with them which might legitimate rather than challenge the status quo. Yet he is clearly not the sort of caricatured 'extremist' with whom Lawton likes to take issue and he takes Lawton's own position sufficiently seriously to want to engage in dialogue about it and its effects. Not all Marxists are 'naïve and simplistic' and Ozolins is merely one of many serious socialist educators who are struggling to understand the complex nature of education under capitalism, to recognise its specificities in particular national and cultural contexts and to devise appropriate strategies of educational and social change. If Lawton and others working along similar lines are genuinely committed to the realisation of social justice, it is to be hoped that they will in future engage in serious dialogue with those on the left who disagree with them, rather than reducing their arguments to caricature.

I now want to make some much briefer comments about the work of those writers associated with the Centre for Applied Research in Education at the University of East Anglia. One of the major criticisms which can be made of Lawton's work is that it remains largely at the level of formal curriculum analysis and is therefore able to avoid confronting the complexity of the real contexts in which educational transactions take place. Culture and curriculum become reified and detached from the contexts of lived experience and hence, also, from the broader structural relations which interpenetrate that experience. The strength of most of the writers associated with CARE lies in their commitment to the integrity of lived experience and their abiding interest in the subjective interpretations of curricular reality made by teachers and pupils.[14] This results partly from the different focus of their interests, for while Lawton (at least until his most recent book) put most of his emphasis on curriculum-planning, the East Anglian group have been more interested in the study of the implementation, evaluation and diffusion of the curriculum. However, while their emphasis on the subjective dimension of curricular change is a useful complement to Lawton's work and certainly a necessary corrective to the crude centre-periphery models of curriculum development imported from the USA[15], it has often attained such a centrality within the work of these school-centred writers that it has served to divert attention away from the broader sociological and political realities of schooling. An understanding of the ways in which curricular meanings are inter-subjectively negotiated and the institutional factors which facilitate or hinder change in schools (Walker and MacDonald, 1976) is absolutely vital to any effective strategy of change but so is an understanding of the ways in which they articulate with the broader power relations of society. The role of teachers' 'habitual and unconscious behaviour patterns' in sustaining traditional modes of pedagogy and the development of self-monitoring techniques amongst teachers as a way of producing and sustaining change (Elliott and Adelman, 1976) are also important areas of work but their real significance can really be grasped only in the context of a fuller exploration of the reasons why teacher behaviour is apparently so generalisable 'across classrooms, subject areas and schools'. In other words, while this work correctly recognises that any realistic strategy of change must address itself to the problem of ideologies *in* education as well as ideologies *about* education (Finn, Grant and Johnson, 1977), it persistently sidesteps the issue of the economic and political conditions in which both exist. It has therefore tended to overemphasise the possibilities for teachers to effect change in schools and for researchers to develop democratic modes of evaluation by bracketing out these wider considerations. Significantly, these writers have, like Lawton, also chosen to ignore the considerable literature generated in the sociology of education on these very issues (Bartholomew, 1974; Whitty, 1974).

This avoidance of broader sociological issues, together with a related distrust of political 'movements' (Stenhouse, 1975), means that such perspectives on the curriculum are, despite their frequent association with liberal and progressive modes of pedagogy, singularly ill-fitted to respond to the current wave of reactionary initiatives in the curriculum field. Barton and Lawn have recently put this case in even stronger terms:

> The CARE unit lays little emphasis on explicating its underlying political assumptions. Where it is evident or implied, one can deduce that there is a strongly optimistic view that revealing information about processes and people will result in increased awareness, partici-

> pation and change by ordinary people. It is radical in that it takes the views of ordinary people seriously, but it can also be seen as conservative in that it does not introduce new questions or challenge the perceptions of the practitioners. Indeed, it may expose in an efficient way its practitioners to the policy-makers and powerful public institutions. It also does not enter into a public debate or theoretical argument which would directly challenge the technological determinism or radical political alternatives evident today.
>
> Perhaps CARE will take note of the warning made by George Orwell in his essay 'Inside the Whale' when he saw in the future a new quietist, passive writing arising which would not fight the world but would be content to 'simply accept it, endure it, record it'. Or will they be influenced, like Mass Observation, which tried to move from a 'naturalistic' to a 'political' perspective because of the political context of the thirties and its crises? Will a siege economy and political conflict in Britain in the 1980s change CARE? (Barton and Lawn 1979, p.14)

While this passage glosses important differences between the various writers at CARE, to which the authors point elsewhere in the paper, it does demonstrate how, although the CARE unit's work differs in significant ways from that of Lawton, it shares his work's ambiguities about the purpose of the enterprise and is even less concerned to place the study of the curriculum and the process of curriculum development within its broader social context. There is, however, already some indication (MacDonald, 1979; Elliott, 1980) that at least some of the writers at CARE are moving into areas of work which will make it increasingly difficult to avoid such issues.

These writers are, as I have suggested earlier, important not only for their own work but also for the influence which they have exerted over the field of curriculum studies in Britain as a whole. Their influence is, as I have said, particularly evident in Open University course E203 (1976) which in turn exerts a major influence over the teaching of curriculum studies in initial and in-service teacher education programmes throughout the country. Even those parts of this Open University course not directly authored by Lawton and the CARE group display characteristics strikingly similar to those identified in their work. The course as a whole exhibits similar ambiguities, a similar optimism about what schools and teachers can achieve and a similar reluctance to address broader structural issues. There are partial exceptions in the contributions of Prescott and Skilbeck but neither really fulfils its initial promise. Thus Prescott raises some important questions about the economic and political dimensions of curricular change in his contribution to unit 5 of the course but concludes rather tamely that they involve 'difficult ideas' which cannot really be pursued in the unit and that it would anyway 'be a pity . . . if this power-political element were to be over-emphasized' (Prescott, 1976). Skilbeck perhaps comes nearest to exploring the relationship between school-based curriculum development and its broader context via a process of situational analysis (Skilbeck, 1976). This certainly combines some of the advantages of the focus of the East Anglian studies with the sort of multi-level decision-making model with which Lawton is now trying to operate. Skilbeck seems to have a rather more developed understanding of the articulation between the various levels he points to but, ultimately, his optimistic 'reconstructionist' outlook on the role of education in social change returns schools to the centre of the stage and diverts our attention away from a more careful consideration of the broader structural context of schooling. Whether the Open University's new curriculum course, being developed in the rather different political climate of the 1980s, will have significantly different characteristics remains to be seen.

I have pointed at various stages of this paper to the institutional separation between curriculum studies as an enterprise and the more established academic disciplines of education. I have also suggested that many of the issues neglected by writers on the curriculum, but of absolutely central importance to the very areas of concern into which curriculum theorists are now beginning to move, have been the subject of considerable debate within the sociology of education over the past decade. Yet there is little sign as yet that those working within the curriculum field in Britain either recognise the significance of those debates for their own work or, where they do, that they are attempting to come to grips with their implications. Thus, they have tended to ignore or caricature such work and have thereby avoided entering into critical dialogue about the nature of education and society and the educational and social policies necessary to change them. Nevertheless, I would want to argue that the whole debate within the sociology of education about the relationship of macro-theories of society and studies of classroom interaction (Hargreaves, 1978, 1980) is directly relevant to the very issues which I have suggested have been consistently neglected or underdeveloped within curriculum studies. Further I would argue that it would be most fruitful to interrogate recent work in curriculum studies with real, as opposed to imagined, forms of Marxist theory.

Thus, for instance, Lawton's model of curriculum decision-making could be explored in terms of those forms of Marxist theory which *do* recognise the specificities and relative autonomies of the different levels with which he is concerned rather than seeing the education system as a monolithic expression of the interests and values of the capitalist ruling class. Such work (e.g. Clarke *et al*, 1979) also addresses questions about the nature of 'lived experience' and the way in which cultures are formed and transformed, issues which relate directly to the interests of the East Anglian group. Must we assume that the reluctance to enter into dialogue with sociologists stems from a fear on the part of the curriculum specialists that a serious confrontation with such questions would lead those of them committed to the pursuance of social justice to advocate rather different practical policies, involving a shift away from narrowly education-centred strategies towards ones which are linked much more directly to other modes of political intervention?

In proposing more of a dialogue between sociologists and curricular theorists, I am not in any way suggesting that curriculum studies would be better incorporated within sociology of education as we know it. One of the great strengths of curriculum studies from the point of view of those committed to social and educational change is that it claims to speak to the worlds of policy and practice and is concerned with developing educational theory as a 'guide [to] action in a desirable direction' (Lawton, 1977). In recent years the sociology of education has sometimes been even more lacking in a sense of purpose than curriculum studies, and observers of theoretical debates in the field could well have been excused for wondering what the whole exercise was for. Yet the issues at the centre of these debates have often had considerable relevance to issues of curricular practice, whether or not practitioners in either field have chosen to recognise it. This is not, I must stress, to suggest that the sociology of education has a set of 'off-the-peg' answers to the problems which curriculum studies has neglected but it has at least tried to address them. It is therefore to be hoped that all those genuinely concerned to explore the relationship between educational practice and social justice in society will seek to overcome some of the suspicion and institutional separation between curriculum studies and the sociology of education. In this we may have something to learn from a number of American writers on the curriculum (Apple, 1979; Giroux, work forthcoming) whose work seems able to transcend the boundaries more easily and fruitfully. It is equally vital that those who see education as part of a broader quest for social justice in society explore more fully how their practice as educators relates to other forms of political action, and this is a task which has scarcely begun on either side of the Atlantic.

Notes

1. The volume does, however, include contributions from some American-based writers who have been associated with the East Anglian group.

2. Lawton's colleagues at London have included Peter Gordon, Maggie Ing, Bill Gibby and Richard Pring, but their work, and his work in collaboration with them, is not discussed in the present paper.

3.The team at the Centre for Applied Research in Education at the University of East Anglia includes Lawrence Stenhouse (director), Barry MacDonald, Rob Walker and Jean Ruddock. Past members include John Elliot, Clem Adelman and David Jenkins.

4. Lawton (1973) and Stenhouse (1975) were amongst the set books for this course; Lawton, Pring, Jenkins, Walker, MacDonald, Elliott and Adelman were amongst the consultants and unit authors.

5. Lawton (1977) has himself argued that 'we have very high quality philosophy of education, sociology of education and psychology, but much less respectable theory at the level of curriculum decision-making'.

6. Lawton is active within the Schools Council and has recently become the Deputy Director of the University of London Institute of Education.

7. Entwistle (1979), on the other hand, mentions this fact (albeit grudgingly) in a footnote but conveniently ignores it in his text!

8. See, for instance, Willis (1977), Young and Whitty (1977).

9. Only a somewhat ambiguous reference to the use of the term 'hegemony' by 'some Marxist writers, following Gramsci'.

10. This last volume (Lawton, 1980) only became available as this paper was being written and my assessment of it should be considered provisional.

11. This may be because he draws heavily in this section of Lawton (1977) on the work of Moore (1974), a philosopher of education. In Lawton (1973, 1975b) greater prominence is given to the role of sociological questions in curriculum-planning. Whether Lawton, himself a former sociologist of education, no longer considers such questions vital is not clear.

12. Ozolins does not, however, see his curriculum as relevant only to working-class pupils. Rather, he claims that 'in the questions it poses, and in the kind of understanding it attempts and the control over one's life that it asserts, it is a universal curriculum, a worthwhile curriculum for any school to adopt'.

13. Lawton's criteria for selection of curricular knowledge in Lawton (1977) combine 'worthwhileness and relevance' (WR) on the same scale. I suspect that Ozolins would regard this as sleight-of-hand, but both concepts seem, anyway, to be more abstract than those utilised by Ozolins.

14. Clearly the various writers at CARE differ in their emphases and these brief comments by no means do justice to the complexities of their work.

15. It would also have to be a vital component of any broader sociological theory which was not purely mechanistic in its conception of change.

Bibliography

Apple, M.W. (1979) *Ideology and Curriculum*, Routledge and Kegan Paul, London

Bantock, G.H. (1968) *Culture, Industrialisation and Education*, Routledge and Kegan Paul, London

Bartholomew, J. (1974) 'Sustaining Hierarchy through Teaching and Research' in Flude and Ahier (1974)

Barton, L. and Lawn, M. (1979) 'Back Inside the Whale: a Curriculum Case Study', unpublished paper, Westhill College, Birmingham; revised version to be published in *Interchange*, Ontario Institute for Studies in Education, Ontario, 1981

Barton, L. and Meighan, R. (eds.) (1978) *Sociological Interpretations of Schooling and Classrooms: A Reappraisal*, Nafferton Books, Driffield

Bourdieu, P. (1971) 'Systems of Education and Systems of Thought' in Young (1971)

Bourdieu, P. (1976) 'Schooling as a Conservative Force' in Dale, Esland and MacDonald (1976)

Bourdieu, P. and Passeron, J-C. (1977) *Reproduction in Education, Society and Culture*, Sage Publications, London

Clarke, J., Critcher, C. and Johnson, R. (1979) *Working Class Culture*, Hutchinson, London

Dale, R., Esland, G. and MacDonald, M. (eds.) (1976) *Schooling and Capitalism*, Routledge and Kegan Paul, London

Elliott, J. (1980). 'Who should monitor performance in schools' in Sockett (1980)

Elliott, J. and Adelman, C. (1976) *Innovation at the Classroom Level*, unit 28 of Open University course E203, Open University (1976)

Entwistle, H. (1978) *Class, Culture and Education*, Methuen, London

Entwistle, H. (1979) *Antonio Gramsci*, Routledge and Kegan Paul London

Finn, D., Grant. N. and Johnson, R. (1977) 'Social Democracy, Education and the Crisis', *Working Papers in Cultural Studies*, 10

Flude. M. and Ahier, J. (eds.) (1974) *Educability, Schools and Ideology*, Croom Helm, London

Giroux, H. (work forthcoming) *Ideology, Culture and the Process of Schooling*, The Falmer Press, Lewes

Hargreaves, A. (1978) 'The Significance of Classroom Coping Strategies', in Barton and Meighan (1978)

Hargreaves, A. (1980) 'Synthesis and the Study of Strategies' in Woods (1980)

Hirst, P.H. and Peters, R.S. (1970) *The Logic of Education*, Routledge and Kegan Paul, London

Johnson, R. (1979) '*Really* Useful Knowledge' in Clarke, Critcher and Johnson (1979)

Lawton, D. (1973) *Social Change, Educational Theory and Curriculum Planning*, University of London Press, London

Lawton, D. (1975a) *Investigating Society*, Hodder and Stoughton London

Lawton, D. (1975b) *Class, Culture and the Curriculum*, Routledge and Kegan Paul, London

Lawton, D. (1977) *Education and Social Justice*, Sage Publications London

Lawton, D. (1979) 'The End of the Secret Garden?', inaugural lecture, University of London Institute of Education

Lawton, D. (1980) *The Politics of the School Curriculum*, Routledge and Kegan Paul, London

MacDonald, B. (1979) 'Hard Times : Educational Accountability in England', *Educational Analysis*, vol.1(1)

Moore, T.W. (1974) *Educational Theory*, Routledge and Kegan Paul, London

Open University (1976) *Curriculum Design and Development*, course E203, Open University Press, Milton Keynes

Ozolins, U. (1979) 'Lawton's "Refutation" of a Working-Class Curriculum', *Melbourne Working Papers, 1979*, University of Melbourne

Prescott, W. (1976) 'Culture and Curriculum – Two Contrasting Approaches' in *Curriculum Change and Social Change*, unit 5 of Open University course E203, Open University (1976)

Rawls, J. (1972) *A Theory of Justice*, Oxford University Press, London

Skilbeck, M. (1976) 'School-Based curriculum Development' in *School-based Curriculum Development*, unit 26 of Open University course E203, Open University (1976)

Sockett, H. (ed.) (1980) *Accountability in the English Educational System*, Hodder and Stoughton, London

Stenhouse, L. (1975) *An Introduction to Curriculum Research and Development*, Heinemann, London

Taylor, P.H. (ed.) (1979) *New Directions in Curriculum Studies*, The Falmer Press, Lewes

Walker, R. and MacDonald, B. (1976) *Curriculum Innovation at School Level*, unit 27 of Open University course E203, Open University (1976)

Whitty, G. (1974) 'Sociology and the Problem of Radical Educational

Change' in Flude and Ahier (1974)
Williams, R. (1961) *The Long Revolution*, Chatto and Windus, London
Willis, P. (1977) *Learning to Labour : How Working Class Kids Get Working Class Jobs*, Saxon House, Farnborough
Woods, P.E. (ed,) (1980) *Pupil Strategies*, Croom Helm, London
Young, M.F.D. (ed.) (1971) *Knowledge and Control*, Collier Macmillan, London
Young, M.F.D. and Whitty G. (eds.) (1977) *Society, State and Schooling*, The Falmer Press, Lewes

3 RADICAL EDUCATION: THE PEDAGOGICAL SUBTEXT

Maureen Clark and David Davies

We intend in this article to discuss the curricular strategies of four radical education journals. We want initially to attempt to 'locate' them in relation to some developments in the sociology of education. We will argue that the 'political' positions and corresponding pedagogical assumptions of these journals are closely bound to the critique which developed within the new sociology of education, of its own radical-libertarian approach to educational issues. This, along with the contradictions inherent in the social-democratic view of educational policy, is at the root of what is widely experienced as *crisis* within education. It is against the backcloth of this crisis that current strategies for curriculum development and the consequences this has for teacher practice must be set.

Recent critiques of educational policy and practice have provided a point of departure for the analysis of radical-socialist practice in the school (Finn, Grant and Johnson, 1977). In this view, there is a crisis within education which is an expression of the crisis within social democracy and it can only be understood in this context. It is symptomatic and an integral part of the more general and pervasive crisis of economy and the state. In situating the educational system in this way it becomes possible to attempt an explanation of the developing and competing strands of education thought which have been typical of the debate amongst educationalists committed to progressive practice in schools. The radical educational journals that we are to examine have, as their declared intention, the aim of making an intervention in this debate at a theoretical and practical level.

Ostensibly, educational policy within the social-democratic tradition aimed to increase access to educational institutions so that a more just and equal society could be achieved. This was to divorce the educational system almost entirely from the expectations and pressures of other societal systems and to give to education an ameliorative function that it could never fulfil.

With the growth and establishment of the Labour Party in British society, the party's chances of being accepted as a legitimate part of the bourgeois state apparatus depended on its gaining political respectability. This could only be grasped by the acceptance of the parliamentary road to a more just society based on meritocratic competition and not on socialism. Reforms were to take place within the given structures of the state; the state and its institutions were accepted as neutral in the struggle between the social classes – they were as potentially capable of being used in the interests of the working class as they had been in the interests of the dominant classes. The main emphasis of Labour Party educational policy was on improving the means of access to educational institutions, but alongside the commitment to meritocratic principles was a belief in the need to make society more egalitarian. These two intertwined but essentially opposed strands – equality and equality of opportunity – reflect the initial development of educational policy within the working class and trades unionism, and also point to the party's reliance for intellectual guidance on Fabian philosophy. An insight into the tension within this philosophy is given by Taylor, Walton and Young (1974) when they write: 'Fabianism attempts the impossible: it tries to create a truly meritocratic society without transforming the property relationships which work continuously to obstruct such a competitive egalitarianism.' The Labour Party, rather than offering a critique of capitalism, concerned itself with extending equal access to elite positions and with developing a welfare state to counteract the more destructive effects of meritocracy.

The educational policy of the Labour Party has remained safely within the confines of the capitalist state; any agitational movements of a socialist nature which developed within the working class and which were seen to challenge this framework were treated with great suspicion and eventually 'voted off' (if indeed they ever appeared) the educational agenda. As far as modern 'labourism' is concerned there has been little attempt to consider working-class needs in relation to education outside of the social-democratic-meritocratic ideology. Whilst the total emphasis remained on the improvement of means of access, of increasing opportunities within the state system, there was little chance that either the content or purpose of education would be given serious attention. These historical tendencies had significant implications for the emergence of 'socialist' and 'radical' education in Britain. It is precisely because within the dominant working-class and Labour movements education was considered a neutral commodity which should be available to all, that a *socialist* theory of the curriculum, of the *content* of education, of schooling and of pedagogy was not developed by the socialist movement. However, as the age of 'affluence' was increasingly incapable of delivering prosperity and opportunity to masses of working people, *education itself*, tthe means by which access to affluence was to be guaranteed, increasingly became the site of dispute and struggle.

The 1960s can be seen as a watershed in British society. This was the period in which the essentially 'provisional' nature of what, following Gramsci (1971, p.12), we might call the hegemonic structure, became clear as increased industrial militancy, oppositional and political movements challenged the authority of dominant groups. It was the period in which the intricate and delicate network of relationships which combine in an ever 'moving equilibrium' began to tear. The shape of the hegemonic structure altered to admit and incorporate into a different set of relationships newly dominant forces. This was a clear response to the changing nature of the deepening crisis of capitalism. It was within this particular conjuncture that educational policy increasingly came to be formulated to meet governmental and societal demands that it should produce a labour force competent enough to fulfil the labour requirements of industry. Yet it was precisely at this period that critiques of conventional schooling were being developed from *within* the teaching profession and state schooling system.

Stuart Hall notes that 'there are long, deep-seated resistances within the philosophy of state education to any attempt to measure schooling directly in terms of the needs and requirements of industry' (Hall, 1979, p.18). During the early days of the Labour Party the aim had been to 'rescue children from the clutches of employers and to define education *against* the demands of employment' (Finn *et al.*, 1977, p.157) but since then the emphasis has increasingly fallen on the need to improve educational attainment so that the needs of the economy can be met. Hall again: 'Clear evidence is supposed to exist that standards are falling: the principal witnesses to this alarming trend are employers who complain about the quality of job applicants: this, in turn, must be having an effect on the efficiency and productivity of the nation – at a time when recession puts a premium on improving both.' (1979, p.18)

During the 1960s teacher autonomy and professionalism were unchallenged (Finn *et al.*, 1977, p. 181). This reliance on the teachers' professional capabilities, coupled with the social concern developing among them as a result of compensatory policies (Karabel and Halsey, p.27), led to what we will call the *radical-libertarian* approach to education. This radical-libertarian approach brought into question the social democratic view that by the equalising of access to educational opportunity a more equal and more economically sound society would result. It also began to question the idea that the curriculum embodied society's most worthwhile knowledge. It moved then from a normative paradigm to an interpretive approach and focused particularly on class-room interaction, the social relations of the school and the content of education.

The ideological consensus which had long been a characteristic of British educational policy was not at an end: the critique of educational knowledge along with the implications this had for an understanding of its relationship to the power structures meant that the social-democratic view of education as unproblematically 'good' was being questioned by academics and by classroom teachers. The focus of research moved from *access*, to the *nature* of education itself within a power structure. The critique of educational knowledge with its roots in the sociology of knowledge led to the questioning of the commonsense assumptions on which the social hierarchy of the school (and society) is based. Teachers and pupils were given key roles in the questioning of the underlying assumptions of everyday life: if knowledge was a social construct they were seen as agents of social change.

This is, of course, the focus of the major criticisms of the new sociology of education: it did not yield a purchase on structural problematics. Its failure to address the historical development of schooling, or the structural relationships of the educational system, and the implications this had for teacher practice, encouraged the belief that radical change could be placed in the hands of the individual. It did not address actual classroom experience which contradicted this belief. It did not offer an analysis by which this might be overcome. Hence Whitty's use of the term 'possibilitarianism' to describe its essentially humanistic approach. Whitty makes the further point that this not only led to individual disillusionment but, perhaps more important, it also encouraged a 'schizophrenic' approach to the practice of teaching. This was noted by Keddie (1975, p.139) and also by Whitty (1977, p.38) himself, who comments on the persistence of positivistic modes of teaching even when acknowledgement is given to the desirability of the practice of freedom in the classroom; Sharp and Green (1976) are useful here, too.

In its early days, then, the new sociology of education was a cultural rather than a political critique. Its roots in phenomenology and ethnomethodology and its relationship to the sociology of knowledge ensured that it focused on the commonsense world rather than on political and ideological structures. The legitimacy or otherwise of societal institutions was outside its frame of reference. Karabel and Halsey make a further point that this critique of education took a cultural rather than a political form because in the late 1960s 'cultural rather than political forms of radicalism influenced the values and life styles of students' (1977, p.49). It was these students who were involved in research leading to the development of the 'new' sociology of education. Perhaps it is in the failure to radicalise dominant forms of social-democratic politics that a reason for the turn towards culturalist 'solutions' lies.

This is not the place to develop these arguments in detail, yet it should be noted that the development of culturalist perspectives took place at a time when, for many radical and socialist teachers, the Labour Party was losing its ability to *defend* working-class culture, let alone advance its interests against those of the dominant class. The increasing importance of the Labour Party and the unions within the state and parliamentary apparatus bore witness, in this view, to the displacement of traditional defensive working-class culture and the incorporation of parts of the socialist tradition into the capitalist system. The authors of a seminal review of the period noted:

> The full absorption of the Labour Party into its parliamentary role within the state (the completion of a long historical trajectory) and the partial incorporation into the state apparatus of the trade unions, on the back of an 'affluent' reading of the post-war situation, had real political consequences for the working class, dismantled real defences. (Clarke *et al.*, 1976, p.38)

Thus the social-democratic view of education was not only incapable of transforming social and ideological conditions – it actually led to the recuperation of potential working-class opposition to the dominant culture. Not only were transformations off the agenda but no struggles could take place on the terrain of education either. The growth of comprehensive schooling, fully supported by the Labour Party, extended the meritocratic principle without calling into question the fundamental material and class inequalities which had provided the impulse for change in the first place.

A further point can be made here. Though comprehensive schooling, as it is presently organised, continues to close off opportunities for the working class *per se*, it has opened up career opportunities for many potentially radical teachers as well as influencing their broader political commitment to meritocratic ideology. The opportunity to develop a curriculum in accordance with progressive principles encouraged teachers to experiment with issues relevant to the local environment of their schools, to involve themselves in multi-cultural studies, or to expend their time, energy and expertise in the pastoral and counselling services within the school. Progressivism and curricula reform were instrumental in binding potentially radical teachers to the social-democratic view of education.

It has been said that the new sociology of education is a developing tradition of enquiry. It moved from its initial interpretive approach to one in which a confrontation with Marxist social theory could not be avoided. It is within this conjuncture, that we situate the journals we are to consider. They are: *Radical Education*, *Teachers' Action*, *Socialist Teacher* and *Teaching London Kids*. Their basic political and pedagogical assumptions can be related to what has already been said: they are the response of radical, politicised teachers to the crisis in meritocratic ideology, to the recognition that liberation and success for the few is dependent on the oppression and failure of the many. Moreover, they are also a response to the limitations of an unpoliticised progressivism, an approach that, whilst questioning traditional relationships within the school and attempting to make education more meaningful to the pupils involved, fails to take into account the wider social and political relationships of the educational system (Bernstein, 1977, p.65). The journals are an attempt by radical teachers to analyse the crisis in society in educational terms and to understand the implications it has for their practice and the lives of their pupils. The social context in which they work is a vibrant one; its dimensions – and the consequences it has for their pupils' life chances – immense. Hebdige (1979, pp. 82-3) sees it thus:

> The widespread disillusionment amongst working-class people with the Labour Party and Parliamentary politics in general, the decline of the Welfare State, the faltering economy, the continuing scarcity of jobs and adequate housing, the loss of community, the failure of consumerism to satisfy real needs, and the perennial round of industrial disputes, shutdowns and picket line clashes, all served to create a sense of diminishing returns which stood in stark contrast to the embattled optimism of the earlier period.

The present debate about and within education is taking place in a context in which the 'diminishing returns' experienced, particularly by the working class, since the latter part of the 1960s has contributed in its own way to a swing to the right in political and educational thought. Informed by 'those three ventriloquist voices of the radical right, the *Mail*, the *Sun* and the *Express*' (Hall, 1979, p. 18), the working class has joined forces with the radical right in their call that progressivism should be abandoned and educational standards re-established.

It is the aim of the radical education journals to explore the means by which a socialist intervention can be made in this debate about and within education. Finn *et al.* note that the debate about education is usually constructed by those not directly involved in the educational system but that it 'forms part of a general political discourse . . . part of a history of hegemony'; these debates 'are a regional instance of the process of bidding for the consent of the governed' (1977, p.148). In their various ways editorial groups and contributors attempt to intervene in these debates by seeking to develop a socialist theory and practice of education. They pose the question whether and with what success their pedagogical practice addresses the politics of schooling. Their practice as socialist teachers is part of a more general response to the political discourse in which schooling is situated. The complex nature of this response is clearly detailed by Paul Willis: 'no institutional objective, no moral or pedagogical initiative, moves in the clear still air of good intention and Newtonian cultural mechanics. Every move must be considered in relation to its context and likely circles of effectiveness within the netherworld (usually to institutional and official eyes) of cultural reproduction and the main world of social class relationships' (1977, pp.178-9).

Just as the level and focus of political analysis varies between journals so do the strategies suggested for curricula innovation. Strategies are often implied rather than made explicit. With the exception of *Teaching London Kids* there is very little discussion of the actual content of curricula, very few examples of lessons taught or materials used, although the reviewing of new books and teaching material is an established part of each journal. Rather a pedagogical *subtext* is inscribed in their analysis of various aspects of the educational system, a subtext which developed in response to the professional and political practices of their contributors. In order to take the analysis further we will attempt to situate the basic perspectives of the journals in relation to critical views of education; in doing so, we will raise questions about the implications of each journal's pedagogical subtext for curricular practice.

The Journals

Radical Education

Radical Education first appeared in the autumn of 1974 and, as a self-confessed general educational journal had two stated aims. The first of these was to work towards the development of a socialist theory of education and the second to counter what they saw as the fragmentation of the eduational 'left'. In their first editorial they argue that, though socialists have ideas about education, they have for too long relied for guidance on the work of orthodox educational theoreticians to inform their classroom practice. Following from this, the need for a coherent socialist theory of education which would stand comparison with that of capitalist economy has not been appreciated. They suggest that the way forward is by a radical critique of the educational process, a critique unhindered by sectional loyalties but made substantive by the application of socialist analysis informed by practice.

A central concern is the analysis of the the social class position of teachers. A simplistic notion of this is rejected in favour of one which recognises that teachers have a particular ideological and political relationship to the state. This has implications for their practice as teachers – they can unquestioningly help to reproduce the status quo or they can develop a sympathetic awareness of the needs of their pupils and can educate them to the *source* of their oppression: an initial choice is required of the teacher.

Radical Education emphasises the professional status of teachers: they have something to offer that is worthwhile. They reject the more extreme notions of progressivism (freedom in the classroom, an undisciplined approach to learning and teaching) whilst seeking to retain many of the gains made by progressive methods, such as teacher autonomy in the classroom and control over curricular developments, because this is not only central to any strategy for change but is a means by which they, as working people, can defend their autonomy. Whilst recognising the place of educational research in curricular development they also insist that developments in pedagogy must be based on actual classroom experience and practice. A change in the social relationships of the classroom and a move towards a collective form of discipline is dependent on this happening. In the face of the Great Debate and the present restructuring of education, *Radical Education* argues that the state has recognised a major strength in the educational system: the power for change which lies within it and therefore within the grasp of teachers and pupils. If the educational system is both the site and stake of the class struggle it is this 'space' which the state has recognised and seeks to redefine and contain.

The need to develop a socialist theory of education and pedagogy is central to the *Radical Education* project; its components are reviewed, analysed and discussed but, increasingly, the focus has become the wider structural crisis in which the educational system is situated: until this is understood in a critical way it seems that little progress can be made.

Teachers' Action

Teachers' Action Collective started publishing in 1975. In one of the earlier issues of their journal (no. 4) they make this statement about their position as teachers in relation to society:

> Teachers' Action believes that the nature of the schooling system is directly attributable to the demands of monopoly capitalism. Just as machine tools are produced for industry so is labour power produced for the same end – capitalist production. We as teachers work on that assembly line and so put ourselves firmly, without pride or guilt, in the category of productive worker.

From this follows their aim in publishing their journal: 'In our journal we want to examine the conflicts in schooling to identify the opposing interests involved in the struggle and to develop strategies and tactics for change.' Some five years later these statements are still central to the Teachers' Action perspective. In issue no. 13 they state:

> We started our activity with a clear analysis of the relationship of schools to the economy and drew conclusions from this analysis coupled with our experience of the classroom, about the class position of teachers, the class position of pupils, the interest and potential of parents, administration and other forces at play in school.

The perspectives summarised here select and inform the educational and societal issues which are the basis of the articles published in the journal.

The approach is essentially political rather than 'educational' but they would argue that the two cannot be separated. Educational practice, i.e., schooling, belongs to the field of political debate and political struggle, and, as teachers, they see themselves as active agents committed to bringing about social change. In order to do this they seek the support of parents and, most importantly, their pupils.

> The classroom teacher must create and participate in a forum at the place of work itself to debate structure and content with students and parents. It is time we translated the political arguments, the social justifications, the educational principles we so heatedly debate in our journals into a language that students and parents understand. (*Teachers' Action*, no. 7, p.17)

Teachers' Action is a forum for teachers consciously engaged in attempting to change their work situation, but this action is very much part of their intention to bring about a change in the social relationships of the wider society. By situating themselves quite unambiguously within the working class as worker-teachers they seek to contribute to and use the collective power of the one class which is historically and strategically placed to bring about change. Their class membership is determined, not by their life style or security of employment, but because of their relationship to the productive process. They are productive workers for capital; they produce labour power for industry; they do this by skilling, grading and disciplining the future workforce. The school then is as much a part of the industrial processes of society as any factory, and teachers, rather than being transmitters of a commodity called education, are organisers and trainers of young people. A teacher, however, has one great advantage over most other industrial workers: he 'can modify the machinery he uses (the curriculum) to process his final product'. Contrary to groups such as Socialist Teachers' Alliance, the aim of the Teachers' Action Collective is not the development of groups of teachers who will seize control of the National Union of Teachers. The union, because of its historic relationship to capital, is not representative of grassroot movements. The future developments of schooling will not therefore be decided at National Union of Teachers conferences: it is 'our conviction that the political battles of schooling are being and will be fought in and around the schooling institution itself' (*Teachers' Action*, no. 13, editorial). This conviction leads them to seek an 'independent teachers' organisation outside the structure of the National Union of Teachers, outside the structure of political parties' (*Teachers' Action*, no. 13, editorial).

The journals chart current examples of these political battles. They reflect the position of teachers as workers in a variety of (mainly) London schools who face redundancies, school closures, compulsory transfers, falling numbers – in other words, the practical outcomes of cuts in government educational spending. Alongside this is the second level of political activity, crucial to Teachers' Action analysis: 'pupils are changing the school institution through their resistance' (*Teachers' Action*, no. 11, editorial). If schooling is about grading and skilling then an increasing number of school students are resisting this function, and, in the process, changing the nature of the institution. The increasing number of pupils in the sixth forms is not an indication of the growth in academic appetite. It reflects an employment situation where the only certainty is such jobs as are available are boring and routine and, also, the recognition by pupils that their CSE qualifications, no matter how 'relevant' the course material might have been, are worthless as far as employers are concerned.

If pupils are active agents of change within the schools, where does this place the socialist teacher? Teachers need to develop a collective strength, and effective strategies for action. They need a strong power base in the staffroom in order to resist decisions being made, without their being consulted, about their place of work, the curriculum they teach or the internal procedures of the school. They must 'combine their strength with that of the kids wherever their interests meet' (Teachers' Action, no. 5, p.5) and discuss with parents the erosion of educational gains. It is from this united base that concrete and effective action will come. Little credence is given to the notion that education within school can be a means of liberation and the contradictory elements present within the transmission of knowledge and control is therefore generally missed. Also missing are theoretical exploration of the potential for change through education and an analysis of the ideological work done by schools.

Socialist Teacher

The first issue of *Socialist Teacher*, the journal of the Socialist Teachers Alliance, appeared in 1977 and set itself two main objectives: the first was to seek to establish unity in action among the mass of teachers around a programme of basic demands; the second to develop a coherent analysis of current educational practice and the role and position both of teachers and of the educational system within the present social framework (*Socialist Teacher*, no. 1).

The journal is essentially about political action as it applies to teachers. Whilst recognising the importance of the Trades Union Movement and the National Union of Teachers it is sceptical about whether they in fact represent the true interests of working people, in general, and teachers, in particular. Whilst encouraging teachers to take an active part in their local branch meetings, they seek the establishment of a strong rank and file movement *within* the union rather than an alternative movement separated from union policies. They seek to defend the advances made in education but argue that they can no longer rely on the Department of Education and Science to do this so they 'must organise independently and build links with the broad Labour and trade union movement'. A constant emphasis is the need to establish left-wing unity and avoid sectarianism. This was an important reason for the establishment of Socialist Teachers' Alliance. They are also concerned to develop political consciousness among classroom teachers – they feel that this can best be achieved by seeking a unity between all those with socialist sympathies. The support of such teachers will develop as the result of 'patient agitation, education and organisation' so that a mass struggle and a deep-rooted conviction will form the basis of the challenge to union policies.

The overwhelming impression gained from the journals is that they are devoted to matters relating to union affairs. However, Faraday and Tyndale are also discussed, together with the implications of falling school numbers, discipline, racism and salary structures; there are also book reviews, and articles on the politics of education, schools in Mozambique and Russia, developments in further education, the Great Debate, class size, APU and Taylor proposals. A wide range of topics interesting to the critical teacher is therefore covered in the journals.

Teaching London Kids

Teaching London Kids is a magazine for classroom teachers, particularly those working in London schools. It explores the pattern of practice and the difficulties faced by teachers, the inter-relationship of school and community, the important part played by language in teaching and learning and 'the way in which the power structure of society affects the orgaisation and curriculum of schools'. Above all else, it is 'concerned with presenting positive strategies for action'. Thus, whilst acknowledging and fully recognising the reproductive role of education in society, *TLK* emphasises that the curriculum can help children to a better understanding of that society and of their potential for contributing to social change. A central concern of this magazine, then, is the practice of progressive-socialist teachers in state schools and how this practice can develop into a positive strategy for action. Its appeal was initially to teachers of English, but under this one subject-heading many areas of experience are discussed. It seeks to address the determining influence of the power structure within society on the organisation and curriculum of schools and the question of how, in spite of this, a curriculum relevant to the needs of working-class pupils can be developed. *TLK* is therefore primarily concerned with teacher action within the classroom and discussions dwell at length on curriculum development: suggestions, ideas, sample worksheets, pictures and reviews of newly published material form the bulk of journal contributions, these being supplemented, and situated in a wider social, political and international context, by interviews and articles which seek to make teachers aware of theoretical as well as practical issues.

Trade union involvement has always been part of the *TLK* platform but it has tended to be implicit rather than a dominant force within the magazine. However, with the mobilisation of teachers over racial issues and with the experience of stringent cuts in education and welfare spending by the government, their commitment to Trade Union activity and political action becomes clear. This is reflected in the editorial comment in issues no. 12 and no. 14, and adds weight to the importance *TLK* attaches to curricular innovation and teacher activity in school. Careful assessment of initiatives taken and progress made will be necessary if *TLK* is to be clear about its strengths and weaknesses, if it is 'to take on the lunacies of the right, and win' (*Teaching London Kids*, no. 14, editorial).

Detailed theoretical analyses of an overtly political nature are lacking, as is any attempt to develop a socialist theory of education. The need for these is implied and political and socialist aims underly the form of the articles and discussions published, but their *raison d'être* is practical rather than theoretical concerns.

Teachers, Social Change and Class Struggle

We now turn to the relationship between teacher activity in the classroom and in society. We also wish to raise questions about the autonomy of pedagogy and the class situation of teachers. This is especially important because it relates to their understanding of the concept of 'struggle' and its relationship to teacher practice and the curriculum. In seeking to detail examples from the journals of the characteristics of a socialist pedagogy, we will attempt to show that, though each journal may well emphasise different levels of involvement, their recognition of the class nature of this struggle is what separates them from the position of the radical-libertarian teacher.

The Schools and the Conjunctural Context

The actual activities of teachers are not irrelevant to socialist or (more accurately) Marxist understandings of the functions and processes of education structures (schools, in particular). But they have been generally ignored by Marxist writers on education who have tended to view schooling as either a reflection or a reproduction of other relationships, located outside the structure of schooling in the economy, labour market or 'social system in general'. Bowles and Gintis have been influential in arguing this position: 'the social relationships of education – the relationships between administrators and teachers, teachers and students, students and students, and students and their work – replicate the hierarchal division of labour' (1976, p.131). Our emphasis would stress that the particularities of teacher activity needs to be recovered and analysed, and understood, not as an automatic *function* for a wider system or an 'essentialist' element within it, but, rather, grasped in terms of its specificity within a *conjuncture*.

Pedagogies and their associated ideologies cannot be simply 'read off' from the logic of capitalism (Willis, 1977, p.178). We must move away from the structural determinism of some approaches, which emphasise a direct correspondence between schooling and the social formation, and seek to identify the particular components of teacher activity which address a particular historical moment and which may have some independence from the determining influence of structure. Willis also notes this possiblity: 'Progressivism and RSLA . . . have actually addressed real problems, have protected kids a little longer from the harshness and inequality of industry, and have helped to give them – in unintended and unexpected ways of course – a definite kind of insight and cultural advance not available to their parents' (1977, p.179).

We are suggesting that what goes on in the classroom is not *just* a reflection of what goes on elsewhere. Pedagogies have their own levels of specificity, but this also raises the problem of the ease with which the mainstream culture can recoup areas which initially were in opposition to it: within the school, areas such as 'women's studies' and 'black studies' – areas which are potentially liberating for pupils – once accepted as part of the legitimate curriculum, can be as readily used to grade pupils as any other, enhancing the teacher's status and devaluing the pupil's.

Gramsci's (1971, p.177) use of the term 'conjunctural' is illuminating here. The conjuctural is an area defined by the 'incessant and persistant efforts' of the ruling group as they seek to conserve and reform a society riven by a deep-seated crisis. The crisis is the 'maturing of incurable contradictions' and a conjuncture arises as a result of 'organic' movements; it is therefore not stable but its nature changes as a result of the shifting relationships and changing combinations of societal institutions. A conjuncture then is a set of 'immediate and ephemeral characteristics' of the economic system and, as far as this paper is concerned, gives rise to debates *about* the school, the content of curriculum, the professional skills of teachers, the need for testing and measurement of attainment and the call for a return to standards. It is, in Gramsci's formulation, on this terrain that the forces of opposition gather to direct their attack.

But this suggests that the ruling group 'define' the area of debate, even though it may be 'predefined' for them by the conjunctural phenomena which are symptoms of the organic movements: their defence tactics, as they seek to maintain hegemony, draws attention to the deep-seated structural contradictions of capitalist society. Within the school, i.e., at the institutional level, teacher practice can operate at a level which points to aspects of everyday experience which are crucial to the maintenance of capitalist social relations but which can be studied in such a way that a critical awareness develops within pupils. If teachers do not actually 'define' an area of debate, they may in fact be instrumental in drafting the initial agenda. They can begin a process which helps make transparent the social relationships of capitalism: the skills needed to decode the taken-for-granted world can be developed within the classroom.

> We did not create the school situation but we go on working within it because we believe that there are possibilities for conveying to pupils the ideas that we think are important and of offering them an alternative existence within the schools . . . We believe that we should try to educate our pupils into recognising the source of oppression and not merely its surface features.' (Radical Education, no. 4, editorial).

Social practices which are essential components of the reproductive mechanisms of capitalism can be detached from mainstream understanding by subjecting them to critical examination in the classroom – their hidden relationships thus become more clear. By taking such everyday practices and making them 'strange' they become 'known' by pupils; they can be activated and turned against their established reproductive function which in turn becomes more readily resisted. It is such examples of the pedagogical subtext that we will discuss.

We have indicated that a major concern of this paper is to raise questions about *how* the school system and the pedagogies it sponsors reproduce themselves. This is to direct attention away from how the school reproduces something else – capitalist social relations for example – and to examine the articulation of other processes within the school. Such processes do not necessarily relate to each other, nor to the reproductive processes of the school for the wider society, in a harmonious way. We thus reject the 'notion of a social formation as a simple structure in which economic factors will be immediately and transparently translated to the political and ideological levels' (Hall, 1979, p. 14) in favour of one which emphasises the need to be sensitive to the various and distinct movements working within a structure at any one historical moment. Hall argues that it is the 'condensation at any particular historical moment' of these contradictions which defines a conjuncture. It is the awareness of these contradictions and the ability to activate them against mainstream definitions which marks out the space within which the socialist teacher can work.

Pedagogies, then have their own level of specificity: they can develop and contribute to a pupil's awareness in a manner which is separate from their reproductive function. If we aim to point to those areas of the curriculum which do not unproblematically contribute to the ideological work of the school, we must also recognise that schooling must be for some children a valid educational experience, and that because its articulation with other levels of the social formation is not static, predetermined or necessarily harmonious, schools can produce those who are critical of its (and society's) processes and meanings.

Attitudes of the Journals

The radical educational journals are written for and by teachers who are practical and political educational activists. Their practice is informed in varying degrees by a critically formulated response to the social relations of capitalism. There is general agreement with the view that meaningful interventions within the context of the politics of education are desirable and possible. *Teachers' Action*, the most anti-theoreticist of the journals we are considering, notes 'the possibility of creating a curriculum wich can assist the process of self-realisation in the working class' (*Teachers' Action*, no. 6, editorial) given that there is a change in the social relationships of the classroom. The emphasis on, and understanding of the nature of the 'struggle' has taken different forms within the broad spectrum of radical education. The roots of the *Teachers' Action* analysis are the class struggle taking place in the classroom and in the need for teachers to recognise within their pupils a potential for revolutionary change: pupils are not deprived citizens – rather they are 'a section of the working class whose exploitation begins long before they receive their first wage package' (*Teachers' Action*, no. 7, p. 23). This approach is inherently critical of the *Radical Education* perspective, 'which leaves the struggle of pupils out of the struggle of the working class'. Further, 'we as teachers must actively engage in the pupils' struggle, recognising its revolutionary potential – if not we are left to teach about 'the struggle' in a traditional and abstract way'.

Radical Education works from the assumption that only if the 'struggle' is understood in all its complexity and its many levels laid bare by detailed analysis can progress be made in the sphere of practical activity. Only with a fuller understanding of the nature of capitalist society will progress be made towards the development of a socialist theory of education. Full recognition is given to the contradictory processes at work and therefore no simplistic definitions of the nature of class relationships or of the relationships between school and society is offered. It is imperative for socialist teachers to detail the areas in which oppositional practices might be developed 'exploiting the gaps and contradictions in the system' and, importantly, developing and fighting for strategies which will 'maximise the possibilities of such a practice' (*Radical Education*, no. 8, p. 25).

There is, then, a significant difference in the approach of these two journals to the concept of struggle, *Teachers' Action* being critical of *Radical Education*'s recourse to what they refer to as sociological theory rather than facing up to the revolutionary potential of school students and to the unambiguous class position of teachers. On the other hand, *Teachers' Action*'s simplistic and structurally deterministic analysis of the relationship of education and the state does not enable them to consider what goes on in schools as potentially liberating, nor to exploit the contradictions present in favour of the working-class pupils. By emphasising the role of teacher as an agent of a state apparatus, to the detriment of her role as an intellectual who can help students gain the intellectual tools necessary to examine critically any number of situations, an important dimension of the socialist teacher's practice is missed, and a significant body of educational and Marxist thought ignored. *Teacher's Action*, then, has a commitment to overt political activism within the school centred round combining with pupils and other workers under threat.

> The groundwork for solidarity in future struggles should begin now and that means beginning in our own schools to build a working relationship between all relevant groups that will not crumble in the face of the opposition we know we shall have to face. (*Teachers' Action*, no. 12, p. 5)

If a commitment to radical educational journals suggests a rejection of the pessimism of the reproductive theories of many contemporary theorists, i.e., there is an implicit belief that something can be done within the school, then the *Teachers' Action* perspective suggests that this will be on the level of actual political activity rather than educational advance.

Teaching London Kids situates 'the struggle' within the classroom; in this respect there is a similarity between their perspective and that of *Teachers' Action*. The journal is about what happens and what could happen within schools. But, whereas the *Teachers' Action* emphasis is on political change as a result of organisation within the staffroom and classroom, change, from the *TLK* perspective, is the result of curricular innovation as a result of teacher practice: '*Teaching London Kids* has always been concerned with practical initiatives which change the curriculum and challenge prevailing views of knowledge. We are also committed to the notion that the best material comes from teachers working with kids' (*Teaching London Kids*, no. 14, p. 13). *Teaching London Kids* then is more interested in developing radical teaching strategies: it makes no claim to be seeking to develop a socialist theory of education. It does not reject the importance of theory but there is an unease with the determinism of current theorists in the sociology of education in comparison with the heady days of the early 1970s when 'theory and practice were within shouting distance' (*Teaching London Kids*, no. 13, editorial) and, difficult though the theories generated by the research of Bernstein, Young, Keddie and Labov might have been, they were tangible. They demanded a dialogue which viewed the teacher as an active, knowledgeable and competent agent in the process of schooling, rather than as an unconscious agent in the reproductive cycle of labour and skill.

Of all the radical journals considered, then, *Teaching London Kids* is alone in setting out to detail the possibilities for critical practice with pupils, i.e., critical practice based on their legitimate role within the classroom. From their point of view there is justification for the claim that the politics of educational practice for socialists is out of step with the critical – Marxist analysis of the capitalist social formation and its utilisation for hegemony of the educational institutions. But, though many activist teachers reject theoretical concerns as only a recipe for defeatism or passivity, *Teaching London Kids* wants to 'revitalise those perceptions about both the curriculum and the structure of education which practising teachers could hear and see so clearly when we began publication' (*Teaching London Kids*, no. 13). They seek a social and socialist alliance of theory and practice.

The two main objectives of Socialist Teachers' Alliance are:

(1) to establish unity in action among the mass of teachers around a programme of basic demands;

(2) to develop a coherent analysis of current educational practice and the role and position of teachers and the education system within the present social framework. (*Socialist Teacher*, no. 1, p. 16)

The area of struggle for Socialist Teachers' Alliance then is both at the practical and theoretical level – the practical referring basically to work within the National Union of Teachers and teachers in higher education. They aim to transform the Trades Union movement by working within it rather than by building up an organisation to compete with it. They seek to organise a mass movement of teachers who recognise the shortcomings of their union over pay and conditions of work, who are critical of the right-wing, social-democratic leadership and who are, significantly, interested in questions relating to the theory and practice of education. There is, then, an attempt by Socialist Teachers' Alliance to combine in a very positive way the two levels of socialist practice in education with that of the organised working class. By working within the trades union movement and seeking to transform it, they aim to make it more responsive to the demands and expectations of its members.

Struggle, then, within the union is of crucial importance to the Socialist Teachers' Alliance and alongside this lies the need to develop a socialist theory of education: from the perspective of the Socialist Teachers' Alliance, one should not exist without the other. Their commitment to a broad-based movement of the left is an attempt to combat the fragmentation of the Labour movement caused by sectarianism and, though they recognise that their aims are reformist rather than revolutionary, this is seen as a strength: they hope to unite teachers with a diversity of political opinions because of their mutual concerns on issues such as pay, class size and an interest in working-class children in schools. Their prime thrust 'must be towards the "middle ground" of people between the far left and the Executive/Communist Party bandwaggon' (*Socialist Teacher*, no. 9, p. 20) so that the left can make a major impact on union policy rather than being isolated 'as a bunch of mindless extremists' (*Socialist Teacher*, no. 8, p. 21) by the executive. At the practical level, then, the area of struggle is defined by social democratic policies contained within the framework of capitalist society. A powerful intervention in this area can only be made by uniting the diversity of political opinion found amongst teachers under certain common concerns and by focusing the militancy of the revolutionary left on these concerns. It is in these areas that the revolutionary left has been most successful (*Socialist Teacher*, no. 9, p. 20).

The broad left base is also seen to be essential in the development of a socialist theory of education: 'So long as we cannot agree on a theory and practice of education, the Left has a huge responsibility to keep all the doors open' (*Socialist Teacher* no. 7, editorial). This area of struggle is also defined by social-democratic educational policy. A socialist theory of education must be defined against this, and particularly against its most recent formulation of progressivism. Whilst recognising the worth of many progressive ideas, e.g., mixed ability teaching, curriculum development etc., ideologically it has contributed to the removal of debates about educational aims and objectives from the political sphere. They were no longer defined as being within an area of struggle because progressivism 'was placed at the service of both social classes, simultaneously promising equality of educational opportunity and economic regeneration' (*Socialist Teacher*, no. 7). There was therefore 'no question of class struggle when class interests on educational issues appeared to more or less coincide'.

The emphasis on 'struggle' takes different forms, then, within the broad spectrum of radical education. But common characteristics are the stress on action and the reading of changes in schooling as victories for the working class – victories defined against the hegemony of ruling groups. This populist approach is significant in the generation of radical educational journals, programmes and pedagogies.

The identification of radical teachers with the experience of subjection that school pupils experience, has itself been sustained by a critical-radical tendency in sociological work on schooling. Some teachers see this subjection very positively, as leading to participation in the class struggle. Teachers' Action Collective consider it to be indicative of wider class relations: school students as a force of the working class make visible the class struggle within the classroom (see, for example,

Teachers' Action, no. 7, p. 24). Support for this perspective is found in the work of Benton (1974, p. 15). Corrigan (1979, p. 43) and Willis (1979, p. 103) show that many working class children experience education as an imposition, an attempt to change their indigenous culture. Willis suggests that 'the specific conjunction in contemporary capitalism of class antagonism and the educational paradigm turns education into control, [social] class resistance into educational refusal and human difference into class division' (1979, p. 103).

It seems then that schooling today continues to be experienced by working-class children as 'an artificial implantation within the working population' (Johnson, 1976, p. 45), but, in spite of this, schools have still not 'acquired the autonomous power that has sometimes been envisaged for them . . . under capitalism, schools seem to reproduce instead of the perfect worker in complete ideological subjection, much more the worker as bearer of the characteristic antagonisms of the social formation as a whole. Schools, in other words, reproduce forms of resistance too, however limited or "corporate" or self-conscious these may be' (p. 52). This view must have the whole-hearted support of socialist teachers. From their experience as classroom teachers, they write that 'discontent *is* a protest against the nature of the school system, and it is the bedrock from which conscious, independent movements of pupils arise (*Teachers' Action* no. 13, p. 17).

Perhaps the commitment to radical education in general as a perspective is indicative of the rejection of the somewhat pessimistic work of the reproductive theorists, who detail no possibilities for either resistance by teachers and pupils or for critical practice with pupils. There is some claim to the point that the politics of educational practice for socialists is out of step with the critical-Marxist analysis of the capitalist social formation and its utilisation for hegemony of the educational institutions.

The radical education journals then recognise that the effects of educational practices at the structural level can be mediated in educationally and politically significant ways by the commitment of teacher activists. To some degree the journals can be 'read' in terms of their understanding of the nature of this action, whether it be direct political activism, the development of a socialist pedagogy, an emphasis on curricular change or the recognition and analysis of the constraints of the ideological and material worlds in which they work. No journal subscribes exclusively to any one of these dimensions – rather, of the series of strands of socialist-radical thought which together form each journal's particular perspective, one or two dominate the nature of the analysis given or the choice of topics presented for information or debate.

Teacher Practice and Curricular Issues

Attitudes of the Journals

The journals have various approaches to progressivism and curricular reform. An important aspect of these is the importance they give to the issues of racism and sexism in the school and society at large. Racism and sexism are recognised as characteristics of bourgeois society, standing alongside social class as indications of the social inequalities of capitalism. There is agreement that neither of the issues can be dealt with in isolation from a much wider political campaign and that both draw attention to a more fundamental division within society: that of social class.

Educational policy within social democracy has had little to say in a coherent way about these issues and their effects within the classroom. The responsibility for dealing with the material effects in the school of the intersection of race, sex and class has rested primarily with classroom teachers. Increasingly, radical and socialist teachers have met together collectively to plan and develop teaching strategies which have sought to make plain the sexism of everyday life and language and the implicitly sexist nature of much teaching material and many books used in schools. Similar efforts have been directed towards the liberal, romanticised view of black culture. The need is to integrate into the curriculum an analysis of the historic and economic causes of racist and sexist practice and to uncover the political bases of these ideas, thus directly challenging the biologism of some popular approaches. In line with their general policy, much of the debate in the journals is informative and analytic, aiming to develop understanding of the relationships and complexities of capitalism so that the teacher is better able to discuss and develop these issues with pupils.

Radical Education. There has been a continuing debate in the more recent issues of *Radical Education* about the merits and weaknesses of progressive forms of teaching. Progressivism has increasingly come under attack by right-wing educationalists and by parents: 'for large sections of the working class the crisis within our schools is immediately attributed to the introduction of "progressive education" ' (no. 12, editorial). Whilst recognising the shortcomings of many so-called progressive methods and teachers, *Radical Education*, no. 13 sees its critique of progressivism as providing the framework for the development of a socialist theory of education. The inroads that progressivism has made into traditional forms of the curriculum and pedagogy marks positive gains for socialist teachers and working-class students: 'Counterpose mixed ability teaching with setted groups, learning through experience with secondhand knowledge, the search for relevance with the old grammar school curriculum and it is clear that progressivism at least in its educational intentions, represents gains for socialist teaching' (no. 13, editorial).

The main body of criticism is directed to progressivism's failure to address class inequalities and conflict: it was not developed within the context of an understanding of society as a whole – rather it sought to bring about social change without threatening the given framework of social democracy. A more just society was to develop because of equality of opportunity in the classroom; a curriculum 'relevant' to children's needs would facilitate this.

> The Labour government made little effort to situate the changes in the educational system within the context of a movement to place power in the hands of the working class. To the contrary Labour sought to offer equal opportunity, in theory, to all within a capitalist society which is fundamentally structured to deny the needs of the majority. (no. 12, editorial)

Without an analysis which recognises this, 'relevancy' is meaningless because it does not address the fundamental nature of class relationships and how these structure pupil experience and the definition of accepted bodies of knowledge. These contradictions 'cannot be resolved without a basic change in the social relationships of the whole of society' (no. 12, editorial).

Thus, using English teaching as an example, *Radical Education* states that: 'progressivism has sought to replace the notion of literature as high culture with one which sees the writings of working-class children and adults as being valid and more relevant to working-class children' (no. 13, p. 5). But restricting working-class children to a curriculum which is 'obviously' relevant might be to deny them access to ideas which, though not speaking directly to their present experience, could be instrumental in leading them to wider understandings. For example, mathematics based on project work may have led to some pupils failing to become conversant with the basic skills needed within a society subject to technological change: 'when a move from valuing goals to valuing process in learning is made and when relevance and learning through experience are stressed, the results may not match the intentions' (no. 13, editorial).

Where then does this leave the socialist teacher? The methodology and content of progressive curricula have been carefully scrutinised to make clear the elements which could form the basis of a socialist curriculum and pedagogy. *Radical Education*, no. 13 makes the following points in an attempt to do this:

(1) The encouragement of collaborative learning.
(2) The search for relevance.
(3) A non-competitive notion of achievement.
(4) An emphasis placed on process in learning rather than the end product.
(5) An emphasis on learning through experience rather than through second-hand information.
(6) The recognition of cultural bias in society and the attempts to take account of it and teach differently because of it.
(7) The use of teacher-produced materials and local resources.
(8) Individualised and resource-based learning.
(9) Mixed ability teaching.
(10) The changed role of the teacher, from the authoritarian imparter of knowledge to the democratic resource in the classroom.

The relationship between individualised and co-operative learning is examined in *Radical Education*, no. 12 along with the need to re-think the pedagogical relationships based on hierarchical authority structures. Resource-based learning, like other progressive methods, has within a social-democratic framework, been used as a method of social control, a means of coping with comprehensive education and mixed ability teaching. There has, therefore, 'been a tendency in the past for many socialist teachers to tackle anti-racism, sexism, working-class culture and history, but to use the same methods as most [reactionary] teachers' (no. 12, p. 14). If resource-based learning, with its emphasis on the process of learning rather than the acquisition of knowledge and on the active involvement of the pupils, is to be of use to a socialist curriculum then pedagogical relationships will need to be examined and changed in the light of socialist principles:

> The framework for resource-based learning, concerned as it is with the development of skills rather than 'fact, fact, facts' – however socialist they are – is a useful starting point for developing socialist analysis and subsequently practices of learning.

There is, then, a need critically to appraise the methods by which people learn and the way in which children organise themselves. The more motivation children have to organise their own learning the fewer disciplinary problems will arise and the greater chance there will be of encouraging students to see beyond studying subjects for examination purposes, to their application outside the school. A methodology of learning is therefore crucial to socialist practice within the classroom because it is the means by which a child will develop confidence in his own abilities to be active outside the classroom: 'Learning thus perceived implies not only active and original research on the part of the school student but the communication and therefore explanation of their findings' (no. 12, p. 14).

Co-operative work and the sharing and communication of discoveries are 'the shadowy beginnings of a model of education where knowledge and action are more concrete, more really useful.' Furthermore, it brings into question the validity of grading and selection as a means of reinforcing and creating elites and elite forms of knowledge: 'The socialist perspective entails the destruction of elites not the creation of new ones' (no. 4, editorial). In this model of learning and the curriculum, discipline comes from involvement in the work in hand rather than from the authority of the teacher. The teacher's position as professional is not denied – 'We believe we have something worthwhile to offer to our pupils' (no. 4, editorial) – but neither is it set in opposition to that of the pupil; rather, she becomes a resource.

The dual nature of professionalism is recognised by *Radical Education*. They argue strongly for their professional role: they believe they 'should try to educate [our] pupils into recognising the *source* of oppression and not merely its surface features' (no. 4, editorial) but recognise that this is at odds with the response of the National Union of Teachers to Department of Education and Science calls for a more efficient educational system, i.e., that a teacher's professional skills should be at the beck and call of the needs of industry and the economy. The model of professionalism set by the NUT is essentially a defensive response to their concerns that other interests attempt to trespass on educational territory rather than critical evaluation of the implications of Department of Education and Science policy.

Radical Education argues for a professionalism based on the practice of their skills, a practice which recognises that 'teachers, students and other sections of the Labour movement have interests in education that are independent of, and opposed to, those of the Department of Education and Science and industry' (no. 10) rather than the restrictive notions of the National Union of Teachers, which, rather than challenging the basis of the attacks on the educational system by government and industry, argues that if the resources are provided the educational system can live up to the expectations of its masters and, perhaps, even outstrip them in their concern to widen the concept of education:

> While an understanding of the workings of the economy is indeed important . . . the schools' curricular objectives need to be broader: the development of mature young adults prepared for the whole of their future lives *which may well include periods of unemployment.* (our emphasis) (no. 10, quoting NUT publication)

While the National Union of Teachers is arguing for curriculum development 'by those with the necessary expertise and teaching experience', *Radical Education* seeks to extend the debate about educational issues amongst the widest possible audience:

> Alliances must be made to strengthen the position of radicals and socialists. One conceivable alliance within the teachers' union is to pressurise the proponents of 'professionalism' away from the purely economistic position into a defence of the right to autonomy and self management of all qualified teachers. In the present situation we believe that we should fight for retaining and increasing decision making by classroom teachers. Obviously teachers are more willing to defend decisions they themselves have made as opposed to decisions passed down from above. They must also take the responsibility of explaining and justifying their educational practice to the parents. (no. 7)

and, further, must struggle to retain control of the curriculum and develop a methodology which is 'based on the experience of classroom teachers who will have to implement them'.

Their professionalism also extends to the upholding of educational standards, despite the comments of the right wing to the contrary:

> We take up the cudgels over standards not because socialist teachers do not have standards, but because they *do* have standards and because they *are* accountable, but not to employers and to the supply and demand mechanisms of the job market.

They must struggle, then, to defend themselves as working people and defend education itself from right-wing attack by a whole series of strategies: ' . . . classroom activity, political control of schools, fighting the National Union of Teachers' collaboration with the government's education and political policies, uniting these various issues in the development of a socialist alternative in educational practice and programme'.

In common with the other journals a central concern of *Radical Education* is the nature of racism, its relationship to the crisis within capitalist society, its practice within schools and, importantly, the responses and initiatives which socialist teachers can give:

> it will be necessary to go beyond the purely 'commentarist' positions which we have had, in common with much of the left in education, over the last few years. The activities of Gould, of Boyson, of the NF show that they understand the importance of focusing their campaigns on particular, agitational issues, which crystallise their general social and educational programmes. We have to do likewise. (no. 10, editorial)

Teacher consciousness is therefore given high priority. Hence the importance of sponsoring certain initiatives that are part of an organised response to the attacks on education, such as the 'All London Teachers Against Racism and Fascism', – its aim being to unite in anti-racist activity all those involved in education.

Discussions about racism in *Radical Education* do not include direct teaching strategies; recommendations of non-racist and non-sexist books and teaching material are included in the journal but classroom practice as such is not within its frame of reference. This is made clear in the first issue: curriculum content is adequately dealt with by other radical teaching journals; their aims are of a different nature – to develop a socialist theory of education and to counter the fragmentation of the educational left.

It is necessary, then, for teachers to respond on two levels of practice: at the level of purely educational issues in schools and the National Union of Teachers and at the level of political debate within the union and the community.

The National Union of Teachers, locked in as it is to government policy, bureaucratic procedures, professionalism and 'political neutrality' is ill-equipped to produce strategies that attack racist practices at their root, i.e., the structural inequalities of capitalism and the subsequent oppression experienced by blacks; rather, it seeks a solution in compensating blacks for their 'disadvantage' by aiming to improve their educational performance. NUT resolutions firmly commit its executive to finding exclusively educational answers to the institutionalised racism of the state. It therefore avoids the need to address racism in general in the curriculum in favour of the development of a school-based, multi-cultural curriculum; it avoids the left's proposal to lend support to the TUC resolution on racism in favour of remaining ouside 'the minefield of sectarian politics' (*Radical Education*, no. 10, p. 21). In the NUT's view educational advancement of all pupils will be dependent on equality of educational opportunity and a relevant curriculum.

Teachers' Action. In spite of recognising the pedagogical advances of progressivism, *Teachers' Action* continues to argue that 'schooling . . . is still a process for grading and disciplining future labour power'. (What is missing, of course, is a clear analysis of why this is so.) Curriculum development must be seen in this 'control' context. The development of a curriculum relevant to the needs of pupils eager to get out of school or to the disillusioned sixth-formers clamouring to come back in, means that an overt emphasis on social control is beginning to take precedence over all other aspects of schooling: curriculum and 'containment' are synonomous.

> Containment, or its junior equivalent, child-minding, has always been a function of schooling . . . New 'exciting' courses are created, 'opportunity departments' set up, work experience instituted, wages for sixth formers proposed and, at the other end of the spectrum, the police presence in schools becomes greater than ever before. If curricular measures fail, nobody is taking any chances. (*Teachers Action* no. 11, editorial)

Although a central theme of many of their articles is the threat addressed by government, LEAs and industry to teacher responsibility for curriculum development, 'teachers' attempts to define what the education of pupils should be about is at stake' (no. 14, p. 12), the underlying causes of curriculum development are to be found in their pupils' rejection of the school system.

> What many kids in our schools do feel is either that education is a con, or that schooling is something which has to be endured . . .

education hasn't got much to offer that is of immediate value so why accept the regimentation of the classroom?' (no. 13, p. 17)

The classroom teacher is, then, in something of a quandary: financial measures are increasingly being used to control and restrict the development of new courses whilst, at the same time, there is state emphasis on the need for more control and discipline within schools. The call is for a return to basics, to essential forms of knowledge and the traditional standards of academic excellence, but without teacher consultation to decide what these particular qualities are. Increasingly, then, the teacher is finding her hands tied. In the past she has maintained equanimity by delving 'into the theory and practice of curricular change to interest them [the pupils], to motivate them, to step away from fact-feeding and involve them in the discipline of learning and "developing" ' (no. 6, editorial). As this practice is increasingly being threatened by state intervention some positive effects are seen to be immanent in its inability to cope directly with pupil disaffection and rejection of the school with its racism and racialist practices: 'by leaving it to the ordinary classroom teacher to solve [these problems, it] has unwittingly allowed us a measure of power which we will not willingly relinquish' (no. 12, editorial).

Generally speaking, then, *Teachers' Action* emphasises the effects of state policy on the forms of schooling, rather than exploring curriculum development as such: 'If microprocessing is introduced on a wide scale, as seems probable, the economy will require the education system to produce a more disciplined, less skilled, more interchangeable work force, headed by a small elite' (no. 13, p. 7). This is leading, they argue, to a return to rigorous forms of selection and the consequent choice by many pupils to opt out of the education system by under-achievement, failure to co-operate, truancy and verbal and physical abuse of teachers and property. Once both teachers and pupils have recognised that the schooling system is loaded against them, the teacher is faced with the unenviable task of 'containment'.

Teachers' Action asks a pertinent question of all socialist teachers in this position. 'Can we be content today to "teach" only those pupils who have no sense of their social power and so buckle under to the disciplines necessary to get 'A' level grades? As a result of long years of struggle and challenging authority the working class now have confidence in their own organised power, and this is increasingly reflected in the classroom. It is this power with which socialist teachers should be seeking to associate themselves, giving practical support to pupils' and parents' organisations rather than 'orientating the whole of the school curriculum and organisation to the emergence of the minority who will eventually enter the professions' (no. 13, p. 18).

The ambivalent position of the socialist teacher to progressivism and curricular reform is highlighted in the response of *Teachers' Action* to the multi-cultural curriculum. On the one hand there is the recognition that progressivism, though failing radically to question the way in which knowledge is transmitted, did lead to the erosion of the traditional hierarchy of the school and did show that mixed ability teaching (for example) could be successful; at the same time, there is the recognition that reformist measures were also a means of recuperating and controlling pupils who were actively rejecting all that the schools stood for.

This is the framework in which the *Teachers' Action* analysis of multi-ethnic education takes place, but it is supplemented by an implicit critique of the reproductive processes at work for capitalism. It is noted that the curriculum has never reflected the culture of the majority of working-class people, that it 'has very tenuous links with the vitality of the ways of life, systems of values, predilections and historical directions of the schooled' (no. 9 p. 5). It is pointed out that much of the 'culture' of blacks which officialdom now wants incorporated into the curriculum is defined *against* white culture, that it 'is a rejection of the position in society that schools prepare them for', that 'blacks have made a culture of action and resistance' and because of this it will 'elude the makers of curriculum'. The multi-cultural curriculum, under the disguise of eliminating prejudice and racial inequality, of enriching white working-class culture, of providing motivation for black pupils and of helping the teacher to form a worthwhile relationship with them, is an attempt to divert attention away from the black experience in Britain. It thus avoids the need to ask blacks about their needs and preoccupations in schools, about their experience of racism, poor housing and work opportunities. 'The multi-ethnic proposals are, in fact, a substitute for a miracle or a social revolution' (no. 9, p. 5; see also an article by Teachers' Action Collective, in *Radical Education*, no. 2).

Teachers' Action has no argument with those teachers who say that the curriculum should be informative but, as far as presenting facts about blacks is concerned, the content will be inadequate unless it develops a political understanding of the divisions within society and the forms of black action and resistance which have grown in response to this. If the curriculum is to be relevant, if it is to reflect society at all, it must 'paint the shifting sands of the balance of power'. And so, whilst emphasising the part played by pupil resistance in curriculum development, *Teachers' Action* is adamant that teacher practice must seek to make plain the nature of a class society. This practice, if confined to the classroom and curriculum, will simply be reproductive of the relationships on which capitalism is based; socialist practice in schools must be informed by participation in struggles which evolve as the result of pupil and parent organisation.

Socialist Teacher. The curricular proposals of the Socialist Teachers Alliance are of a similar nature to those of *Radical Education*. They each recognise that educational theory must be linked with classroom practice – left wing educational theorists must be drawn into 'a relationship with us in the development of a counter theory and practice' (*Socialist Teacher*, no. 2, p. 15) – as well as with developments in the relationship between the educational system and other societal systems. There is also the need to link 'ideas for genuine educational change with the forces fighting for the transformation of society' (no. 2, p. 14). This latter point is a crucial one for Socialist Teachers' Alliance because the arena in which this link will be forged is that of trade unionism. Although its broad-based approach gives credence to the revolutionary left, essentially *Socialist Teacher* emphasises active trade union involvement as the means of confronting the offensive from the right.

It is argued that this offensive indicates that the educational system is not 'efficiently and absolutely performing its role for capital' (no. 2, p. 14), that there are possibilities for the relative autonomy of the educational system to develop further and that therefore socialist teachers should seek to make clear these possiblities and also to retain the ground gained during the era of progressivism in schools. The responsibility for curriculum development must, then, lie with the classroom teacher rather than with 'experts' appointed by the National Union of Teachers or with employers as suggested by the Taylor Report. The curriculum should be developed, not in isolation from the education process itself, 'but through a process of maximum consultation with the organisations of the working class as well as with as yet unorganised sections of teachers, students and working class parents' (no. 2, p. 18). It is important to note, however, that the reformist methods of progressivism must not be uncritically taken on board; rather, 'socialists should be blending what is truly progressive in these methods with a critique of what education could be like under socialism, what forms and content of education are in the genuine interest of the working class as a whole' (no. 2, p. 14).

A socialist pedagogy must, then, recognise the school as an area of class conflict and that educational practice has ideological and political implications for teachers and pupils. It must also recognise that whilst working class interests cannot *predominate* in the school at the present time 'they can certainly be expressed – the school does not directly and monolithically serve solely the interest of the dominant class' (no. 7). The argument is for a *transitional* pedagogy which will bring to the fore an 'adequate formative education for the working class' supplemented by a rejection of racist and sexist ideas. It will encourage collective rather than individual achievement, and by extending the rights of children will challenge the ideology of childhood. The critical appraisal of the images of work presented in the school will be central to this pedagogy, thereby demystifying the relations of production (and their reflection in the school) and ethnocentrism will be discouraged by developing an internationalist perspective amongst school students and teachers. Such a curriculum must also enable relevant questions to be asked about political and social life.

These basic ideas are designed to confront the world-view usually presented by the school. They address a society which increasingly is seeking a utilitarian function for schooling but which also has within it an increasing number of young people who not only 'reject what the school offers but demand that it reflects their own concerns'. The transitional pedagogy (importantly for the Socialist Teachers' Alliance perspective) also recognises a new element in the teaching profession: an increasing number of teachers, many without a formalised political allegiance, who are introducing into the curriculum areas of social concern which are directly critical of capitalism. Studies of racism, sexism, working-class history and imperialism all may come within this category.

In view of this, and because textbooks continue to be used extensively in schools, *Socialist Teacher* regularly reviews newly published material and also offers analyses of texts and other resources currently available. These are evaluated according to their usefulness in mixed ability classrooms, whether or not they reproduce the racist and sexist images of bourgeois culture, whether the material emphasises a euro-centric perspective, and whether they make more clear the social relations of capital. With this in mind it is useful to consider the Socialist Teacher critique of curriculum material about racism.

Tankits, 'as the first direct intervention by the organised left into the content of the curriculum' (no. 7) are given serious attention. *Tankits* are packages of resource material compiled by Teachers Against the Nazis. They deal with a range of anti-racist and anti-fascist topics and have been developed to be used in both primary and secondary schools.) It must be restated that the contributors to and readership of *Socialist Teacher* are practising teachers who take their professional skills seriously. They seek to educate their pupils, develop categories of thought which will allow them to understand more precisely the causes of the oppression experienced. Pedagogically, *Tankits* are found to be inadequate: there is an 'over-reliance on emotive images and slogans', there is a 'lack of historical depth in some sections [which makes] little allowance for the students' own queries and initiative' and, because of the closed nature of much of the texts, they do not allow students to pursue their own lines of enquiry or provide enough 'jumping off points into controversial areas'. The critique may seem damaging, particularly in view of the fact that racism and fascism are areas of deep concern to socialist teachers and that there is a dearth of critical material available. However it points to the professional concerns and integrity of *Socialist Teacher*'s readership: there is a rejection of 'premature and simplistic answers' in favour of careful analysis and documentation of evidence; pedagogical considerations are of prime importance:

> One of our functions as socialist teachers is to provide students with the opportunities to reflect on ideological processes at work . . . Presenting complex and possibly unpopular political ideas in such starkly simple forms induces cynicism in students, and certainly runs counter to [the] learning processes. (no. 7)

Teaching London Kids. An article 'Have you done poverty this term?', in *Teaching London Kids*, no. 3, points up the dilemma of the radical teacher. In spite of well developed social consciences, in spite of the righteous indignation they experience and can develop within their pupils during the study of socially relevant topics, as educationally successful members of the middle class, they are distanced from their pupils by that success, by their lifestyle, by the social relationship of the school. The social problems discussed because they are 'relevant' are, for many pupils, part of everyday life rather than neat categories of 'experience' incorporated into the curriculum in order to encourage social awareness. The writer goes on to suggest that 'we cannot by the very nature of our position and the process offer an alternative'.

The unease expressed by this writer – 'It is clear that we are trapped whether we are happy with the situation or not' – underlies that experienced by many teachers operating within a radical-libertarian perspective and discovering its shortcomings. The point is developed further by Doug Holly, in his discussion of progressivism. Arguing that socialist teachers must defend the gains made by progressivism, he emphasises that curricular reforms and more liberal pedagogical relations will not, of themselves, bring about change within society:

> we should never trust isolating reform, however brightly packaged. Strenuous efforts by curriculum-mongers to change the nature of lesson content and classroom practice deliberately ignored wider social and political issues – which is why they aroused so little opposition at the time. They were safe because insulated within 'educational' discussions and sponsored by institutional bodies. (*Teaching London Kids*, no. 14, p. 22)

There is, then, a need for teachers to develop a self-conscious purpose about their practice, to take arguments about the nature and content of education outside the staffroom and to associate with parents and other members of the community in an attempt 'to show the connection between their preoccupations and the interests of people at large'.

Paul Willis, in another issue, suggests that teachers should be seeking closer links between Education and Industry and with the organised Labour movement so that strong links can be forged for the left rather than leaving the ground open for the restricted ideological purposes of the right. His view of what goes on in schools would seem to undermine the emphasis placed by *Teaching London Kids* on the important contribution curriculum innovation can make to social and political change. He says that a teacher's 'immediate activity in the institutions we now have is not critical to socialist outcomes' but argues for the importance of socialist teachers supporting their practice with socialist aims (no. 12, p. 21). He does not, then, appear to give much 'space' to the socialist teacher though he recognises the importance of certain forms of knowledge for working-class pupils. This is often rejected by these pupils because of 'the structural relationships in which it is provided and because of the cultural forms of struggle against what the kids perceive the school to be *prior to any specific communication*. What role, then, can the socialist teacher play in this seemingly deterministic and pessimistic view of education?

Teaching London Kids believes in the existence of a viable working-class culture which needs recuperating: it is there, outside their schools: 'we have to say that . . . history teaching should begin to acknowledge that just outside the school real people live and work and have ideas and have a history' (no. 3, p. 7). Coming to terms with this history is a means of casting off the restricting nature and predetermined outcomes of socially prescribed knowledge and replacing it with forms of knowledge relevant to the development of class consciousness within pupils:

> working-class students themselves using their own local resources, perceiving their own neighbourhood, families histories and themselves – in short, their own *class* – as relevant and proper material to form a basis of knowledge and ideology, has blasted through the moss-covered walls of the old knowledge.' (no. 14, p. 24)

The aim, then, of *Teaching London Kids* is to develop a curriculum which is genuinely working-class and which will help that class grasp power. The content of this curriculum will relate directly to working-class experience within their locality and will try to uncover the way that experience develops and is understood: 'in our lessons we would try to focus on the social structures which shape our lives and on the ways in which we acquire our ideas about the world and our sense of identity' (no. 10, p. 1). Although an historical perspective is seen as crucial if any understanding of processes and structure is to be gained, it is necessary 'wherever possible [to] link up with the present so that the struggle is not seen to be over' (no. 6, p. 26).

Their teaching has an explicit political content. It may start with encouraging research in the immediate locality of the school but is not restricted to this:

> Next year we plan to move out of the local community to explore struggles in the Third World. Children with origins outside the East End will then be able to recreate their own history and local children will have much to learn too. (no. 6, p. 26)

Sexism and sex stereotyping comes in for much discussion and the economic and personal difficulties likely to be encountered when 'stepping out of role' (no. 10, p. 15) are explored. They recognise that they cannot in their journal tackle all areas of curriculum development in depth nor offer perfect solutions to all classroom situations, but they aim to establish and open up areas of debate, areas of which understanding is essential if socialist aims are to be achieved.

Whereas within education generally the political content of what counts as knowledge is denied, *Teaching London Kids* actively seeks to recreate forms of knowledge which will be the bedrock of political awareness and action and in this way it differentiates itself from radical progressivism: 'It is important to disassociate genuine socialist education in the classroom from the often laissez-faire attitudes of progressive education which can degenerate into aimless projects and collages' (no. 7, p. 6). Fundamental to their approach to curriculum content is the importance of language development and the skills of literacy. These are weapons in the struggle, and skill and familiarity of use are essential if children are to not only demystify the social relations of capital but instigate change – if they are to confront their class enemies as equals. Failure to develop these skills within children will allow their continued control by societal forces totally opposed to their interests and, further, will hinder them as they seek to make alliances with others. Perhaps, then, because they are teachers of English (although undeniably this must be a concern of socialist teachers regardless of specialisation) there is a concern with the consequences of the Bullock Report, with helping the child to make '(his) own language rich, flexible and adaptable' (no. 7, p. 17), to extend its dimensions so that his ability to act in and understand many different situations is increased.

There appears to be some difference of opinion over such hoary topics as the importance of 'correct' spelling: this is seen by some contributors as being of symbolic rather than functional importance (no. 7, p. 17), but others, again, believe that even this is a weapon in the class struggle and that therefore their pupils should be equipped in every way possible to enter this struggle with every advantage. Freire is quoted to support this belief: 'literacy is a quality of consciousness and that "lack of consciousness is the fate of oppressed groups everywhere and discriminatory social structures rely on this state of mind to prevent changes and challenges"'. But we are again left with the question, particularly in view of the determining theories of some contemporary writers (see no. 13, editorial), of how the declared intentions of the teacher activists who subscribe to and write for *Teaching London Kids* are to be put into practice. Chris Searle states (no. 7, p. 6):

> The only way I can really operate successfuly is to take advantage of the contradictions within the classroom and to try thereby to

> persuade the children of the contradictions in society. We can't escape the fact that I am a teacher, paid by the state, to fulfil a certain function – to turn the children I teach into a fairly docile labour force. But we also can't escape the fact that neither myself nor the children I teach are prepared to accept that. The contradiction is that I'm working in an impure situation in order to transform it, and within a continuing power structure of which I disapprove, but which I am determined to subvert and transform. (no. 7, p. 6)

In order that these contradictions may be fully exploited in the interests of the working class, and in view of the disturbing and reactionary turn of events as a result of a Tory government being returned to power in May 1979, the *Teaching London Kids* editorial group insist that the debate about progressivism and socialist education must continue.

Conclusion

It would seem, then, that the radical teaching journals have moved beyond the 'possibilitarian' stance of the new sociology of education. The halcyon days when societal change was to come about because of change in classroom relationships and 'relevant' curricula have been replaced by the other sober realisation that an oppositional pedagogy and curriculum must take seriously the implications of the political nature of knowledge. A socialist formulation must recognise that the society in which teachers work is a class society, that the interests of the two major levels of social class cannot coincide, that it is in the interests of the ruling groups to maintain their grasp on what shall be defined as knowledge and that overt class conflict will develop at times when the organic weaknesses of capitalism mature.

There has also been a movement away from the deterministic forms of some analyses to a growing realisation that social crises, although fundamentally economic in origin, are an immanent characteristic of capitalism and as such 'create a terrain more favourable to the dissemination of certain modes of thought and certain ways of posing and resolving questions involving subsequent development of national life' (Gramsci, 1971, p. 184). The awareness and analysis of this terrain, by revealing points of least resistance, enables initiatives to be taken by opposing forces. Teachers can have crucial roles to play in this opposition – both as teachers and as political participants. Gramsci writes:

> The decisive element in every situation is the permanently organised and long-prepared force which can be put into the field when it is judged that a situation is favourable (and it can be favourable only in so far as such a force exists, and is full of fighting spirit). Therefore the essential task is that of systematically and patiently ensuring that this force is formed, developed, and rendered ever more homogeneous, compact, and self-aware. (1971, p. 185)

This then is the arena in which socialist teachers must situate themselves; it is this form of activity and self-awareness which distinguishes them from radical libertarians and advocates of progressivism.

Whilst recognising the complexity and density of schooling and pedagogies as reproductive agents *and* as a field of ideological struggle with areas of autonomy and intervention for teachers, we are still left with the question of *schooling for whom and for what?* From a socialist position the question becomes transposed into whether, and in what sense, socialist and radical pedagogies actually transform the framework within which education in the form of state schooling occurs. We have already argued that progressivism and liberal education reforms within social democratic limitations generally have failed to do this and, further, have successfully removed debates about the content and form of education from the political sphere.

If we consider Williams's suggestion that we should revalue the idea of determinism, moving away from 'the notion of an external cause which totally predicts or prefigures, indeed totally controls a subsequent activity' to 'a notion of determinism as setting limits, exerting pressures (1976, p. 202) and place this alongside a conception of determination inhering in men's own activities, we can perhaps begin to think in terms of a socialist theory of education which seeks, as an initial aim, the halting of the 'given' inevitability of the capitalist process. This then gives great importance to struggles within the conjunctural. Should this opportunity for struggle not be taken then the forces of reaction have time to re-establish their hold on superstructural elements and the chances of change within society diminish.

We have then, as central, the notion of people's actions determining the course of struggle, taking advantage of deeply seated organic crises within capitalist society. We can then place socialist teachers in this struggle: as well as giving active support to fellow workers, they contribute their own particular professional skills to the struggle. The societal framework in which schooling takes place is not then transformed at a stroke but neither is it the overwhelmingly restrictive structure some theorists' work has suggested.

However this does bring us to a further point Williams makes when discussing alternative and oppositional cultures: when a cultural form 'becomes oppositional in an explicit way it . . . gets approached or attacked' (1976, p. 207). A socialist curriculum which attempts to penetrate the dominant system of values must face this possibility. Its strength will lie in the establishment of a dialectical form of relationship with other oppositional movements; it must move alongside, accompanying and complementing all other forms of socialist struggle.

Bibliography

Benton, T. (1974) 'Education and Politics' in Holly, D. (ed.), *Education or Domination*? Arrow Books, London

Bernstein, B. (1977) 'Education Cannot Compensate for Society' in Cosin, B.R., Dale, I.R., Esland, G.M., Mackinnon, D. and Swift, D.F. (eds.), *School and Society: a Sociological Reader* (a course reader) Routledge and Kegan Paul for the Open University Press, London

Bowles, S. and Gintis, H. (1976) *Schooling in Capitalist America*, Routledge and Kegan Paul, London

Clarke, J., Hall, S., Jefferson, J. and Roberts, B. (1976) 'Subcultures, Cultures and Class: a Theoretical Overview' in Hall, S. and Jefferson, T. (eds.), *Resistance though Rituals: Youth Subcultures in Post-war Britain: Working Papers in Cultural Studies*, nos. 7-8, Hutchinson for the Centre for Contemporary Cultural Studies, London

Corrigan, P. (1979) *Schooling the Smash Street Kids*, Macmillan, London

Dale, I.R., Esland, G.M. and MacDonald, M. (eds.) (1976) *Schooling and Capitalism: a Sociological Reader*, (A course reader) Routledge and Kegan Paul, London

Finn, D., Grant, N. and Johnson, R. (1977) *Social Democracy, Education and the Crisis: Working Papers in Cultural Studies*, no. 10, University of Birmingham, Centre for Contemporary Cultural Studies

Gramsci, A. (1971) *Selections from the Prison Notebooks*, Lawrence and Wishart, London

Hall, S. (1979) 'The Great Moving Right Show' in *Marxism Today*, January

Hebdige, D. (1979) *Subculture: The Meaning of Style*, Methuen, London
Johnson, R. (1976) 'Notes on the schooling of the English working class, 1780-1850' in Dale *et al*. (1976)
Karabel, J. and Halsey, A.H. (eds.) (1977) *Power and Ideology in Education*, Oxford University Press
Keddie, N. (1975) 'Classroom Knowledge' in Young, M.F.D. (ed.), *Knowledge and Control*, Collier-Macmillan
Sharp, R. and Green, A. (1976) *Education and Social Control* , Routledge and Kegan Paul, London
Taylor, I., Walton, P. and Young, J. (1974) *Critical Criminology*, Routledge and Kegan Paul, London
Whitty, G. (1977) 'Sociology and the Problems of Radical Educational Change: Notes towards a reconstruction of the "new" sociology of education' in Young, M. and Whitty, G., *Society, State and Schooling*, The Falmer Press, Lewes
Williams, R. (1976) ' "Base and Superstructure" in Marxist cultural theory' in Dale *et al*. (1976)
Willis, P., (1977) *Learning to Labour: How Working Class Kids Get Working Class Jobs*, Saxon House, Farnborough

Journals Discussed

Radical Education, 86 Eleanor Road, London E8
Socialist Teacher, 221 Westcombe Hill, London SE3
Teachers' Action, 2 Turquand Street, London SE17
Teaching London Kids, 40 Hamilton Road, London SW19
Tankits can be obtained from: J. Hurford, Teachers' Club, 61 Noll Avenue, Cosher Walk, London N7

Part Three

NEW DIRECTIONS

INTRODUCTION

This section is constructed to introduce the reader to three areas of curriculum work which are being revitalised by, amongst others, our three writers. Each of the following contributors represents a particular field of interest – existentialism, Marxism, and humanistic deliberation – and makes his or her own distinctive contribution to the relevant field. They are attempting here to explore their choice of research area by autobiographical accounts which serve to illustrate their development and dissatisfactions. The section will not only serve as a useful commentary on their previous work and guide to their future research but it will also indicate current developments in the field of curriculum. The three writers are united by their opposition to the technological determinism that has characterised the field and they represent points of view that have been neglected by the dominant paradigm in the post-war period. They reflect here upon their development as researchers and teachers and are united by a desire to explore their ideas in relation to the ideas inherent in other perspectives.

The central concern of this book is the polarity and tension between self and structure in curriculum studies. All three writers represent positions which are concerned with dialogue and not exclusivity.

Madeleine Grumet has developed a teaching and research interest based on an autobiographical method which was in turn developed from the method of William Pinar, called *currere*. No radical change of the curriculum is possible, she argues, unless it stops being a reflection of ourselves and we engage in a critical reflexivity to retrieve and understand our past histories. Through *currere*, the curriculum could be reconstructed and a practical curricular discourse developed. She emphasises that this is not a narcissistic or subjective process but a move to escape solipsism by creating a theoretical discourse based on public meanings.

Michael Apple began his inquiry into curriculum studies with a concern for social justice and a gradual belief that education was part of a wider, exploitative system of social relations. His work in exploring the ideological and cultural reproduction of society that takes place in schools and the curriculum has now led him to move away from a fundamentally determined view to one focusing on schools as sites of ideological production, resistance and contestation. His recent work is committed to explaining the mediation of state or industrial power in the area of the curriculum and the struggles to avoid deskilling by 'groups of human actors'.

Reid distinguishes humanistic deliberation from the existential and Marxist perspectives. He takes an evolutionary approach to curricular problems, bound by the need to understand and improve human society. His ideas are based on the importance of endeavouring to improve good decision-making through rational discourse and avoiding tailor-made solutions to curriculum problems. It is a process, therefore, that starts with the problem, not the theory.

The purpose of this work is to develop a concern in curriculum studies for the individual or groups of teachers, and the societal structure and culture with which they are interacting in terms of a theoretical and practical enterprise. The contradictions and tensions between the writers should lead to a fruitful and exciting discourse.

4 RESTITUTION AND RECONSTRUCTION OF EDUCATIONAL EXPERIENCE: AN AUTOBIOGRAPHICAL METHOD FOR CURRICULUM THEORY

Madeleine R. Grumet

Because curriculum is the collective story we tell our children about our past, our present and our future, curriculum enquiry requires acts of interpretation as well as observation. This essay provides a rationale for the use of autobiography as a form of curriculum enquiry. If the design and analysis of curriculum is to escape the automatic imprint of our own educational experience, we must engage in the critical reflection that permits us to reclaim our own histories and to surpass them through the acts of remembrance and interpretation.

Remembrance is the dominant form of autobiographical writing. Although it is usual that we think of autobiographical accounts as memoirs rather than as anticipations, such an attribution of experience to either the past or the future is temporal reductionism. It is the temporal ambiguity that attends autobiographical method that makes it a sufficiently flexible frame for curriculum discourse. How does my present situation influence my understanding of the past? How do my hopes and dreads determine what it is in my past that I remember? How does my past veil the present? How does it provide the future? What is it that we find when we reclaim our experience? Similarly, curriculum theory is threaded on time. Of course this is hardly extraordinary, as all human action takes place within temporal horizons. But, as curriculum theory strives to clarify the relations of the known to the unknown, of subject and object, of generations to each other, its propositions, whether they address the doctrine of eternal forms, or career education, assume distinct positions on a continuum of past, present and future.

When William Pinar first described this autobiographical method of curriculum theory he called it *currere*, employing the Latin root of curriculum to emphasise the course, not in terms of the race, nor in terms of the readiness of the runner (1975). He subordinated the perspectives of past and future to the immediate experience of one particular runner, on one particular track, on one particular day, in one particular wind. Both he and I have written extensively about the paradox that develops as soon as we try to seize that moment. We cup it in our hands, holding it gingerly. We cannot see it, but feel it moving, tickling our palms. Yet, as soon as we spread our fingers to look at it, it falls to pieces, fragments of past and future. And so the autobiographical method we outlined was an attempt to reveal the ways that histories (both collective and individual) and hope suffuse our moments, and to study them through telling each other stories of educational experience.

From the inception of this work, the method has always had both phases, the evocative and the analytic, although it may be that, at the outset, it was the first phase that we articulated most clearly rather than the second. Well it *was* the *first* phase, and so received the privileges of primogeniture. It was also a repudiation of the highly instrumental and rationalised approaches to educational practice that followed the 1960s. Autobiographical method was a project of restitution, wresting experience from the anonymity and generalisation that had dominated the social sciences and even literary interpretation in the heyday of structuralism and systems theories, and returning it to the particular persons who lived it. Perhaps we did hand our stories of educational experience around, delighting in their shapes, their colours, their textures, their taste. They were like those foil-wrapped chocolate apples that separate into sections as soon as the cellophane is removed. Only in sections can they be eaten, only in sections shared. Criticism of these stories has always been an integral part of this method, and it is this analytic phase of the process that I wish to emphasise here, discussing specifically the concept of subjectivity that is the foundation for this method for the first person and the possible contributions that this method may make to curriculum theory's fund of doubt. Because the method bears the stigma of narcissism and privatisation and the field confidently asserts that reconstruction will evolve from practice, both illusions, the privacy of the method and the pragmatism of the field need to be exposed and corrected.

My first task is to rescue autobiography from its association with the self, the alias that has given subjectivity its bad name.

The Ojibwa, a North American Indian tribe, teach their chidlren to fast so that they may receive powerful visions. These visions are valued in this Indian society: the ability to have them, hold them and finally to communicate them is honoured. Nevertheless, children are taught to keep their visions to themselves:

If a child seems about to discuss his vision with his father, the latter

> will halt him, saying, 'This is yours. You must keep it close to you. Do not talk about it. Make it so real to yourself that you can almost touch it and hear it.' (Mead, 1937, p. 118)

So, Mead tells us, the child who has once dreamed is admonished so that he will continue to dream.[1]

The children who are my students have forgotten their dreams. They have neither time, nor place, nor signs for their telling. Even though their dreams, like the dream of the Indian child, are shrouded in secrecy, the privacy that sustains one vision destroys the other. For each culture the private vision is associated with information, feelings and ideas that can be classified as latent rather than mainfest content. The manifest content in our culture displays itself in our laws and rules, in our language, our customs, our conventions. It is palpable and concrete. The latent content is more mysterious. It is the content that rarely comes to form, the signs that flicker and whisper for a moment, and then, just as we turn our heads to catch them, slide back into the silence, into the darkness. Prelinguistic, preconceptual, ambiguous, idiosyncratic, they elude the common code. I would never tell my dreams, here, to you. Well, that's not really true. I am prepared to do just that, but I will cleverly disguise them, drain them, bleach them, fold and sort them and deliver them to you as rational discourse.

In contrast, the Indian child is taught to hold on to his dreams and to cultivate them as a resource. Indian culture aims at integrating what is obvious with what is hidden and in acknowledging that combination as a ground for human action. Hallowell (1953) reports that the Ojibwa consider their dreams to provide important information about their daily subsistence activities. In the morning adult members of a family will gather to recount their dreams to each other; the dreams will be interpreted by the group and then decisions concerning the day's activities will often be influenced by the group's interpretation of this latent content.

But not us. Hear Joan Didion: 'Only the very young and the very old may recount their dreams at breakfast, dwell upon the self, interrupt with memories of beach picnics and favorite liberty lawn dresses and the rainbow trout in a creek near Colorado Springs. The rest of us are expected, rightly to affect absorption in other people's favorite dresses, other people's trout' (1961, p. 136). Didion's suspicion that the telling of dreams is a sign of weakness tolerable only in those we categorise as impotent is supported by the Frankfurt School's critique of individuality, more recently developed in the particular terms of American culture by Christopher Lasch (1978) and Eli Zaretsky (1976). The argument, which I will present briefly (assuming that you are already familiar with it) suggests that individualism is a product of the economic and social conditions that accompanied the development of capitalism. It associates the rise of the middle class with the concept of the individual, a person who, emancipated from the determinism of inherited wealth or poverty would make his own way in the world, and would, accordingly, perceive this passage through the world as evidence of his own intentionality and achievement. As capitalism left the phase of entrepreneurship and family business and passed into our present monopoly and corporate forms, we find the middle class still wedded to a concept of individuality, trying to make daily experience coincide with this idea of a self that social and economic experience could no longer sustain. And so the bourgeois, who had, at the onset of capitalism, experienced his individualism by seeing it mirrored in the transformations that he, himself, wrought in his family's social and economic world, now, in advanced capitalism, was exiled from the economic and social worlds to other zones of experience to gratify this enduring appetite for a sense of direction, of movement and identity. Collectively, this appetite fed on romanticism, nationalism and, ultimately, fascism.

And so it is no coincidence that Didion's images of dreams are beach picnics, liberty lawn dresses and rainbow trout in a creek near Colorado Springs. These are souvenirs from the last days of ingenuous, winsome capitalism. They are the nostalgic scenes from the 1920s: flashbacks of imported English frocks, sea-shore vacations, communion with the wilderness, relics from the lost worlds of Fitzgerald and Hemingway. These are not dreams to be read into the record. They cling to faded postcards, stacked in antique shops, to dusty photo albums. They are the reflections of a culture that severed work from play, material from spirit, value from feeling.

Like the Indian father we also teach our young to withhold their dreams. But, I fear, our motives are different from his. Whereas the Indian is eager not to subordinate the vision to the reality and strives to maintain the distinction of latent from manifest content so that their eventual integration will contain all the richness of the dialectic, we have no use for our visions. In our own helplessness, we see so little promise of bringing our dreams into the discourse of daily life, that we designate them as private in order to disavow them. We are not preserving them so that we may hear their songs or feel their textures. Either we seclude our visions in museums, diaries and prayers, or we encapsulate them in a sterile fantasy of the 'self'. Recent expressions of the bourgeois notion of selfhood are identified as the stigmata of what Lasch has called the culture of narcissism, the valorisation of therapy, physical culture, media fantasy and religious cultism. These competing, but equally monological ideologies of autonomy and the whole person promote a casual bonding of expressiveness and authenticity that tethers subjectivity to the status quo. 'Do your own thing', 'let it all hang out' ignore the conditions that force selected portions of our experience into expression and silence or disguise the rest. Celebrating selfhood and wholeness, we forget that it is not the fusion but the tension and struggle of feeling and form that releases subjectivity. There are no formless feelings, no neutral forms, and whenever we identify subjectivity with either form or feeling we surrender its capacity for negation to the silent partner of that dialectic.

Given that false consciousness is the national state of mind, it is surprising that our notion of subjectivity still bears the stigma of solipsism. The reveries that Didion describes have been absorbed into outdoor survival programmes and Freddie Laker has colonised the remaining beaches. We turn inward, listening for our inner voices to find that we have tuned in Woody Allen and Jane Fonda. And if the contemporary cant of the 'self' is transparently social, so is the notion of subjectivity within contemporary educational theory.[2] Asserting the social ground of subjectivity is not new to curriculum theory. John Dewey continually framed human action, whether it was ethics, art or enquiry within a social and public context. Dewey, locating our paramount reality in the world of everyday life, celebrated the continuity of manifest and latent content rather than their disassociation:

> We dream, but the material of our dream life is the stuff of our waking life. Revery is not . . . wholly detached from the objects of purposeful action and belief . . . Its objects consist of objects of daily concern subjected to a strange perspective, perverted in behalf of a bias. Such empirical facts as these are fatal to any theory which seriously asserts the wholesale irrelevance of the material of consciousness to the things of the actual world. Irrelevance exists, but it is relative and specifiable. (Dewey, cited in Webb, 1976)

Dewey's stance amidst this dialectic is hardly neutral. Subjectivity is presented as a 'strange perspective', its logic perverted, biased. Dewey extends a hospitality to latent content that is similar to the welcome extended to black students bussed out to white suburban schools. They are embraced so long as they deny what keeps them separate from white, middle-class culture, so long as they surrender their resistance. Dewey's conciliatory approach to the tension between the individual and society precluded his deep understanding of Freud's insight that society is maintained at the price of repression. 'The greatness of Freud', wrote Adorno, 'consists in that, like all great bourgeois thinkers, he left standing undissolved such contradictions and disdained the assertion of pretended harmony where the thing itself is contradictory. He revealed the antagonistic character of social reality' (Jacoby, 1975, p. 28). My criticism of Dewey parallels Russell Jacoby's criticism of the Adlerians and neo-Freudians.

Jacoby argues that those of Freud's followers who investigated the relationship of the individual to the particular norms and values of contemporary society under the banner of ego psychology, became apologists for the repressions of contemporary culture. Jacoby scores the neo-Freudian concept of the self for failing to sustain Freud's profound grasp of the conflict of nature and civilisation. Freudian concepts exposed individualism as an illusion by showing us that what the person discovers when he experiences the latent content of his own subjectivity are the distortions that are the response of his humanity to the repressions of society. Critical theorists maintain that the 'self' and the 'individual' that Adler, Fromm and their contemporary exponents promote is hardly the passionate, instinctual humanity that Freud's analysis sighted on the horizon of our collective neuroses, but an ersatz identity, a 'second-nature', thoroughly infiltrated with those assumptions of the society to which it is, supposedly, a dialectical alternative. Jacoby cites Marcuse to make the distinction between the neo-Freudian and Frankfurt School notions of the dialectical relation of the individual and society:

> Either one defines 'personality' and individuality' in terms of their possibilities within the established form of civilization, in which case their realization is for the vast majority tantamount to successful adjustment. Or one defines them in terms of transcending content. This would imply transgression beyond the established form of civilization to radicaly new modes of 'personality' and 'individuality' incompatible with the prevailing ones . . . This would mean 'curing' the patient to become a rebel. (Marcuse in Jacoby, 1975, p. 35)

While Jacoby's full critique of conformist psychology is too detailed to be fully developed here, I introduce his argument to suggest its implications for curriculum theory, particularly in re-examining the pragmatism of Dewey and in developing a position from which we can distinguish our sense of the relation of the individual to the curriculum that would substitute a vital dialectic for the ultimate isomorphism of his conception. To the degree that Dewey's emphasis on integration and on the paramount reality of everyday life functioned to stabilise and reinforce the status quo, a consequence of his theory carefully documented by Feinberg (1975), it provides a basis, despite its liberal rhetoric of reconstructionism, for curriculum theory that is confined within the society it is given. It is a philosophy of adjustment, not transcendence, and reminds us that Dewey's project was different from ours. He was struggling to repair the Cartesian bifurcation of experience, to integrate idealist and materialist epistemologies and thus invest philosophic enquiry with the wholeness that he knew to be the pervasive quality of human experience. It is this very quality of wholeness that is the problem that concerns me here.

Because the Indian father I spoke of at the outset of this discussion shares Dewey's conviction that the daily world of work, of social life, of immersion in physical activity, is the paramount reality, *he* teaches *his* child to cultivate visions. Suspicious of wholeness that is limited to manifest content, he cultivates dreams. Dewey, wary of the division of spirit from matter, of thought from action and knowledge from experience, asserts, with some optimism, that enquiry and understanding will evolve out of the daily doubts and questions that spring from the situations we live through. This is the confidence we must resist. Dewey's faith that experience, the full participation of the individual in the work, art and governance of his society, would engender the reconstruction of that society is a false and misleading promise. According to Marcuse (1964) we have relinquished this access to doubt to the one dimensionality of technical rationality. In his critique of modern culture he has argued that the tensions and transformations that formerly characterised the relations between the psychic and social structures have collapsed into an immediate identification of the individual with his society, into a *mimesis* that reduces subjectivity from a radical challenge to an empty posture. Generational tensions have given way to peer group influence; working-class negation has been co-opted by the homogenisation of culture, and by solicitous but insidious social services. Rebellious subjectivity has been enervated by the processes of 'repressive desublimation'. This is Marcuse's term for the objectification of human activity; it is an interaction of person and milieu that permits the speedy and efficient gratification of desire.

> The organism is thus being preconditioned for the spontaneous acceptance of what is being offered. In as much as the greatest liberty involves a contradiction rather than extension and development of instinctual needs, it works *for* rather than *against* the status quo of general repression. (Marcuse, 1964, p. 74)

If curriculum theory is to be anything other than a reinforcement schedule of the status quo, if it can also define its project as the revelation and realisation of possible worlds, then it must rigorously root out optimism. It must see integration as a blight, for I fear our capacity to dream, to pervert, invert, subvert diminishes with the creation of every new open classroom, every career orientation programme, every group dynamics, sex education, bilingual, head-start, mainstreaming initiative. Progressive education collapses into the most insidious form of co-optation unless accompanied by deep suspicion of our most cherished and most comfortable ideologies. It is suspicion that this autobiographical method cultivates. Doubt is a response to a problem. Suspicion is a response to a solution.

The problem of studying the curriculum is that we are the curriculum. It is we who have raised our hands before speaking, who have learned to hear only one voice at a time, and to look past the backs of the heads of our peers to the eyes of the adult in authority. It is we who have learned to offer answers rather than questions, not to make people feel uncomfortable, to tailor enquiry to bells, buzzers and mods.

Unlike Dewey, I have little hope that the reconstruction of the school or of society or of the curriculum will evolve from the immersion and active participation with our fellows in these places. The process that I will describe I have called the restitution and reconstruction of educational experience. It is a method of curriculum research that employs autobiography to restore the visions that have been muted by years of schooling. The vision is rarely revealed in the text but hovers in and around it. The narrative, an autobiographical account of educational experience serves to mark the site for excavation. What is returned in the process of excavation is hardly the original experience but broken pieces of images that remind us of what was lost. What is restored is our distrust of the account, as the experience, pieced together and reassembled, fails to cohere. There in the interstices, the spaces where the pieces don't quite meet, is where the light comes through. What the restoration returns to us is doubt in the certainty of our own assumptions, and without that doubt reconstruction dwindles into reification.

Paul Ricoeur's description of the dialectic of written communication as an interaction of distanciation and appropriation offers us a way of understanding how these texts of educational experience may serve as wedges that we may drive between the layers of that experience. Distanciation is achieved as the written text edges away from the original intention of the author and the reception of his original audience and makes sense without being limited in reference to the original context of the dialogical situation from which it emerged. Appropriation is achieved by the reader who takes to himself what was once alien. Ricoeur is careful, however, to distinguish this process from the romantic ideal of coinciding with the author's intention or psyche, or the historicity that would require this reader to identify the original author's intention, the original audience's response, nor, and this is most important, with the range of experience and imagination (a personal *a priori* of self-understanding) that the reader brings to the text.

Appropriation of the text that requires a coincidence of the reader's experience with that of the original author, reader, or with her own history would merely be an act of *mimesis* that refers back to old, already accomplished meanings. Interpretation of texts fails to contribute to an enlarged understanding of the world if it merely corresponds to that world as concretely lived by the original communicative dyad and their contemporary eavesdropper. Rather, Ricoeur argues, the text projects the possibility of new worlds by offering sense that, though drawn from the dialectical interplay of actual contexts, transcends them, leaving the reader with the possibility and option of finding within himself and his community the capacity to realise the world the text signifies.

In the past few years William Pinar and I have been working with autobiographical accounts of educational experience as a mode of curriculum enquiry. In other pieces we have described the method of writing and analysis that we have used. The schemes have varied, but in each case they repeat this rhythm of appropriation and distanciation, claiming and estrangement. (Pinar and Grumet, 1976; Grumet, 1978, 1979a, b). The methods that we have employed in working with our own texts and with those of others are akin to psychoanalytic and phenomenological methods. Our project is less ambitious than either of its progenitors. As curriculum theory pursues the relationship of the knower and the known we have been less demanding of the knower than psychoanalysis, avoiding where we could, the cultivation of intense transference relationships and revelation of unconscious wishes. Similarly, our phenomenological impulse has been tempered, and we have forsaken the search for the ground of certain knowledge that was Husserl's goal, content to investigate the genesis of the categories that pertain to curriculum theory within the educational experience of the writers. The dialectic of distanciation and appropriation inheres in our approach to the generation and interpretation of autobiographical texts of educational experience. The method provides a channel for curriculum discourse that undermines the pat and facile generalisations of the deadly curriculum while it rescues subjectivity from its self-indulgent privatised exile from human affairs and restores it to the critical function of simultaneously reconstructing its own understanding and the objects of that understanding.

Now in this process the original author, the original audience and the contemporary reader are one and the same person. This person is asked to write an essay that presents three narratives that the author categorises as educational experience. Students are instructed to defer the definition of that category as long as possible, focusing first on the stories that come to mind and are freely associated with the phrase, 'educational experience'. This injuction is enunciated in order to disarm the writer. First of all, we must remember that the student usually writes this essay as a requirement of the education course in which he or she is enrolled and for which I am the instructor. Years of banking education and of survival in educational institutions have taught the student to figure out what is expected and to deliver the order as neatly, quickly, and obsequiously as possible. If these authors were to work deductively, the definitions of educational experience they would devise would never be their own. They would be drawn from Piaget, from Cremin, from Holt or Plato (or from Grumet if they had been attending class).

Now the definitions that they draw from the narratives they compose are also not their own. Even if no definition of educational experience is developed in the text, the stories themselves are saturated with theory. The difference between the definition that precedes the narratives from the one that follows them, is that while neither is original with the author, she knows the former is borrowed and disclaims responsibility for it, while she often doesn't realise that the latter is borrowed as well, and will claim it as her own. It is here that the dialectic of distanciation and appropriation first emerges, although it is appropriation that emerges first. What the student reclaims is her own version of the curriculum. Most often the context of the tale is not the school, and even when it is the classroom, instruction and materials are rarely featured. Time and space, ways of knowing, of teaching and learning pervade the texts although they may not be identified as its formal content. So curriculum here can refer to a discussion at the dinner table, a sailing trip, the first day in kindergarten, the death of a parent. These events, dispersed through a kaleidescope of contexts that constitute our daily experience and revealed through our forms of perception, organisation and interpretation disclose epistemological, ontological and ethical presuppositions that we share. It is these suppositions that are extended into the so-called learning outcomes that present themselves as the goals and, collectively, as the rationale for curriculum choices.

I suppose that I do con the students. For the invitation to write such an essay confirms the illusion that they harbour an utterly unique and private subjectivity, and they turn to the writing with a desperate eagerness to rescue their past educational experience from the alienation of their transcripts and old notebooks and to penetrate all the public talk about education with their own private truths. So they think that they are appropriating their own pasts when they produce these autobiographical texts. Now and then someone is wise to the ruse. 'I'll write the essay,' he tells me, 'but you'll never know, never be able to really understand this experience of mine. The words can't give it to you.' Sometimes I mourn the solipsistic fallacy that insists that you can never understand my experience, convincing this student that theoretical discourse can never be a medium for his visions. Ricoeur acknowledges this rift between experience and expression as do Husserl, Merleau-Ponty and Laing, but celebrates the capacity of language to make private experience public.

> Language is the exteriorization thanks to which an *im*pression is transcended or becomes an *ex*pression or in other words the transformation of the psychic into the noetic. Exteriorization and communicability are one and the same thing for they are nothing other than this elevation of a part of our life into the logos of discourse. There the solitude of life is merely, a moment away, illuminated by the common light of discourse. (Ricoeur, 1976, p. 19)

Nevertheless, what this first phase of appropriation discloses to the writer is that this apparently private event is pervaded with public meanings. Now it can be argued that to find words for the event is to violate the rich layered moment of lived experience, filled with ambiguity, feeling, intuition, and to bleed that instant when past, present and future fuse in meaning into the linear, monological forms of written discourse. It can be argued that as experience is drained into written discourse it leaves its life behind and is channelled into forms that impose alien and public meanings upon its unique but silent truth. When the Indian child is ordered to keep his visions to himself it is implied that the rebellious subjectivity of the vision will dissipate in its telling. I have not dreamed the Indian boy's dreams, nor have I danced his dances, planted his corn or herded his sheep, and I cannot judge the distance that separates his stories from his visions. I would venture to say that for me and my students, the forms that our experience takes in this narrative and the forms that experience takes in our silent visions are fairly congruent. The 'self' that we discover when we reflect on our experience is as Sartre (1972) has argued, a construct, an interpretation that we make after panning for meaning in the stream of our experience and trying to identify the rocks that gleam through the silt. The 'self,' the Madeleine Grumet whom I find in the dreams pulled throught the skein of sleep into the fabric of the day, into the habitual breakfast, single poached egg on dry wheat toast, into the echo of the child's voice singing as we drove to school, into the polite exchange of greetings at the post office, into the comments violating the margins of the student's essay, that Madeleine Grumet is no more apodictic than the definition of educational experience drawn from the narrative accounts that the students have written. That self and that definition are still the intentional objects of consciousness and my perception of those objects is as partial, perspectival and inadequate, historical and contingent as is my perception of this chair, the Iran crisis and your response to this paper. So the first phase of this so called appropriation, this narrative of educational experience, this rendering of private experience, produces a text, an object that is the precipitate of the author's intentional activity.

Once the student transforms this object, her educational experience into a text, she has achieved the opportunity to distance herself from it. The next phase subjects the text to various forms of analysis. The first search of the text resembles Marcuse's category of 'critical remembrance', an analysis that seeks to combat the one dimensionality of the account by referring the author back to the experience that she is trying to draw from impression into expression. The author is asked why some aspects of the experience are articulated and others are ignored. The author is asked to estimate the distortions that the narrative form has imposed on the experience. The author is asked to examine discontinuities between the details and the generalisations of the account. The author is asked to compare the patterns of actions that may be common to all three narratives, noting thematic correspondences or contradictions. Finally, the author is asked to account for the discrepancies that can be noted in the definition of educational experience and the particular narratives from which it is drawn.

Most important, however, is the point that the text is not taken as a sign of what is or was. The very act of interpretation suggests that the text points to the future as it reveals what the text has concealed, or forgotten and begins to bring these submerged intimations to expression. The stringing together of three distinct narratives loosens our immersion in any one of them and permits us to carry the momentum of our movement between them, beyond them. When the story shows us what is missing, when three apparently disparate stories all seem to portray the same theme, the same pattern of actions, when the three stories announce themselves as congruent but contain details that jar the smooth assertion of continuity, we are surprised. This is the astonishment that Ernst Bloch discovers in story telling (Jameson, 1971). The dialectic of memory and story is recovered in interpretation and restores both doubt and promise to what appeared to be closed accounts. Jameson cites Bloch's praise of story telling to show how 'an implicit or explicit perception of the future is concealed within that which exists; it already carries within itself a story line, the trajectory of the not-yet-finished, the struggle of the incomplete to free itself from the as-yet-formlessness of the present'. (Jameson, 1971, p. 124).

> In short, it's also good to think in fables. For there is much that fails to be exhausted by taking place, or even by a good telling of it. Things have an odd way of keeping on going, there's a problem there somewhere, its pointing this way of beginning to strike. Such stories are not only re-counted [erzählen] you also count up [zählen] what is making itself heard through them, or you perk up your ears. Who goes there? An unexpected Mark! emerges from perfectly ordinary circumstances; or else a Mark! that was already there turns up traces of its presence in all kinds of insignificant incidents. They draw attention to a More or Less that ought to make us reflect while we're telling stories, or tell stories while we reflect; one that isn't quite right, because it's out of tune with us and with everything else. So much can be grasped only through such stories. (Bloch, cited in Jameson, 1971, p. 124).

While revelation is supported by the distanciation that the written text achieves, it discloses subjectivity as a process rather than as a content. Autobiographical method shows the author of the piece the way in which he has construed his experience and reveals the ways in which curriculum has invaded his own perceptual lens. It reveals that this apparent subjectivity is a highly socialised one, and carefully tailored to the assumptions about time and space, community, knowledge, and power that are the dominant ideologies of our society. It discovers the future that has been hovering in and around the past and provokes the student to name both the silent and the silencers.

This process is disquieting. It is as if the student has gathered all her courage to come forward and to dramatically rip off her mask, only to find underneath it another, and to feel its taut rubber surface when she had expected to feel the familiar texture of her own skin. It is because the text never completely coincides with the experience it signifies that interpretation is a revelatory enterprise. Intimations, half-truths, contradictions, distractions hover around every tale we tell. Excluded from the text, they are the phantoms its author meets when he reads his own story. That is why we dread reading our own essays. What has been said is only an index to what we were too frightened, or too lazy to say.

Well, subjectivity does not come easy. Once more the student returns to the text, once more appropriating it, but this time attempting to restore the distinctions between essence and appearance, potentiality and actuality, the social and the natural, the essential dualities that critical remembrance struggles to reclaim from the flatness of the original text. It is this final phase of analysis that introduces subjectivity into the dialogue, and it is ironic that this release of subjectivity is mediated by others. I have responded to the text with questions as have other students when the narrative was read aloud. Our questions do not establish the substance for later analysis but provide a model for distanciation to help the writer become the 'other' that his own reflexive dialectic requires. For it is the reflexive attention that takes its own intentional act as the object of its understanding that discloses the freedom of rebellious subjectivity and resuscitates doubt. Only when curriculum is reclaimed from the very processes of interpretation that we apply to our experience can we cease to promote the status quo despite our rhetoric of reconstruction. The fundamental structure of curriculum inquiry is complicity and only the rigorous dialectic of distanciation and appropriation can inform our project of restitution and reconstruction.

Notes

1. I am endebted to Daniel Williams, a student at Hobart and William Smith Colleges, for bringing this material to my attention.

2. William Schubert has recently argued that the practical orientation of Dewey's educational thought, most recently interpreted for current curriculum theory by Schwab, penetrates current projects of curriculum research (Schubert, 1980). Schubert argues that this practical theme binds enquiries in policy deliberation, ethnomethodological studies, qualitative evaluation and reconceptualist critiques into a cohesive approach to curriculum theory. While the methodology proposed in this paper participates in this theme, through its focus on lived experience, it cultivates a suspicion of the organisation and descriptions of that experience and subjects the category of 'the practical' to critical scrutiny.

Bibliography

Didion, Joan (1961) 'On Keeping a Notebook' in *Slouching Toward Bethlehem*, Dell, New York

Feinberg, Walter (1975) *Reason and Rhetoric*, Wiley, New York

Grumet, Madeleine (1978) 'Songs and Situations: the Figure/Ground Relation in a Case Study of *Currere*' in G. Willis (ed.) *Qualitative Evaluation*, McCutchan, Berkeley

Grumet, Madeleine (1979a) 'Supervision and Situation', *Journal of Curriculum Theorizing*, vol. I, no. 1, Fall

Grumet, Madeleine (1979b) 'Autobiography and Reconceptualisation'. *Impact*, New York State Association for Supervision and Curriculum, Development, (ASCD) vol. 14, no. 3, Spring

Hollowell, A. Irving (1955) 'The Self and its Behavioural Environment' in *Culture and Experience*, Univ. of Pennsylvania Press, Philadelphia, pp. 75-110

Jacoby, Russell (1975) *Social Amnesia,* Beacon Press, Boston

Jameson, Frederic (1971) *Marxism and Form*, Princeton University Press, Princeton

Lasch, Christopher (1978) *The Culture of Narcissism*, W. W. Norton, New York

Marcuse, Herbert (1964) *One Dimensional Man*, Beacon Press, Boston

Mead, Margaret (1937) *Cooperation and Competition Among Primitive Peoples*, McGraw-Hill Book Company, New York

Pinar, William (1975) '*Currere*: Toward Reconceptualization' in Pinar (ed.), *Curriculum Theorizing: the Reconceptualists*, McCutchan, Berkeley

Pinar, William, and Grumet, Madeleine (1976) *Toward a Poor Curriculum*, Kendall-Hunt, Dubuque

Ricoeur, Paul (1976) *Interpretation Theory*, Texas Christian University, Fort Worth

Sartre, Jean-Paul (1972) *The Transcendence of the Ego*, Forrest Williams and Robert Kirkpatrick (trans.) Octagon Books, New York

Schubert, William (1980) 'Recalibrating Educational Research: Toward a Focus on Practice,' *Educational Researcher*, vol. 9, no. 1, January, pp. 17-24

Webb, Rodman B (1976) *The Presence of the Past: John Dewey and Alfred Schutz on the Genesis and Organization of Experience*, University Presses of Florida, Gainsville

Zaretsky, Eli (1976) *Capitalism, the Family and Personal Life*, Harper and Row, New York

5 SOCIAL STRUCTURE, IDEOLOGY AND CURRICULUM

Michael W. Apple

Introduction

It is not inconsequential that a central thrust of radical criticism of our institutions during the last decade or so has been on the school. It has become increasingly obvious over this same time period that our educational institutions may serve less as the engines of democracy and equality than many of us would like. In many ways, this criticism has been healthy since it has increased our sensitivity to the important role schools – and the overt and covert knowledge within them – play in reproducing a stratified social order that remains strikingly unequal by class, gender and race. As individuals as diverse as Bourdieu, Althusser, and Baudelot and Establet in France, Bernstein, Young, Whitty, and Willis in England, Kallos and Lundgren in Sweden, Gramsci in Italy, and Bowles and Gintis, myself and others in the United States have repeatedly argued, the educational and cultural system is an exceptionally important element in the maintenance of existing relations of domination and exploitation in these societies.

While there may be serious disagreements among these people about how this goes on, still none would deny the importance of examining the relationship between schooling and the maintenance of these unequal relations. And, while some of us may also disagree with parts of the logic of each other's analysis, we simply cannot look at the schools, and the knowledge within them, in quite the same way as we did before this corpus of work appeared. These economic and cultural criticisms of schools, and what this means for the field of curriculum, will be the subject of this chapter.

While this criticism has been healthy, it has perhaps had two side effects that are, paradoxically, the opposite of each other. On the one hand, it has caused us to give too much importance to the school. We may see the school as *the* issue, instead of as part of a larger framework of social relations that are structurally exploitative. That the issue is much larger can be seen in the recent study by Jencks *et al.* (1979). It documents the fact that not only are economic returns from schooling twice as great for individuals who are economically advantaged to begin with, but for, say, black students even finishing high school will probably not bring any significant benefits. Thus, even if we could alter the schools to equalise achievement, the evidence suggests that it might not make a significant difference in the larger framework in which schools exist. (See also Wright, 1979).

The second side-effect is nearly the mirror image of the possible over-emphasis on the power of the school. This is the rather pessimistic stance that says that since schools *are* so integrated into this larger framework and since they seem to mirror basically what a 'society needs', then they can be ignored. Nothing of value can be gained by acting in them because they are fundamentally determined institutions. Both of these side-effects can have negative consequences, I believe. As I present my arguments here, we shall need to be cautious of these effects. Behind my own sense of this lay these two cautions, therefore: the realisation that understanding and acting on schools is not enough, but also knowing that ignoring them is simply wrong. It is the result of an incorrect analysis and is misguided politically. As I shall argue, in fact, the educational system – because of its very location within a larger nexus of social relations – can provide a significant terrain over which serious action can evolve.

In this essay I shall be forced to speak rather generally at times, skating over what are serious issues and controversies within structurally oriented economic and cultural scholarship on schools. How does one summarise one's work over a decade, as well as other people's efforts, when that work has grown in sophistication considerably over those years? How can one trace the rapid developemnt of critical ideas about what schools do, without at the same time showing how these ideas about what happens within schools have been fundamentally influenced by one's political practice and by the intense debate going on now within the leftist community on the relationship between culture and mode of production? Obviously, all of this can't be done. Therefore, I have chosen to handle this problem in three ways. First, I shall lay out what Marxist-oriented curriculum scholarship is about by making some general points about how one should interpret the issue of reproduction. I want then to trace the development of my own thinking on these matters by illuminating the concerns I had during the years when I wrote *Ideology and Curriculum* (1979a). In so doing, I want to show how my analysis has progressed in more recent work, a progress that, again, has been strongly influenced by the exceptional work being currently done within Marxist literature and by my own involvement in political activity. Possible action will, finally provide the third aspect of this chapter.

Since I cannot give a sense of all of the debates that are continuing to influence the work of people like me, I shall indicate in my notes and bibliography some of the major controversies that remain unsettled. This will leave a good deal unsaid, for in order to show how, say, my own political work – with poor, black, white, and hispanic groups to secure their and their children's economic and cultural rights, with politically progressive workers on the development of materials for political education, on economic justice, etc. – has been so important in my latest analyses, I would have to transform this chapter into an autobiography. For the present, I shall leave that style to others. I do want to stress, however, that none of what is written here can be thoroughly understood without reference to the concrete practice of the men and women with whom I act.

Curriculum and Reproduction

For the major part of this century, the curriculum field has devoted a good deal of its energy to the search for one specific thing. It has searched long and hard for a general set of principles that would guide curriculum-planning and evaluation. In large part, this has reduced itself to attempts at creating the *most efficient method* of doing curriculum work. One need only trace the internal history of the dominant traditions in the field – from Thorndike, Bobbitt and Charters in the early years of the twentieth century to Tyler and the even more vulgar behaviourists and systems managers today – to begin to realise how strong the emphasis on curriculum as efficient method has become (Kliebard, 1971, pp. 74-93).

The focus on method has not been without its consequences. At the same time that process-product rationality grew, the factual concept that curriculum is through and through a political enterprise withered. By the questions we asked we tended to divorce ourselves from the way in which the economic and cultural apparatus of a society operated. A 'neutral' method meant our own neutrality, or so it seemed. The fact that the methods we employed had their roots in industry's attempts to control labour and increase productivity, in the popular eugenics movement, and (more particularly) in class and status group interests was concealed by the stunning lack of historical insight in the field (Apple, 1979a; see also: Selden, 1977; Braverman, 1974; Collins, 1979). At the same time, we seemed to assume that the development of this supposedly neutral method would eliminate the need to deal with the issue of whose knowledge should be or already was preserved and transmitted in schools. While a number of alternative traditions continued to try to keep this kind of political question alive, by and large the faith in the inherent neutrality of our institutions, the knowledge that was taught and our methods and actions was ideally suited to help legitimate the structural bases of inequality.

The key to this last sentence is the concept of legitimation. Like Wittgenstein, I am claiming that the meaning of our language and practices lies in their use. And the use in this case has tended to be twofold. The traditions that dominate the field assist in the reproduction of inequality while at the same time serving to legitimate both the institutions which recreate it and our own actions within them. This is *not* to claim that individual children are not often being helped by our practices and discourse; nor is it to claim that all of our day-to-day actions are misguided. It is to claim that macro-economically our work may serve functions that bear little resemblance to even our best intentions.

How are we to understand this? A fundamental problem facing us is the way in which systems of domination and exploitation persist and reproduce themselves without being consciously recognised by the people involved (Di Maggio, 1979, p. 1461). This is of particular import in education, where our commonly accepted practices so clearly seek to help students and to ameliorate many of the 'social and educational problems' facing them. On the face of it, such a focus on these 'problems' should seem helpful. Yet it ignores something that has been made rather clear in recent sociological literature.

The essentials of this literature are stated rather pointedly by Di Maggio when he argues that commonsense classification of individuals, social groups, or 'social problems' tends to confirm and reinforce these structurally generated relations of domination. For 'purposeful, reasoning, well intentioned actors' often contribute – simply by pursuing their own subjective ends – to the maintenance of these structural relations (Di Maggio, 1979, pp. 1461-2). These purposeful, reasoning, and well intentioned actors, hence, may be latently serving ideological functions at the same moment that they are seeking to alleviate some of the problems facing individual students and others. This is as much due to the linkages between economic and cultural institutions – what many Marxists have called (not unproblematically) the relationship between base and superstructure[1] – as it is to the personal characteristics of these people. Thus, one can examine schools and our action on them in two ways: first, as a form of amelioration and problem-solving by which we assist individual students to get ahead; and secondly, on a much larger scale to see the patterns of the *kinds* of individuals who get ahead and the latent outcomes of the institution. These larger social patterns and outcomes may tell us much about how the school functions in reproduction, a function that may tend to be all too hidden if our individual acts of helping remain our primary focus.

So far I have been using words like 'function' and 'reproduction'. These concepts point to the role of educational institutions in preserving what exists. But they also imply a good deal more that deserves our attention if we are not to be utterly mechanistic.

What do we mean when we look at how schools 'function' to reproduce an unequal society? Unlike sociological functionalism, where order is assumed and deviance from that order is problematic, Marxist and neo-Marxist analyses signal something else by that term (or at least they should). Rather than a functional coherence where all things work relatively smoothly to maintain a basically unchanging social order, these analyses point to 'the *contested* reproduction of a society's fundamental relations, which enables society to reproduce itself again, but only in the form of a dominant and subordinate (i.e., antagonistic, not functional) social order' (Hall, n.d., p. 6). For schools are not 'merely' institutions of reproduction, institutions where the overt and covert knowledge that is taught inexorably moulds students into passive beings who are able and eager to fit into an unequal society. This account fails in two critical ways. First, it views students as passive internalisers of pre-given social messages. Whatever the institution teaches in either the formal curriculum or the hidden curriculum is taken in, unmodified by class cultures and class (or race or gender) rejection of dominant social messages. Anyone who has taught in working-class schools, in schools located in our inner city ghettos, and elsewhere knows that this is simply not the case. Student reinterpretation or, at best, only partial acceptance and often outright rejection of the planned and unplanned meanings of schools are more likely. Clearly, schools need to be seen in a more complex manner than simple 'reproduction'.

The 'reproduction' account is too simple in another way. It under-theorises and hence neglects the fact that capitalist social relations are inherently *contradictory* in some very important ways. That is, just as in the economic arena where the capital accumulation process and the 'need' to expand markets and profits generates contradictions within a society – where, for example, rising profits and inflation create a crisis in legitimacy in both the state and the economy (O'Connor, 1973) – so, too, will similar contradictions emerge in other dominant institutions. The school will not be immune to these.

For instance, as a state apparatus schools perform important roles in assisting in the creation of the conditions necessary for capital accumulation (they sort, select, and certify a hierarchically organised student body) and for legitimation (they maintain an inaccurate meritocratic ideology and, therefore, legitimate the ideological forms necessary for the recreation of inequality).[2] However, these two 'functions' of schools are often in conflict with each other. The needs of capital accumulation may contradict the needs for legitimation. In the school we can see this in the relative overproduction of credentialled individuals at a time when the economy no longer 'requires' as many high salaried personnel. This very overproduction calls into question the legitimacy of the ways in which schools function. (See Bourdieu and Passeron, 1979, p. 81; Collins, 1979). On a more concrete level, we can see the contradictions of the institution in the fact that the school has different ideological obligations that may be in tension. Critical capacities are needed to keep our society dynamic; hence schools should teach students to be critical. Yet critical capacities can challenge capital as well.[3] This is not an abstract idea. These ideological conflicts permeate our educational institutions and are worked out every day in them.

The emphasis on working out contradictions in the last few paragraphs is not just important for thinking about how schools may be caught in conflicts of accumulation and legitimation not necessarily of their own making. It also provides a fundamental principle for thinking about how ideology works, a working that has been a constitutive part of my own enquiries.

Just as the school is caught in contradictions that may be very difficult for it to resolve, so too are ideologies filled with contradictions. They are not coherent sets of beliefs. It is probably wrong, in any case, to think of them as only beliefs. They are, instead, sets of lived meanings, practices, and social relations that are often internally inconsistent. They have elements within themselves that see to the heart of a society's inequalities and, at the same time, tend to reproduce the ideological relations and meanings that maintain the hegemony of the dominant classes (Johnson, 1979, p. 73). Because of this, ideologies are contested; they are continually struggled over. Since ideologies have both 'good and bad sense' within them, people need to be won over to one side or the other, if you will. Particular institutions become the sites where this struggle takes place and where these dominant ideologies are produced. The school is crucial as one of these sites.

Here it is not just the institution that is important. Actors – real people – must elaborate dominant ideologies. As Gramsci – one of the most influential figures in the analysis of the relationship between culture and economy – notes, this has been one of the prime tasks of 'intellectuals', spreading and making legitimate dominant ideological meanings and practices, attempting to win people over and create unity on the contested terrain of ideology (Mouffe, 1979, p. 187). Whether we accept it or not, educators are in the structural position of being such 'intellectuals' and, therefore, are not isolated from these ideological tasks (though many of them may struggle against it, of course). Again, Gramsci's insights are helpful. The control of the cultural apparatus of a society, of both the knowledge preserving and producing institutions and the actors who work in them, is essential in the struggle over ideological hegemony.

All of these general comments about how recent scholarship has looked at ideology and reproduction raise some exceptionally complex issues, of course. Reproduction, the state, legitimation, accumulation, contradiction, ideological hegemony, base/superstructure, all of these are strange concepts to a field involved in creating efficient and neutral methods. Yet, if we are to take seriously the political nature of curriculum and the unequal benefits and results of schooling (see Karabel and Halsey, 1977; Persell, 1977), they are essential. By and large, then, if we conceive of the internal qualities of schools and the knowledge found within them as being intricately connected to relations of domination, what is it that the use of these concepts entails in an analysis of schools and the curriculum?

In his discussion of the various ways in which Marxists have looked at schooling (and these ways are not all alike: they *do* differ radically),[4] Stuart Hall captures the essence of part of the approach taken by those of us who have been influenced by this scholarship and, in particular, by the original work of Gramsci. A quotation from one of his longer passages summarises part of the background of this position rather clearly.

> [This position] attributes the fundamental determination in securing the 'complex unity' of society to the relationships of the economic structure, but regards the so-called 'superstructures' as having vital, critical 'work' to do in sustaining, at the social, cultural,

> political, and ideological levels, the *conditions* which enable capitalist production to proceed. Furthermore, it regards the superstructures as having the role, above all, of drawing society into 'conformity' with the long-term requirements and conditions of a capitalist economic system (for example, in the work of Gramsci). This suggests that, though the superstructures are more determined than determining, the topography of base/superstructures is not so important as the relatively autonomous 'work' which the superstructures perform for the economic structure. This is regarded as difficult, contested 'work', that operates through opposition and antagonism – in short, by means of class struggles which are present at all the various levels of society – where simple correspondences are hard to come by. Far from assuming a simple recapitulation between the various structures of society, this approach sees the 'work' which the superstructures [like schools] perform as necessary precisely because, on its own, the economic system cannot ensure all the conditions necessary for its own expanded reproduction. The economic system cannot ensure that society will be raised to that general level of civilization and culture which its advanced system of production needs. Creating an order of society around the fundamental economic relationships is just as necessary as production itself; the relations of production alone cannot 'produce' such a social order. Here, then, the relationship is not one of correspondence but of coupling – the *coupling* of two distant, but interrelated and interdependent spheres. Gramsci is one of the outstanding theorists of this position. The nature of the 'coupling' envisaged is described in Gramsci's phrase, the 'structure-superstructure complex'. Again, simplifying, we may call this the paradigm of *hegemony*. (Hall, n.d., p. 7).

Notice what is being argued here. 'Superstructural' institutions such as schools have a significant degree of relative autonomy. The economic structure cannot ensure any simple correspondence between itself and these institutions. However, such institutions, the school among them, perform vital functions in the recreation of the conditions necessary for ideological hegemony to be maintained. These conditions are not imposed, though. They are, and need to be, continuously rebuilt on the field of institutions like the school. The conditions of existence of a particular social formation are rebuilt through antagonistic relations (and sometimes even through oppositional forms, as we shall see when I discuss my own genesis through these concepts and positions, in the next section of this essay). Above all, hegemony does not simply come about; it must be worked for in particular sites like the family, the workplace, the political sphere and the school.[5] And it is just this process of understanding how hegemony comes about, how it *is* partly produced, through the day-to-day curricular, pedagogical, and evaluative interactions in schools, that has been my primary concern.

Ideology and Curriculum as a First Approximation

What emerges from this general discussion of the way in which we might interpret schools? No simple one-way, conflict free, base/superstructure model will do. Contestation is central to reproduction. Even concepts like reproduction may be inadequate. It is easier for me to say this now, and to begin fully to understand the significance of what this perspective articulated by Hall implies today, than it was even three years ago when I was completing the work on *Ideology and Curriculum*.

To be honest, all of these points about reproduction, contradiction and contestation did not dawn on me all at once; nor was I able to appreciate either how they could be employed or what they might mean. Given my own interest, and that of people like Bowles and Gintis, Bourdieu, Bernstein, and others, in *reproduction* – an interest that was critically important, I believe, at that particular historical moment, but an interest that at the beginning tended to exclude other elements of what might be happening in schools – these points have had to be struggled with, worked through, and have ultimately been slowly incorporated. At times, this involved (and still does) serious self-criticism of my own previous work, building on and correcting mistakes, and fleshing out what now seems too simple and mechanistic.

Given this painstaking movement away from a focus on simple reproduction by a number of people like myself, in what follows I would like to employ the development of my own work as a paradigm case for understanding how the exceptional growth of literature on how such things as, say, reproduction, contradiction, and contestation are accomplished has influenced scholarship that seeks to situate the school within a larger nexus of social relations.

In my previous work I focused on the role school curricula played in the creation and recreation of the ideological hegemony of the dominant classes and class segments of our society. In essence, the fundamental problematic that guided my work was the relationship between power and culture. While I was not totally clear on it, I intuitively grasped the fact that culture has a dual form. It is lived experience, developed out of and embodied in the day-to-day lives and interactions of specific groups. Yet it also has another characteristic. Here I am referring to the ability of certain groups in society to transform culture into a commodity, to accumulate it, to make of it what Bourdieu has called 'cultural capital'. In many ways, it seemed to me that cultural capital and economic capital could be thought about in similar ways.[6] Yet both of these senses of culture – commodified and lived – were partly underdeveloped in my original investigations, perhaps because of the debates and issues into which I wanted to intervene.

Much of my analysis of schooling in *Ideology and Curriculum* concentrated on two issues: (1) a debate with liberal theories of the curriculum and of education in general, by attempting to show what is actually taught in schools and what its ideological effects might be; and (2) a debate within leftist scholarship in the educational field about what schools do.

The first of these two issues grew out of my general agreement with individuals like Bowles, Gintis, Althusser and others that schools are important agencies for social reproduction. Our attempts at reforming these agencies tended to be misguided, in large part because we misrecognised the socio-economic functioning of the institution. Along with these other individuals, I set out to document how this functioning actually went on. The kinds of questions I asked were unlike those which tended to dominate our efficiency-minded field. Rather than asking how we could get a student to acquire more curricular knowledge, I asked a more political set of questions. 'Why and how are particular aspects of a collective culture represented in schools as objective factual knowledge? How, concretely, may official knowledge represent the ideological configurations of the dominant interests in a society? How do schools legitimate these limited and partial standards of knowing as unquestioned truths?' (Apple, 1979a).

These questions provided the fundamental set of interests guiding my work. As I mentioned earlier, I was taken with the fact that, in our long history, from Bobbitt and Thorndike to Tyler and, say, Popham and Mager, of transforming curriculum into only a concern with efficient methods, we had almost totally depoliticised curriculum. Our search for a neutral methodology and the continuing transformation of the field into a 'neutral instrumentation' in the service of structurally non-neutral interests served to hide from us the political and economic context of our work. The kind of political-economic scrutiny I was engaged in was very similar in many ways to that being done by Katz, Karier and Feinberg, in the history and philosophy of education, by Bowles, Gintis, Carnoy and Levin in the economics of education, and by Young, Bernstein, and Bourdieu in the sociology of education. While there were similarities, however, there were and are serious disagreements among many of us on the left who examine and act on educational institutions. These disagreements provided the context for the second issue I noted above.

All too much of this of neo-Marxist scholarship treated the school as something of a black box and I was just as dissatisfied with this as I was with the dominant tradition in curriculum. It did not get inside the school to find out how reproduction went on. In many ways, oddly, it was an analogue of the Tyler rationale in curriculum, in that the focus tended to be scientistic and to place its emphasis on input and output, consensus, and efficient production. The interpretations placed upon the school were clearly different from those of Tyler and the efficiency-minded curriculum 'experts', yet schools were still seen as taking an input (students) and efficiently processing them (through a hidden curriculum) and turning them into agents for an unequal and highly stratified labour force (output). Thus, the schools' major role was in the teaching of an ideological consciousness that helped reproduce the division of labour in society. This was fine as far as it went, but it still had two problems. *How* was this accomplished? Was that *all* schools did?

I spent a good deal of time in *Ideology and Curriculum* attempting to answer these questions. I interrogated schooling using a variety of techniques – historical, economic, cultural, and ethnographic. In the process, it became clear that at least three basic elements in schooling had to be examined. These included: the day to day interactions and regularities of the hidden curriculum that tacitly taught important norms and values; the formal corpus of school knowledge – that is, the overt curriculum itself – that is planned and found in the various materials and texts and filtered through teachers; and, finally, the fundamental perspectives that educators (read in here Gramsci's points about the role of intellectuals) use to plan, organise, and evaluate what happens in schools (Apple, 1979a, p. 14). Each of these elements was scrutinised to show how the day-to-day meanings and practices that are so standard in classrooms, while clearly there to help individual children, tended to be less the instruments of help and more part of a complex process of the economic and cultural reproduction of class relations in our society.

One word in this last sentence highlights the question, 'Is that all schools do?' – the word 'cultural'. Like Bernstein, Bourdieu, and, especially Gramsci, it was evident to me that schools were cultural as well as economic institutions and examining the reproduction of the social division of labour would not exhaust how schools contributed to the creation of ideological hegemony. Thus, once again, the form and content of the curriculum became of great significance if we were to see how cultural domination works and how 'unity was created'. What the investigators who dealt almost totally with the problem of economic reproduction were neglecting was the culture preserved, transmitted, and rejected within the institution. The way the curriculum was organised, the principles upon which it was built and evaluated, and, finally, the very knowledge itself, all of these were critically important if we were to understand how power was reproduced. Here I meant not just economic power but cultural power as well, though the two are considerably interwoven (Collins, 1979).

Yet the focus on curriculum and culture still left out one very important aspect of schools, and it was here that I also tried to go beyond the theorists of economic reproduction such as Bowles and Gintis. They attempted to see the school as a place where economically rooted norms, dispositions and values were taught, something I had also documented in both the ethnography of what is taught in kindergartens and in the analysis of social studies and science curricula reported in *Ideology and Curriculum*. This position tended to see schools and their overt and hidden curriculum as part of a mechanism of *distribution* only. This was all well and good. After all, schools do distribute ideological knowledge and values. However, it neglected an essential factor of what our educational apparatus also does. I wanted to argue that the educational system constitutes a set of institutions that are fundamental to the *production* of knowledge as well. This was and is a key element in my argument about how we should interpret curriculum. Schools are organised not only to teach the 'knowledge that, how, and to' required by our society, but they are organised as well in such a way that they ultimately assist in the production of the technical/administrative knowledge required, among other things, to expand markets; control production, labour and people; engage in the basic and applied research needed by industry; and create widespread 'artificial' needs among the population (Apple, 1979b; Noble,

1977). This technical/administrative knowledge was able to be accumulated. It acted like a form of capital, and, like economic capital, this cultural capital tended to be controlled by and serve the interests of the most powerful classes in society.[7] Economic and cultural capital were inextricably linked. The kinds of knowledge considered most legitimate in school and which acted as a complex filter to stratify groups of students was connected to the specific needs of our kind of social formation.

Thus, I began to see the need to interpret schooling as both a system of production and reproduction. Our analysis of what gets into schools and why, of what counts as legitimate knowledge and values, would be incomplete unless we saw the complex and (as I have argued in later work that goes beyond the original outlines found in *Ideology and Curriculum*) contradictory roles schools play. As some of the 'new' sociologists of education argued, schools process both people and knowledge. But the 'processing' of knowledge includes not only its differential distribution to different kinds of people, but also its production and ultimate accumulation by those in power.

While all of this may seem horribly abstract, its roots were in something much more concrete. As someone who had taught for years at both elementary and secondary level and who had worked continuously with teachers and administrators as a professor, I was searching for ways of understanding my and their actions. Teachers, for example, blamed themselves as individuals (or their pupils) for the failures of students, just as I did. It more and more, however, seemed to me not to be a question of the amount of effort teachers and curricular workers put in. Indeed, few groups work harder and in more uncertain, difficult and complex circumstances than teachers and adminstrators. Rather, it became clearer that the institution itself and the connections it had to other powerful social agencies generated the dominant rules and practices of educators' lives. Blaming teachers, castigating individuals, was less than helpful. Figuring out how and, especially, why the institution did what it did in ways that went beyond these individual actions, that constrained these actions in ideological and material ways, seemed much more ethical. In this way we could make much better decisions on warranted curricular and pedagogical action. While an understanding of control was but a small step in challenging that control, it was a step that I felt was essential if we were ever to see the control for what it was and to begin to realise the differential benefits – both economic and cultural – that resulted from it.

At the same time, as I became even more aware myself of these differential benefits and the structures in which education found itself, it altered my own practice politically. The analysis, while still deficient in ways I was beginning to grasp, was compelling in other ways. It required an even deeper involvement in socialist politics and action at a variety of levels, thus, ultimately, reacting on my original analysis. My original work did not seem adequately to 'theorise' the kinds of things either I myself, or the groups of workers, parents and progressively orientated teachers, with whom I was working, were doing. This became all the more pressing.

Conflict and Contradiction in Labour and Culture

After reading the initial general section of this chapter – the one about simple reproduction theories and their problems – it is probably clear to you that part of the problem was the very fact that the dominant metaphor behind most of the analysis that went into *Ideology and Curriculum* was the idea of reproduction. I had broadened it to include cultural as well as economic considerations and I had argued for a notion of the school as a productive, as well as reproductive, apparatus. However, the orientation here still remained at too functional a level. It saw schools, and especially the hidden curriculum, as successfully corresponding to the ideological needs of capital; we just needed to see how it was really accomplished. What was now more obviously missing in my formulations at this time was an analysis that focused on contradictions, conflicts, mediations and, especially, resistances, as well as reproduction. For, while I had argued against mechanistic base/superstructure models where economic form totally determines cultural form and content, and while I wanted to show that the cultural sphere had some degree of relative autonomy, I had a theoretically underdeveloped notion of determination. It was a notion that led me to drift back to the logic of functional correspondence between what schools taught and the 'needs' of an unequal society and one that could not fully account for what else might be going on.

In struggling with this problem, my colleague Erik Olin Wright's work on the nature of determinations became quite helpful. He identified a number of basic models of determination, some of which indicated a situation where an institution or a practice simply reproduced a given ideology or social order. But he also showed how a good deal more could be going on. There could be meanings and practices that contradicted the overt and covert interests of a dominant class. There were important 'institutions' – such as the state – that mediated the interests of capital. And, most importantly, there could be concrete actions and struggles, though sometimes not conscious ones, by real groups of human actors that existed and which might be both mediating and transforming existing structures and meanings in significant ways (Wright, 1978).

I began to realise that functionalist accounts of the hidden curriculum – accounts that sought to demonstrate that students, like workers, were effectively socialised – were part of the very process of ideological reproduction I wanted to struggle against. This meant that I had to examine two areas – resistances at both the school and the workplace. If Wright (as well as my own personal experience) was correct, then I should be able to find contradictory processes at work in these institutions, not only a correspondence between what industry wants and what goes on. As I argued:

> [Such] overly deterministic and economistic accounts of the hidden curriculum are themselves elements of the subtle reproduction, at an ideological level, of perspectives required for the legitimation of inequality. What I mean to say is simply this. The analyses recently produced by a number of leftist scholars and educators are themselves partial reproductions of the ideological vision of corporate domination. By seeing schools as total reflections of an unequal 'labor market,' a market where workers simply do what they are told and passively acquiesce to the norms and authority relations of the workplace, these analyses accept as empirically accurate the ideology of management. (Apple, 1980b)

This growing awareness of the way contestation and resistances operated, and my own political work with people involved in factories, schools and offices, led me to examine the rapidly growing research on the day-to-day control of labour. Something quickly became rather apparent. When one examines the labour process, the actual life of men and women in our offices and factories, it becomes clear that what is found is a more complex picture than one has been led to expect from the literature on the hidden curriculum where simple correspondences between the school and the economy emerge in some straightforward fashion. This complexity is quite important since the truth of correspondence theories is dependent upon the accuracy of their view of the labour process. Rather than finding workers at all times being guided by the cash nexus, by authority, by expert planning, and by the norms of punctuality and productivity, however, the actual organisation and control of the labour process illuminates the extent to which workers at all levels often resist and engage in action that is rather contradictory.

> Rather than the labor process being totally controlled by management, rather than hard and fast structures of authority and norms of punctuality and compliance, one sees a complex work culture. This very work culture provides important grounds for worker resistance, collective action, informal control of pacing and skill, and reasserting one's humanity . . . Men and women workers seem engaged in overt and informal activity that is missed when we talk only in reproductive terms. (Apple, 1980b)

Clearly, then, workers resist. They often contradict and partly transform modes of control into opportunities for resistance and maintaining their own informal norms which guide the labour process. Whatever reproduction goes on is accomplished not only through the acceptance of hegemonic ideologies, but through opposition and resistances. We should remember here, though, that these resistances occur on the terrain established by capital, not necessarily by the people who work in our offices, stores, and industries.

We need also to remember a point I noted earlier. These informal cultural resistances, this process of contestation, may act in contradictory ways that may ultimately tend to be reproductive. By resisting and establishing an informal work culture which both recreates some sense of worker control over the labour process and rejects a good deal of the norms to which workers are supposedly socialised, workers may also be latently reinforcing the social relations of corporate production. Yes, they can partly control the skill level and pacing of their work, but they do not really impinge on the minimal requirements of production; nor do they effectively challenge the 'rights' of management. Resistances on one level may partially reproduce the lack of control on another.

All of these analyses of life in our workplaces were of no small import to me. My work on 'the other side of the hidden curriculum', on what the labour process actually looked like, had given me a considerable amount of insight into the way oppositional cultural forms developed in day-to-day life. My interest in ideology and the relative autonomy of culture remained strong, for if resistance and contestation were real, then they could be employed for serious structural change as well. They could be used to 'win' people to the other side, if you will. Base/superstructure models were clearly too limiting here both theoretically and politically and I was going beyond them in some important ways now. My attempts to go further – to deal with culture as well as economy more seriously, to articulate the principles of the production as well as the reproduction of knowledge – were also stimulated by something else, however. A significant amount of progress was being made on the very topic of cultural production and reproduction, especially by Marxist ethnographers.

Recent ethnographic investigations, in particular those carried out by people such as Paul Willis at the Centre for Contemporary Cultural Studies in the University of Birmingham, provided critical elements which enabled me to apply some of what I had learned about the labour process to the school. Willis and others demonstrated that, rather than being places where culture and ideologies are imposed on students, schools are the *sites* where these things are produced. And they are produced in ways which are filled with contradiction and by a process that is itself based in contestation and struggle (Willis, 1977; Everhart, 1979). Once again resistance and the importance of lived culture came to the fore. The general points I laid out in my earlier discussion about reproduction were now no longer mere abstractions. The heritage of mechanistic perspectives was now being further pushed aside.

These ethnographic investigations helped make it abundantly plain that there was no mechanistic process where the external pressures from an economy or the state inexorably mould schools and the students within them to the processes involved in legitimation and in the accumulation of economic and cultural capital. Students themselves act in contradictory ways, ways that both support this reproductive process and partially 'penetrate' it.[8] As Willis showed, for example, groups of working-class students often expressly reject the world of the school. The official knowledge and the hidden curriculum considered legitimate by the institution bear little resemblance to the actual world of work, to the life on the street, to the facts of generalised labour that many students experience through their parents, friends and their own part-time jobs. By rejecting the 'legitimate' culture within the school, by affirming manual work and physicality, the students affirm their own subjectivity and, at the same time, act in a way which constitutes a realistic assessment that, *as a class*, schooling will not enable them to go much further than they already are.

This partial penetration into the role of schooling in economic and cultural reproduction is paradoxical, however. By rejecting school knowledge, the students are in essence rejecting mental labour. They, thus, harden the distinction between mental and manual labour. While they are affirming and acting on the strengths of particular aspects of a lived working-class culture, they are caught in a real structural contradiction by hardening one of the major principles guiding the articulation of the social relations of capitalist production. On the one hand, they are learning to 'work the system' by developing rather creative ways of dealing with the demands of the school so that they can get out of class, inject humour into the formal curriculum, control the pacing of the work, and so on. On the other hand, while this will prepare them to have some power in the world of work and represents a penetration into the reality of the work these students will probably face, it reproduces on an ideological level the categories required to maintain work as it is.

Other studies in the United States showed similar things. For example, Robert Everhart's ethnography of junior high-school students illuminates how these predominantly working-class youths spend a large amount of their time 'goofing off' and recreating cultural forms that give them some degree of power in the school setting (Everhart, 1979). While these students do not totally reject the formal curriculum, they give the school only the barest minimum work required and try to minimise even those requirements. These students, like the lads in Willis' work, resisted. They gave only what was necessary not to endanger the possible mobility some of them might have. Yet, they already 'knew' that this was only a possibility, one that was not guaranteed at all. Most of them would, in fact, remain within the economic trajectories established by their parents. The elements of self-selection, of cultural forms of resistance, that both reproduced and contradicted the 'needs' of the economic apparatus, all of this demonstrated the relative autonomy of culture. It also provided a critical element in any serious evaluation of what schools do. For without getting inside the school, without seeing how and *why* students rejected the overt and hidden curriculum, and without linking this back to non-mechanistic conceptions of reproduction and contradiction, we would be unable to comprehend the complexity of the work that schools perform as sites of ideological production (Apple, 1980b)[9].

The notion of a specifically Marxist ethnography was very significant here. For, unlike vulgar representations which look for the imprint of economic ideology on everything, a more sophisticated approach would see ideology differently. It was not a form of false consciousness 'imposed' by an economy. Rather it was part of a lived culture that was a result of the material conditions of one's day-to-day practices. It was a set of meanings and practices that, indeed, did have elements of good sense as well as reproductive elements within it. And because it had these elements of good sense, just as in the case of the workers whom I had examined, that made it objectively possible to engage in activity centred on political education that would challenge the ideological underpinnings of the relations of dominance and exploitation in the wider society. The objective possibility of political education is something to which I shall return in the final section of this chapter.

As all of this was going on, as I began to make much better sense of how a more refined conceptual framework could help me understand the political and cultural practices I was seeing (and engaging in), I began to realise that I now could also begin to answer more coherently even some of the more traditional questions which plagued the curriculum field. If I wanted to understand why our efforts at reform often failed, why even our most creatively designed curricula seemed not to be able to reach many of the most 'disadvantaged' students, the research tools and conceptual framework which emerged from Marxist-oriented ethnographies provided major insights (Apple, 1980a; see also Apple, work forthcoming, a). We were much closer to fully understanding this because of these studies of resistance, contestation and lived culture.

Ideology and Curricular Form

So far I have talked about the labour process and the hidden and overt curriculum in two sites. I have described how ideologies work in contradictory ways in both the workplace and the school. At the same time, I have argued that the usual ways in which the left has examined these sites has tended to be somewhat limited. Even given the movement of my own thinking over the last years, we should be careful not to overstate the case against reproduction metaphors. For I do not want to imply that the logic and ideology of capital do not enter into the school and its curriculum in some very powerful ways. In fact, as I have tried to document in my most recent work, such a logic is having a profound impact on day-to-day school practices (Apple, work forthcoming, b). In order to understand this, we need to return to the idea of culture not as a lived experiece, but as commodified form. This provides an opening into how schools act as sites of ideological production and reproduction.

Throughout my enquiries over the past decade, I have maintained that if we are to fully understand how ideologies work in schools we need to look at the concreta of day-to-day school life. Of immense import here currently is the way the logic and modes of control of capital are entering the school through the *form* the curriculum takes, not only in its content. That is, as a number of cultural analysts have indicated, ideology can be seen most impressively at the level of form as well as what the form has in it. (See, for example, Jameson, 1971; Apple, 1978.)

In order to understand this we should remember that schools are also places of *work*. This is something we tend quite regularly to forget. Yet stressing this is a key to laying out possible actions within schools and among teachers. For this very realisation opens up a door to our understanding of what happens in schools and provides us with a key building-block in our analysis. How? Let us discuss this a bit more. Certain principles have guided the organisation and control of places where people work in corporate economies. These principles have entered not only into the shop floor in factories but have found their way more and more into all aspects of the productive apparatus of society. Blue and white collar labour, manual and mental labor, selling and assembling – yes, even teaching – have slowly but surely been incorporated into the logics of these forms of organisation and control; In ways that are not inconsequential, teaching is a labour process, one that, to be sure, has its own specific characteristics that are not reducible to working on a shop floor, in an insurance company office, or as a sales person, but one that is a labour process none the less.

As we saw in my discussion of recent Marxist ethnographies, particular processes and modes of control tend to guide the corporate production process. The separation of mental from manual labour, the divorce of conception from execution, each of these is a constitutive element in organising work in our society. However, they are usually accompanied – as the exceptional research of Braverman, Burawoy and Edwards has shown (Braverman, 1974; Burawoy, 1979; Edwards, 1979) – by other things. Managers attempt to change the control of what actually goes on in one's work so that they have more knowledge than the actual worker himself or herself. Deskilling also goes on, where the skills that employees used to need are 'taken from them', broken down, and prespecified at the level of conception and then given back to the employee. The employee's work is rationalised. His or her role is transformed into merely an executor of someone else's plans. With this comes what has been called reskilling. That is, while the employee loses important skills and control to management, new skills are taught that often result in contradictory results.

Managers have attempted various modes of control to bring all this about; a quite fruitful one has been what has been called *technical control* (Edwards, 1979). This implies that the forms of control are embedded in the machinery of the job itself. No one has to tell you what to do. What you are to do is neatly programmed into the way the 'technology' operates.

In a number of ways, this is exactly what is happening to teachers. In curricular areas such as mathematics, reading and science, for example, the form the curriculum takes is more and more prespecified and 'prepackaged'. It is often 'individualised' according to the rate at which a student proceeds through it, with each student given a set of commercially produced work sheets or 'appropriate skill level' material. Many of these curricula are 'systems', which have diagnostic and achievement tests already built into them. They often have the actions to be taken by the teacher and the responses of the students almost totally prespecified as well. All of this is determined outside the classroom. Conception is strongly separated from execution. While observations have shown that some teachers do not fully accept what is clearly a process of deskilling, these observations also indicate both the rapid growth of the use of this kind of material, its increased acceptance, for a variety of internal and external reasons, and the difficulty of not employing it given the growing strength of an ideology of accountability, cost effectiveness, and meeting 'industrial needs'. It is actually a rather sophisticated embodiment of technical control.

At the same time that teachers are being deskilled by these procedures, they are being reskilled. Since the fundamental aspects of curricula are being taken out of their hands, their role is transformed into that of a manager; hence, the search for and teaching of 'efficient' management techniques such as behaviour modification and the like. Thus, we are faced with an exceptionally interesting set of circumstances. The work of teachers is being increasingly 'proletarianised' in many ways, as these kinds of commodified curricular forms enter into schools, while at the very same historical moment the skills of curriculum planning and deliberation that teachers may tend to lose because of this are replaced by the techniques and ideologies of management. It is an inherently contradictory situation and one which will have to be worked out by many teachers in their everyday lives.[10]

This process of technical control and the deskilling of teacher actions has important implications for people besides the teachers, of course. Students themselves interact every day with this kind of 'individualised' curricular form. The effects of such continued interaction may be ideally suited to 'reproduce' one of the sets of ideologically saturated social relations which dominate our society – that of the unattached individual. This, clearly, may not be a neutral set of social practices. Notice that I have set off the word 'reproduce' by inverted commas. For, once again, it is necessary to recall my earlier point that the school will not simply impose either this rationalisation on teachers or this ideological vison of the individual on students. Neither of these groups are mere *homunculi* whose strings are only pulled by the abstract powers of an economic system. Teachers have work cultures; students have class cultures. Contradictory pressures of lived culture can lead to contradictory results.

These concerns are not divorced from practice. If the jobs of men and women are being increasingly deskilled, if even 'professional' jobs are being more thoroughly rationalised, then we would expect that, as at other places of work, this will create resistances there also.[11] If, with the growth of rationalisation in the labour process, the conditions of teachers' work are – like those of other workers on the mental side of the mental/manual dichotomy – best described as becoming more 'proletarianised', then *this also opens up the possibility of political intervention and political education*. It gives us spaces in which to act. And it is to some possible forms of action that I shall briefly turn in the concluding section of this essay.

Educational and Political Practice

In the final part of this chapter I cannot hope to lay out all of the kinds of educational and political practices that might be generated out of the preceding pages. What I shall do, then, is to provide a range of actions – some concerning scholarship, others concerning more practical action – that should be considered. There may be disagreement about the efficacy of these suggestions, just as there has been debate over some of the arguments I have presented throughout this essay, as I have tried to show in the notes to this chapter. But the very fact that they may be argued over can increase the possibility that a more thoughtful programme can evolve.

There is an immense amount of concrete curricular work that needs to go on. While this cannot substitute for political and economic organisation and action to alter the structural conditions we face, it is still essential that certain things go on where they can in schools. No institution, no ideology, is totally monolithic and this includes our educational institutions.

Part of our task is historical. We have restricted the notion of education to that organised around the region of the state. However, there were models of, for example, working-class education that were quite generative during and even after the years when schooling became more and more monopolised by the state (see Clarke *et al.*, 1979; Apple, work forthcoming, a). We need to recapture what a genuine socialist alternative would be; first, to help us think and work through the issues surrounding new models of curriculum and teaching, and, secondly, to place education again on the socialist agenda.

Working-class history is significant in another way. The history that is presented to students in schools is nearly devoid of extended and serious treatments of labour. There is no sense that it was (and is) legitimate for workers to challenge the way in which corporate production is organised and controlled, for example (Anyon, 1979). Yet, as David Montgomery has documented (1979), working men and women have had a long history of successfully controlling production, a history that is lost to ourselves and our children. It is not only the history of workers in general, but the histories of the concrete and long-term struggles and culture of women, minority groups and so on that are the victims of the 'selective tradition.'[12] If students are to see that alternative sets of social arrangements are legitimate and possible, the struggle by ourselves as educators to get honest material on these topics into schools is imperative. This can be best accomplished not by educators alone, however, but through close working relationships among groups of progressive educators, students, parents and organised workers.

Some of this is going on already, as many of you know. There are teachers and administrators who are *currently* engaged in the hard work of creating more democratic institutions, in putting democratic and socialist pedagogical and curricular models into practice, and in creating material that is not reproductive of the ideologies of existing class, race and gender relations. We have much to learn from these individuals and should support them. However, a serious effort is necessary to reduce the isolation (and sometimes, unfortunately, elitism) of educators engaging in this kind of practical work. Here, again, linkages can be made between people at colleges and universities, groups of committed teachers and administrators, and labour, minority and women's groups.[13]

This is not meant to imply that 'reforming' curricula is enough. Obviously it is not. However, as Gramsci reminds us, the fight against existing relations of domination and exploitation needs to be waged on a variety of fronts. It is not limited to 'the economy', but needs to be carried out on the terrain of the state, the workplace, the cultural apparatus, the family and elsewhere. The real issue is not reforms or 'compromises', but how they are understood and where they lead.

Not all reforms are to be opposed. Instead, what is necessary is that we begin to take much more seriously the notion of *non-reformist reforms*. These are reforms that are worth fighting for because they can do one or both of two things. First, they can ameliorate present conditions and are linked to a broader programme of structural change. And/or, through the struggle over them, they can educate people about political strategies, create lasting progressive political coalitions and create a momentum toward more long-lasting alterations. Obviously, any 'reform' that can do both of these – serve as a link to a larger structural programme and serve to educate and build group cohesiveness – is best (Apple, work forthcoming, a).[14] Since schools are local institutions that people are deeply concerned about because of their very nature, they are often ideal places to focus upon for both of these things.

Throughout the previous section of this essay, I stressed the nature of contestation and resistance. While we can romanticise these things too much, both in scholarship and political and educational practice (and I do not necessarily mean to separate the two) much more work needs to be done on the resistances of teachers and students. This needs to be thought through more clearly, and more consciously connected to the specifics of race, class, and gender, since resistances may tend to differ along each of these axes.

Why should student resistance be considered? The lived culture of students needs to be understood more thoroughly or we shall merely recapitulate the experience of student rejection of curricula. Furthermore, as Willis has noted in *Learning to Labour* and as activists in the black and latino communities have demonstrated, for instance, the resistances and the lived culture of students can be effectively employed as material for both educational and political 'literacy'.

While studies such as those done by Willis, Everhart and others have given us a provocative picture of 'ideological' conflict and resistance between groups of students and the school, we actually know little about the life of teachers. (Grace's work (1978) is, however, at least a first step in this direction.) If I am correct that the actual conditions of the work of teachers are increasingly becoming more like other kinds of work, then we should expect particular kinds of resistances to evolve. These forms of contestation will be mediated by the ideology of professionalism and by teachers' contradictory class position, but the resistances will arise in ways that may be quite consequential to political work among teachers as well.

Hence, if we remember that there are elements of good sense in ideologies, with the increased rationalisation of teachers' work, they also may begin to 'penetrate' into the reality of control in our society. These elements of penetration and good sense need to be expanded. It will not be automatic that, as the conditions of their work become more like the work of other employees in blue and white collar labour, teachers will flick a switch and all of a sudden turn into supporters of socialist politics and practice. What it implies, however, is that there is a potential for winning people over to a broader movement. Concrete work in the political and organisational spheres, based on the deteriorating conditions teachers face in schools every day, is essential. They can be led to see (as many of them have already seen and taught me, for instance) that the same forces affecting their lives affect the lives of a large portion of people employed in other workplaces. And the crisis all of them face is dependent on a larger crisis of accumulation and legitimation, of unequal benefits and control, in the dominant institutions of our society.

Finally, educators do have skills that are required outside of the formal school setting also. Curricula for labour education need to be written. The skills of educational design can be applied to the problems of political education. Here too, this entails a close working relationship between both progressive educators and organised groups of workers, women and other groups. By making these linkages, by becoming 'organic' members of these groups, the skills that educators have developed over many years can be shared. At the same time, these skills will be applied to situations that are part of a long term programme of social change. Of critical importance here are not only the skills involved in designing and evaluating materials, but, equally, the skills of, say, analysing ideological reproduction in the existing pedagogical, curricular and evaluative practices of the schools. Just as it is essential for investigations of the relationship between ideology and curriculm to continue, so, too, is it necessary that this be carried out by people outside as well as inside academic settings. How one does this kind of analysis can and must be shared with these very same groups of progressive people.

Throughout this essay, I have talked about the possibilities for action. I have tried to show, through my own personal genesis, how this has affected my own work. I have noted that the real, lived conditions of men and women in our factories, stores, and offices – and, I have strongly suggested, more and more in our schools – provide distinct opportunities for winning people over to a concern for widespread social and economic justice. The processes involved in the control of culture and labour and the resistance this engenders, the *contested* reproduction shown by many workers, teachers, students and others, the oppositional practices that emerge when one looks carefully at day-to-day life, all of these mean that pessimism need not dominate our outlook. In this concluding section, I have briefly noted only a very few general areas of the possible actions we might engage in. The focus should not remain only on possibilities, however, but on actualities. For possibilities are nothing until they are acted upon.

Notes

1. The debate over the relationship between base and superstructure is exceptionally intense at present. See, for example, Barrett *et al.* (1979), Clarke, Critcher and Johnson (1979), Hirst (1979), Sumner (1979) and Williams (1977). I have summarised part of what this means for educational investigations in 'Analyzing Determinations' (1980a) and 'Class Culture and the State in Educational Intervention' (work forthcoming, a).

2. I have argued actually that there are three functions of the state – legitimation, accumulation and production. See Apple and Taxel (work forthcoming).

3. Personal communication from Ron Aminzade. The literature on what is implied by the school's role as a state apparatus is increasing rapidly. It does, however, tend towards a functionalism that may not do justice to the contradictions and competing class interests both within the state and between the state and the economic and cultural spheres of a society. See Dale (work forthcoming).

4. On the debate engendered by these differences, see Apple (1980b).

5. The argument here is similar to that of Finn, Grant and Johnson (1978, p. 4), when they state that one's analysis must 'grasp the relations between schools and other sites of social relations . . . within a particular social formation'.

6. It is important to keep in mind, though, that capital is *not* a thing, but a set of relationships.

7. Here I was arguing in part with Bourdieu, since he did not go far enough into the way cultural capital was produced. See Apple (1979b).

8. There is a danger in employing concepts like 'penetration', however, especially given the manner in which sexist words and images dominate our linguistic usage.

9. There are other important ways of conceiving of cultural production as a process of production *per se*. See, for instance, the essays in Barrett *et al.* (1979), Coward and Ellis (1977) and Wexler (work forthcoming).

10. I have given only the barest outline of my argument here. The situation and the current conditions are quite complex. See Apple (work forthcoming, b).

11. Of course, the claim that teachers are workers can lead to a rather vulgar position – one that automatically places them within the working class and gives them interests that are necessarily opposed to capital. This is simply too easy an assertion. It is probably more accurate, as Erik Olin Wright has argued (1979), to see teachers as having an inherently contradictory class location. They 'stand between' the bourgeoisie and workers, with ideological interests allied to both.

12. Some of the major research on how the selective tradition operates is summarised in Apple and Taxel (work forthcoming).

13. Sassoon's point about how the lack of unity around a coherent alternative socialist political (and educational) proposal makes it easier for governments to play off one group against another is pertinent here and points again to the need for connections to be made between educators and other progressive groups. See Sassoon (1978, p. 39).

14. See also Sassoon's discussion of the political efficacy of certain kinds of 'compromises' (1978), as well as Wright's treatment of the potential of action within the state (1978).

Bibliography

Anyon, Jean (1979) 'Ideology and United States History Textbooks', *Harvard Educational Review*, 41, August, pp. 361-86

Apple, Michael W. (1978) 'Ideology and Form in Curriculum Evaluation' in Willis, George (ed.), *Qualitative Evaluation*, McCutchan, Berkeley, pp. 495-521

Apple, Michael W. (1979a) *Ideology and Curriculum*, Routledge and Kegan Paul, London

Apple, Michael W. (1979b) 'The Production of Knowledge and the Production of Deviance in Schools' in Barton, L. and Meighan, R. (eds.), *Schools, Pupils and Deviance*, Nafferton Books, Driffield, pp. 113-131

Apple, Michael W. (1980a) 'Analyzing Determinations', *Curriculum Inquiry*, 10, Spring, pp. 55-76

Apple, Michael, W. (1980b) 'The Other Side of the Hidden Curriculum: Correspondence Theories and the Labor Process', *Journal of Education*. CLXII, Winter, pp. 47-66

Apple, Michael W. (work forthcoming, a) 'Class, Culture and the State in Educational Intervention' in Everhart, Robert (ed.), *The Predominant Orthodoxy*, Ballinger, New York

Apple, Michael W. (work forthcoming, b) 'Curricular Form and the Logic of Technical Control, *Journal of Economic and Industrial Democracy*

Apple, Michael W. and Taxel, J. (work forthcoming) 'Ideology and the

Curriculum' in Hartnett, Anthony (ed.), *Educational Studies and Social Science*, Heinemann, London

Barrett, Michele, *et al.* (eds.) (1979) *Ideology and Cultural Production*, St. Martin's Press, New York

Bisseret, Noëlle (1979) *Education, Class Language and Ideology*, Routledge and Kegan Paul, London

Bourdieu, Pierre, and Passeron, J-C. (1979) *The Inheritors*, Univ. of Chicago Press, Chicago

Braverman, H. (1974) *Labor and Monopoly Capital*, Monthly Review Press, New York

Burawoy, Michael (1979) 'Towards a Marxist Theory of the Labor Process: Braverman and Beyond', *Politics and Society*, VIII, nos. 3 and 4

Clarke, John, Critcher, Charles and Johnson, Richard (eds.) (1979) *Working Class Culture*, Hutchinson, London

Collins, Randall (1979) *The Credential Society*, Academic Press, New York

Coward, Rosalind and Ellis, J. (1977) *Language and Materialism*, Routledge and Kegan Paul, London

Dale, Roger (work forthcoming) 'Education and the Capitalist State: Contributions and Contradictions' in Apple, Michael W. (ed.), *Cultural and Economic Reproduction in Education*, Routledge and Kegan Paul, London

Di Maggio, Paul (1979) 'Review Essay: on Pierre 'Bourdieu', *American Journal of Sociology*, LXXXIV, May

Edwards, Richard (1979) *Contested Terrain*, Basic Books, New York

Everhart, Robert (1979) *The In-Between Years: Student Life in a Junior High School*, Univ. of California Graduate School of Education, Santa Barbara

Finn, D., Grant, N., Johnson, R. *et al.* (1978) 'Social Democracy, Education and the Crisis', mimeograph. Univ. of Birmingham, Centre for Contemporary Cultural Studies, Birmingham

Grace, Gerald (1978) *Teachers, Ideology and Control*, Routledge and Kegan Paul, London

Hall, Stuart (n.d.) 'The Schooling-Society Relationship: Parallels, Fits, Correspondences, Homologies', mimeograph

Hirst, Paul (1979) *On Law and Ideology*, Macmillan, London

Jameson, Fredric (1971) *Marxism and Form*, Princeton Univ. Press, Princeton

Jencks, Christopher *et al.* (1979) *Who Gets Ahead?*, Basic Books, New York

Karabel, Jerome and Halsey, A.H. (eds.) (1977) *Power and Ideology in Education*, Oxford University Press, New York

Kliebard, Herbert (1971) 'Bureaucracy and Curriculum Theory' in Haubrich, Vernon (ed.), *Freedom, Bureaucracy and Schooling*, Association for Supervision and Curriculum Development, Washington, DC, pp. 74-93

Montgomery, David (1979) *Workers' Control in America*, Cambridge Univ. Press, New York

Mouffe, Chatal (1979). 'Hegemony and Ideology in Gramsci' in Mouffe, Chatal (ed.), *Gramsci and Marxist Theory*, Routledge and Kegan Paul, London

Noble, David (1977) *America by Design*, Knopf, New York

O'Connor, James (1973) *The Fiscal Crisis of the State*, St Martin's Press, New York

Persell, Caroline Hodges (1977) *Education and Inequality*, Free Press, New York

Sassoon, Anne S. (1978) 'Hegemony and Political Intervention' in Hibbin, S. (ed.), *Politics, Ideology and the State*, Lawrence and Wishart, London

Selden, Steven (1977) 'Conservative Ideologies and Curriculum', *Educational Theory*, XXVII, Summer, pp. 205-222

Sumner, Colin (1979) *Reading Ideologies*, Academic Press, New York

Wexler, Philip (work forthcoming) 'Structure, Text and Subject: a Critical Sociology of School Knowledge' in Apple, Michael W. (ed.) *Cultural and Economic Reproduction in Education*, Routledge and Kegan Paul, London

Williams, Raymond (1977) *Marxism and Literature*, Oxford Univ. Press

Willis, Paul (1977) *Learning to Labour: How Working Class Kids Get Working Class Jobs*, Saxon House, Farnborough

Wright, Erik Olin (1978) *Class, Crisis and the State*, New Left Books, London, New York

Wright, Erik Olin (1979a) *Class Structure and Income Determination*, Academic Press, New York

Wright, Erik Olin (1979b) 'Intellectuals and the Class Structure of Capitalist Society' in Walker, P. (ed.) *Between Labor and Capital*, South End Press, Boston, Mass. pp. 191-211

6 THE DELIBERATIVE APPROACH TO THE STUDY OF THE CURRICULUM AND ITS RELATION TO CRITICAL PLURALISM

William A. Reid

In this paper I set out to do three things: first, to describe a number of approaches to the study of the curriculum; secondly, to consider in some detail the approach I label as 'deliberative', and, thirdly, to examine its potential for enabling curriculum studies to avoid the extremes of dogmatic monism on the one hand and unrestricted relativism on the other.

Perspectives on the Curriculum

The core of the paper is a consideration of the deliberative approach to the study of the curriculum but, before I enter on that, I will note some assumptions that underlie my discussion, and sketch out a view of the general range of perspectives and approaches within which the deliberative approach takes its place. My first assumption is that anyone who reflects on broad questions about the curriculum of the school, does research on it or teaches about it, acts as a kind of social philosopher. Social philosophers are concerned to understand the nature of human society and how it intersects with the lives of its members, and also to visualise ways in which that understanding could be used to improve the quality of society and of the lives of the individuals who compose it. My second assumption is that 'social philosophising' is a role attribute. 'Practising' is also a role attribute. Although we should expect social philosophy to relate to practice, we should not expect social philosophers to behave like practitioners, or *vice versa* – though they can, and often do, exchange roles. Further assumptions will emerge in the ensuing discussion, or will be discovered by the reader.

In any attempt to analyse the character of various contributions to the study of the curriculum, we have to steer a doubtful course between two contrasting and equally untenable positions. On the one hand, it is plain that the approaches of individual writers and theorists are not just idiosyncratic; on the other, it would be just as nonsensical to claim that there is a limited number of schools to which everyone must belong. Yet both propositions contain an element of truth. Here, for my own rhetorical purposes, I shall act as if there were more truth in the second one. The reader must remember, where necessary, to enter the qualification: 'But all these people are also unique.'

One characteristic which distinguishes 'types' of curriculum theorist is the degree to which they identify their interests with those of the school system (using that term in its broadest sense to include schools, institutions that administer and influence schools and people who work in the schools and associated institutions). There are those who lean towards the system and see their work as being directed to improvement through helping people within it solve their problems. They do not, however, form a unitary group, and, for the purposes of my present analysis, I shall in fact invoke a distinction which excludes many theorists of this kind from consideration altogether. My reason for doing this relates to the basic assumption I stated at the outset: my concern here is with the curriculum theorist in the role of social philosopher, and many theorists who work closely with schools do not act as social philosophers. They have no consistent view of the relationship between their position on particular issues and an overall conception of what curriculum theorising is, or how it relates to broader questions of the nature and purposes of man in society. This is not to make a criticism of such theorists, but to point to a difference in function and motivation. My reason for excluding them from the discussion is not that I regard them or their views as of little importance, but that they do not fit into the particular frame of analysis that I want to employ. However, even those system-oriented theorists who do, implicitly or explicitly, reveal a recognisable social philosophy range along a very wide spectrum from unquestioning support for established authorities and structures to a commitment to work for change, perhaps in some ways quite fundamental change, through gradualist action.

In the opposite camp we find those for whom the school system is either an instrument of bourgeois exploitation which should not be supported, or something which has no central relevance for the kind of attack on curriculum questions they want to make. In the case of those who are indifferent to, or opposed to the established school system, we need be less concerned about distinguishing the social philosopher from the pragmatist. Almost by definition, such theorists cast themselves as social philosophers, extending, in this case, from committed Marxists, for whom nothing less than a total transformation of society will suffice, to the more tender-minded whose concern for self-fulfilment through 'consciousness raising' allows them to be tolerant of present evils.

The second discriminating characteristic I want to identify is the extent to which theorists subscribe to over-riding principle or procedure. This might be tagged 'a priorism'. Those whose concerns lie at the 'macro' level, whether in that they work to support current structures, or in that they want to revolutionise them, tend to be united by a relatively closed view of what the interesting problems are, and what practical or intellectual tools should be brought to bear on them. Those theorists who exhibit a lower degree of 'a priorism' are, by definition, not so dogmatic. They cannot give administrations their unqualified support, nor believe that they know exactly how they should be transformed. Such people tend to be more exploratory in their behaviour, more provisional in their judgements, less attached to generalisations, abstractions and over-riding principles. Their concern is more with individuals than with systems, though they may disagree over the extent to which such concern should be related to people in their public roles, as teachers and learners, or to the more private aspects of their intellectual and emotional development.

The groups I want to distinguish on the basis of the two characteristics I have described are: the 'systemic', consisting of those who accept current structures and write about ways of conceiving curricular ends and means in terms of *a priori* notions of control, planning and innovation; the 'radical', compromising theorists who trace connections between curricular forms and structural inequalities in society; the 'existentialist', embracing writers who, starting from the standpoint of the individual who is the subject of the curriculum, discuss its relationship to his or her personal growth, and the 'deliberative', covering those who emphasise curriculum decision-making as transactions between morally engaged individuals in the context of social institutions. These represent respectively: system-oriented 'a priorists'; system-opposing 'a priorists'; system-indifferent explorers, and system-supportive explorers. The simplification is crude, but useful.[1] And, in spite of the crudeness, the groups I have formed do, I think, represent important and enduring positions on questions of social philosophy. It is precisely because I see them as enduring positions that I have avoided the use of labels such as 'traditionalist', or 'reconceptualist'. These represent what is transient: the relative social or academic standing of a given school of thought at a given time.

In the following section, I shall elaborate the four major perspectives and make comparisons between them, using as themes: the purposes they attribute to curriculum studies, notions they have about appropriate subject-matter, their preferred methods, and their underlying principles and assumptions.[2]

The Systemic Perspective

People who work and write within the systemic perspective are typically quite articulate about purposes. For them, one of the main objects of curriculum studies is to find the most efficient and effective ways of planning, implementing and evaluating curricula. For more specific definitions of these purposes, they tend to be dependent on initiatives taken by politicians and administrators. Frequently they are hired by government agencies to work on policy issues. Of necessity, the frame of reference within which they operate reflects established administrative structures and the procedural rhetorics which inform them. Often, systemic theorists concern themselves with very large-scale rationalisations of the nature of the school curriculum, which are then used as the basis for more specific procedural theories at the level of planning.

The subject-matter to which system-oriented theorists address themselves is twofold: on the one hand it consists of certain kinds of data about schools and school systems. These data are 'objective' in character: measures of abilities and attainments, logistics of school and classroom organisation, statistical representations of trends and relationships; on the other hand, the subject-matter comprises the content-free paradigms and models which are used for conceptualising the system, for analysing data, and for solving systemic problems. Much writing within the systemic perspective is concerned with the elaboration of such universal paradigms and models which may then find their way into curriculum textbooks as matter to be learned. In quoting examples of work of this kind, I reiterate my previous warning that all individuals depart from the 'ideal type'. However, the position I am characterising can readily be associated with books such as *Curriculum Theory* (Beauchamp, 1975), *Curriculum Design and Development*, (Pratt, 1980), or *Curriculum Process* (Wheeler, 1967). The exemplary list should also contain supportive psychometric texts of the type of *Foundations of Behavioral Research* (Kerlinger, 1964), and strongly empirical work on instructional design, such as *Human Characteristics and School Learning* (Bloom, 1976).

Subject-matter and method are closely linked: the paradigms which are the object of study take their place as vehicles for the scientific diagnosis and solution of problems. It is assumed that diagnosis can have a factual reference, and that the solution of problems is dependent on rational procedures which are universally applicable. Method is construed as the application of abstract, analytical constructs to concrete, objective data.

On the matter of underlying principles and assumptions, systemic theorists do not often make explicit statements, probably because they see themselves as working within a tradition with well-established credentials ('doing normal science', to use Kuhn's phrase). Arguments for such an approach in terms of deep-level commitments are more likely to be found in nineteenth-century than in modern writers. The systemic philosophy assumes, typically, that curricular questions can be treated in a value-free way, by technical means, and that the warrant for the method lies in its scientific character. Discussion of the underlying value assumptions of the perspective have, in recent years, been initiated by outside critics such as Wise (1977) and Kliebard (whose relevant papers are collected in Pinar, 1975). These assumptions are stated to be: that educational purposes are not deeply controversial, that human and institutional qualities can be abstracted and measured, that education is concerned with measurable effects, that there is no problem about the location of power, that social systems can be controlled by administrative action and that the curriculum theorist is a kind of scientist.

The Radical Perspective

While systemic thinking is rooted in existing social forms, radical thinking is related not only to what exists, but also to what would exist in the aftermath of fundamental social change. Hence, there is a duality in radical statements about purposes, subject-matter and methods. Since method and purpose are claimed to inhere in concrete situations (rather than universal paradigms) and the post-revolutionary context is thought of as having little in common with the current one, radical programmes often exhibit qualities of relativism, in contrast to the absolutist qualities favoured by the systemic theorist. Within a capitalist society, the radical curriculum theorist has typically pursued two main purposes: first, to show how curricula serve to reproduce the structural inequalities of that society and, second, to bring about curriculum change by working for its necesssary precondition – a transformation of society itself.

In most radical writing on curriculum theory, the stress has been on the former purpose. For example, Kallós and Lundgren (1976) state: 'Curriculum studies cannot primarily be focussed on *how* a curriculum should be constructed or developed, but must primarily explain the determinants of the curriculum.' Instances of such radical critiques include *La Réproduction* (Bourdieu and Passeron, 1970) and *Ideology and Curriculum* (Apple, 1979). These serve, apparently, the subsidiary purpose of raising 'revolutionary consciousness' as a first step towards the transformation of society. Only beyond that point will it become possible for a radical theorist of strongly Marxist persuasion to concern himself with procedural matters of curriculum design. To do so now would be to work for the preservation of the present 'concrete reality' since, for the radical thinker, planning theory can only be a function of the reality that the planner confronts.

The stress on demonstrating the reproduction of social inequalities through the curriculum points to the appropriate subject-matter and methods. The subject-matter is any situation, past or present, which can be analysed to show the existence of these relationships which are considered, *a priori*, to hold good. Many radical theorists, especially in the United States, have worked from historical records. *Schooling in Capitalist America* (Bowles and Gintis, 1976) is perhaps the best-known example. Alternatively, recent and contemporary settings are analysed through the statistical or observational methods of the sociologist or anthropologist. This has been the favoured approach of European researchers such as Willis (1977), Sharp and Green (1975) or Chamboredon and Prévot (1973). What is distinctive about such radical analyses is not so much the method, as the linking of method to purpose. Thus, *Schooling in Capitalist America* can rely on data gathered by administrators, as does also the interesting Chamboredon and Prévot paper, 'Le "métier d'enfant"'; moreover, the handling of the data is done through conventional statistical techniques which would recommend themselves to researchers in the systemic tradition.

The assumptions underlying such work, in so far as they emerge from the writing, are: that no worthwhile curriculum improvement is possible without a radical transformation of social and political institutions; that abstract concepts like 'class', 'capitalism' or 'hegemony' are, in some way, 'real' and provide the key to what is wrong with society; that the needed remedies are already known, at least in principle, and that the function of research and theorising is to increase the power of already known facts. I say 'in so far as they emerge' because of the point I made earlier that the immediate purposes and methods of radical theorists are context-dependent and may obscure rather than illuminate deeper commitments.

The Existential Perspective

While radical and systemic theorists tend to approach curriculum questions through the macro-structures of society, those of an existential persuasion concentrate their attention on the mind of the individual who experiences a curriculum. For them, the reality of life consists not in classes, capitalism or hegemony, on the one hand, nor in administrative processes and established structures, on the other, but in the relationship of the individual consciousness to the external world. When radicals speak of consciousness, they tend to conceive of a shared consciousness from which general qualities can be abstracted. For the existential thinker, however, consciousness is always unique, always to be explored in its own terms, not in the terms of some wider collectivity. The purposes of existential analysis might be summed up, crudely, but with some justice, by adapting Sartre's dictum that: 'the proper function of psychology is to improve the biography of the individual'. Here it is the function of curriculum that is at issue, but the shift in focus is not major. Existential curriculum theory, as I understand it, is essentially psychological in character. It is allied to the humanist, introspective psychology which is the polar opposite of the objectivist, psychometric psychology favoured by systemic theorists.

The subject-matter of the perspective is, therefore, the individual consciousness as revealed to the actor and to others. The method is the ordering of experience through frames provided by biography, psychoanalysis, existential philosophy and mysticism. This ordering is undertaken in a tentative and exploratory way. The truth is never to be demonstrated, always to be discovered. Paths of discovery lead in unknown directions. Examples of research undertaken within this perspective are offered by Huebner, Greene, Grumet, Macdonald and Pinar.[3]

Since the work of existential curriculum writers has this strong exploratory character, it is hard to pin down the positive assumptions that shape it, though these would obviously include a belief in the primacy of the individual and in the centrality of the life of the mind. It is easier to see what must be rejected in principle. Excluded is belief in social engineering of the right or the left, in rational planning, or in projects of justifying curriculum decisions through empirical generalisations.

The Deliberative Perspective

Theorists who adopt this position (which is more closely considered in the next section of the paper) share the exploratory outlook of the existential writers. Where they disagree with them is in the emphasis they would place on the need to conceive of curriculum studies as having a relationship to schools and to practice. While Pinar has stated that although 'curriculum must be planned, described in brochures, . . . it can hardly be a matter of serious scholarly and theoretical attention' (1975), the deliberative theorist would argue that the central concern of curriculum studies should be precisely to improve people's capacity, both individually and collectively, to make good decisions about teaching and learning, and that it is possible for this to be done in a scholarly and theoretical way.

It may be that, in making his statement, Pinar had in mind the kinds of prescriptions for planning that are put forward by systemic theorists. When the deliberative theorist claims that there should be a focus on practical questions, such as how to plan a curriculum, he has in mind the application to planning of a humanistic frame of reference, and would reject the idea that curriculum studies was, or ever could be, either a science or a body of universally applicable techniques. Such a humanistic frame could accommodate at least some of the interests of existential writers, though the fact that it was being used to address central questions of policy- and decision-making would direct it more naturally to empirically based truth strategies, and more traditional styles of humanistic reasoning.

The assumptions of the deliberative position are diametrically opposed to those of the radical perspective, being broadly allied to those of classical liberalism. They comprise an emphasis on the individual as a morally responsible person, a belief in the possibility of improvement through working with present institutions, and in the efficacy of consensual approaches to the identification and solution of problems.

The discussion so far has concentrated on establishing unique identities for the four perspectives I have identified. It would be an equally possible and equally rich enterprise to write about the links that exist between them and and about what they hold in common. I might also have talked about people who do not fit well into any of the categories. This is a theme to which I shall return briefly at the end of the paper.

The Deliberative Approach: a Detailed Account

My more detailed account of the deliberative approach is also more personal, more speculative and more diffuse than any of the tidy portraits I have offered so far. The label 'deliberative' is not self-evidently descriptive, nor does it draw attention to some aspect or focus of the position that could be the rallying point of a cause. To be deliberate is to show a concern that is broad and careful. Deliberative theory is evolutionary in its social philosophy and pragmatic in its conception of how knowledge should relate to policy and action. But it has clearly-articulated value commitments and a distinctive method.

I begin with a personal account of what I see as valuable in the deliberative perspective, then consider how theorists within the tradition respond to a particular issue in curriculum and, finally, review some objections which have been, or could be raised to its style and method.

When people are asked why they support certain positions and reject others, they usually point to some kind of logical justification. Often, however, this fails to produce an advance in understanding. Logical systems tend towards closure. If you are in them, everything hangs together quite nicely. If you are outside them, the logic is opaque. It is rather like having someone show you how he won his game of chess when you don't know the moves. An awkward paradox comes into play: only the expert can really have a 'feel' for the system within which he operates, but his very familiarity puts a barrier between him and the outsider looking for enlightenment. A deeper question is why people 'buy into' particular systems in the first place, and that is, literally, a deeper question, in that the reasons (if indeed it makes sense to speak of 'reasons') are hidden even to the individuals concerned. Partly they inhere in character, partly in the accidents of experience, and even that kind of distinction may not hold up very well. If I were asked why I favour the deliberative approach, I could, for example, point to some personal preferences: I am independently minded and am not attracted by theoretical positions that handle human problems through gross generalisations, or abstract principles; I am peaceable and don't like social philosophies that stress power and conflict and I am inclined to favour logical ways of resolving problems (using logical in a broad sense). As far as the accidents of experience are concerned, I have, by chance as much as choice, studied European literature from classical to modern times in original texts, including such byways as the dark ages and the early medieval period. Such a background induces a degree of scepticism when faced by the kind of 'ahistorical' thinking that has characterised curriculum studies in recent years, with its talk of modernity, development and innovation. Finally, I spent ten years teaching in secondary schools and this leaves a strong sense of the reality of learning and teaching in the classroom.

When, in 1969, I moved from schools to work on funded research projects (I would now refer to what I was doing as 'curriculum research', but I don't think I used the expression at that time), I started to explore the literature of curriculum studies. Most of what I found ranged from fairly straightforward commonsense at one extreme (not too much of that), to pure fantasy at the other (simplistic talk about objectives, systems, feedback etc.).[4] The first paper I came across that said it was about curriculum and actually seemed to be talking about real things but in a way that transcended commonsense was Schwab's 'The Practical: a Language for Curriculum' which, coincidentally, was published in 1969. I'm not sure I understood much of it at the time, and I certainly knew nothing of the background from which it came. But it seemed to be saying things about curriculum which responded to my concerns.

First, I liked the idea that it was possible to talk, theoretically, about practice without that sacrifice of its messy uniqueness which resulted from the use of procedures divorced from subject-matter, or analytical abstractions at odds with the complexity of the real world. The problem about practicality was not solved for me by Schwab's paper, but a way was shown by which it could be conceived and productively worked on. His resolution of the problem depends on an assertion that 'the practical' and 'the theoretic' are essentially different and cannot be assimilated to one another, but that, nevertheless, one can theorise about the practical, just as one can theorise about the theoretic: 'the expression of practical philosophies depends, despite their quest for concrete foundations, on the formulation of a theory which takes its place among other theories' (McKeon, 1952, p. 79). What one cannot do is take over the kind of theorising that belongs to the latter and apply it to the former: and this is precisely where most attempts on the part of curriculum theorists to demonstrate their concern for the practical break down.

The second thing I liked about the paper was its plea for eclecticism and for tolerance of ambiguity. Schwab's rejection of subscription to over-riding principles and procedures struck a sympathetic chord. Much of what I saw being put forward as 'curriculum theory' seemed to be directed towards the establishment of closed, axiomatic systems – an extension of positivism to areas where even philosophers such as Russell would not believe its writ could run. And why should anyone want to do that? My sense of the history of ideas and my experience of schools suggested that, if we were seriously interested in the improvement of the curriculum, we should be looking for styles of theorising that confront the ambiguities inherent in curriculum decision-making, not styles that eliminate them by axiomatic pronouncements, or bypass them by abstracting only those qualities from situations which can be measured with an apparent lack of ambiguity. The problem was not, I thought, to find theories which claimed to provide answers to questions, but theories which could help us towards a productive search for answers. This was the promise of Schwab's paper. The theorising was not tight. It did not preclude search by setting up axioms, or by imposing stipulative definitions. It encouraged enquiry, and left unresolved questions for the researcher to work on.

A third attractive feature of Schwab's writing was that it was not dominated by momentary concerns. Much of the output on curriculum in the late 1960s and early 1970s, both in England and the United States, was bound up with a limited and temporary reality that belonged to curriculum developers, to administrators, to some extent, but to schools and teachers hardly at all. Research and development money freed advocates of modernism in the curriculum from the restraints associated with the real decision points in schools and classrooms, and projected them into a 'never never land' where all kinds of innovation-oriented activities could flourish. But when the results were fed back into the schools, these new forms of life died, or went through painful adaptations in order to survive. Yet it was the developer's activities that became the commonplaces of curriculum writing. Analyses of a hothouse culture were seriously put forward as a contribution to the improvement of life in the barnyard. Schwab, though active in curriculum projects, seemed untouched by all this. What he had to say about the curriculum seemed to have a genuinely universal relevance. It was true as much of the nursery school as of the university, of the conventional classroom as the curriculum project. Even when he addressed himself to current controversy (Schwab, 1969a) his analyses and his remedies had a timeless quality.

This should not be taken as a summary of all that is to be found in 'the practical', still less of all that is to be found in Schwab. But it distils the points that were immediately striking, and provides the grounds on which I can address some of the deeper notions underlying the central theme of 'the practical'. First of all, some apparent contradictions have to be dealt with. How is it possible to see qualities of universalism in something that responds to contingent reality? One could turn that problem round. How is it possible to believe in universal principles that do not apply in any particular case? The problem is a problem as long as the theoretical search is guided by an aspiration to axiomatic or empirically demonstrable truth. It ceases to be a problem when we accept the notion of the practical which follows rules of its own domain. Secondly, I have been a critic of theories which claim to offer procedures for carrying out curricular tasks (planning by objectives and so on); how then can I praise Schwab for building curriculum theory around a core of method? The answer lies in the distinction I would want to make between 'procedure' and 'method'.

Procedure is to be understood within a context of axiomatic thinking. Within that context, procedure is an end-point of enquiry. Working from first principles, one arrives at a formulation which can be applied universally when a particular kind of problem has to be solved. The logic of the process is to be understood not in terms of the mind of the user, or of the material situation that has to be confronted, but in the goodness of fit between the finished procedure and the principles that gave rise to it. Method, on the other hand, has to be understood within the context of deliberative thinking. This starts, not from principles, but from problems. The essence of methodic enquiry is to initiate and sustain a process through which the nature of a problem is exposed and a solution converged upon . Each step is contingent on preceding steps: at each moment, method and subject-matter interact. Method is not an end-point of enquiry. It guides enquiry in an open-ended way. Its existence is guaranteed, not by abstract formulae which can be recorded, but by personal skills that have to be learned. At every point its use is subject to the judgement of individuals, and only retrospectively can its course be charted. Its logic is continuously reconstructed as it interacts with its subject-matter. The answer to anyone who says: 'But that is very esoteric!' is: 'Nevertheless, that is what we do all the time. That is how we deal with the demands of everyday life.' Such responses illustrate how we have become trapped in the very problem we want to solve. The practical concerns of life are at once too trivial and too esoteric to be encompassed by the kinds of theories that it is academically 'respectable' to talk about. On a philosphical level, the issue is well summed up by Brown: 'The attempt by logical empiricists to identify rationality with algorithmic computability is somewhat strange, since it deems rational only those human acts which could, in principle, be carried out without the presence of a human being' (1979, p. 148).

Conceptually, then, notions like 'the practical', like 'enquiry', like 'deliberation', are difficult. Our capacity for understanding them has been undermined by the vast success and academic prestige, in recent history, of scientific theorising and research. The ideas we meet in

Schwab are, in large part, ideas that were once commonplaces of scholarship, but were submerged in the onrush of positivist science. Only now are they beginning to be revived as ideas with force and application, rather than as the preserve of esoteric philosophers and critics. In order to appreciate them, it is necessary to engage them closely, and to enlist the help of a variety of writers who use them in order to break the barrier of unfamiliarity which surrounds them. To assist in the process of appreciation, some brief analysis of how they relate to the general course of development in Western thought is necessary.

If we begin at the present day, and look for writers who have, in recent years, brought a deliberative perspective to the study of the curriculum, we do not find very many, though they include one of unique stature in Dewey.[5] Other educational writers I would identify with the perspective are Digby Anderson, Michael Connelly, Joseph Schwab, Decker Walker and Ian Westbury. (I think Pinar was missing a great deal when he categorised these two latter as 'conceptual-empiricists' in his preface to *Curriculum Theorizing* (1975).) Others who seem to me to have affinities with the perspective, though they might not identify themselves with it, are Douglas Barnes, Elliot Eisner, Ernest House, Lawrence Stenhouse and George Willis. Critics and philosophers who have held positions compatible with deliberative curriculum theory are Wayne Booth, R.S. Crane, Richard McKeon and Geoffrey Vickers.[6] It is an interesting fact that, of the names I have mentioned, about half are of people who are or have been faculty members or students (or both) at the University of Chicago. The exact connections of the University of Chicago with what has been described as the 'neo-Aristotelean' tradition remain to be traced, but a start has been made in *Science, Curriculum, and Liberal Education* (Westbury and Wilkof, 1978), an essential text for anyone wishing to study deliberative styles of curriculum theorising.

These references to Aristotle provide an essential key to the understanding of the deliberative method. The connection to be made is not simply with Aristotle himself, but with the Aristotelean scholastic curriculum which dominated European scholarship through the post-classical and medieval periods and broke down as late as the eighteenth century. Within that tradition, no strong distinction was made in social philosophy between matters of fact and matters of value. The humane disciplines were conceived of as arts and methods which should guide our practice 'for the attaining of our true good and happiness'.[7] And, since whatever had consequences for good and happiness was intrinsically moral in character, the conduct of those arts and methods was something to be undertaken by moral agents guided by the realities of the concrete situation, and not by a set of abstract principles. Opposed to the arts of the practical were the sciences, which were theoretic and directed to the discovery of knowledge of the truth considered speculatively. The subject-matter of science was restricted to the phenomena of the natural universe. In the late renaissance, however, spectacular success in theorising within the realm of the natural sciences severely undermined the whole structure of scholastic thought and method. It suggested that Aristotle's scientific ideas were mistaken[8] and it provided the impetus for the extension of scientific theorising into the realm of the practical. '[I] n Bacon and Descartes, for the first time . . . the tradition of linguistic and literary studies which had constituted the basis of the humanities in the Renaissance comes into sharp conflict with the claims of natural philosophy to the possession of both a superior method of enquiry and of superior possibilities of utility to man' (Crane, 1967, p. 67). The power of the scientific method seemed to reside in its search for facts and in its ability to use facts to demonstrate law-like relationships between events. This method was taken up as a method of treating the subject-matter of political economy and ethics, which it could do only by separating what had previously been inseparable: questions of fact and questions of value. Writers like Bentham popularised the idea that a scientific calculus could be applied to human affairs. Theorists distanced themselves intellectually from the practical, and began to behave as moral judges or critics, able to rely on *a priori* principles, rather than as moral agents who have to be engaged with the particularities of cases. But what had been a strength in the pursuit of the theoretic, became a weakness in the pursuit of the practical. 'Bentham's relation to the principle of utility is what Newton's would have been to the law of gravity, had Newton established that law by persuading the planets to obey the inverse square relationship in their own interest' (Gillispie, 1960, p. 154). McKeon points to the essential difference when he says of Aristotle's *Politics:* 'Its purpose was practical, to lead men to perform good actions, not theoretic, to discover and demonstrate the final good (McKeon, 1977, p. 208).

Faith in the scientific method grew stronger through the nineteenth century. Political theorising was dramatically influenced by it. Marx was, in the view of Engels, 'the first to discover the great law which governs the march of history . . . the more or less clear expression of struggles between social classes . . . This law bears the same relationship to history as the law of the conservation of energy bears towards the physical sciences'. Human studies such as anthropology were launched under the aegis of scientific method. Tylor, in his preface to *Primitive Culture* (1871) states: 'To many educated minds there seems something presumptuous and repulsive in the view that the history of mankind is part and parcel of the history of nature . . . But let us take this admitted existence of natural cause and effect as our standing ground, and travel . . . as far as it will bear us. It is on the same basis that physical science pursues, with ever increasing success, its quest of laws of nature'. In the present century, the development of disciplines related to curriculum, such as sociology and psychology, have been subjected to similar influences.[9]

Today, however, general disillusionment with the results of 'rational' or 'scientific' planning in fields such as housing and welfare, as well as curriculum, adds practical necessity to the theoretical discontents which have stimulated searches for alternative ways of construing the principles that guide the study of practical affairs. The basic problem we face is the one which is central to all questions of social significance: how to relate matters of fact and value. When we confront this issue we should not neglect, as a way of responding to it, the possibility of recapturing something of the spirit which informed the humanities before they were changed, under the influence of Cartesian 'method' from 'disciplines conceived as arts and methods to disciplines conceived as fields and established bodies of knowledge' (McKeon, 1967, p. 175). The barrier we face is the difficulty we experience in trying to conceive of academic subjects or policy-related studies as other than collections of facts and theories on the one hand, or as systems of axiomatic principles on the other. We see the unfortunate consequences of this in, for example, teacher 'training' courses which consist of admixtures of disconnected information and latitudinous prescriptions, and which only incidentally, or accidentally, help students engage with the concrete realities of their art (Westbury, 1977, pp. 9-10). Writers such as Dewey, Schwab, and Westbury suggest how we might develop a method in curriculum that allows for particularity, is under the control of people, and regards them as acting in morally committed ways. The consequences of working with such a view of method can be illustrated by reference to a specific example.

As an instance, I shall use the issue of 'accountability'. This is a topical concern, in relation to the curriculum, of politicians and administrators in both England and North America. It is suggested that schools and teachers should be more accountable both for what they decide to include in their curricula, and for the results of teaching them, in terms of student achievement. Here is grist for the mill of curriculum studies. What are we to make of it? In the case of radical theorists, it is a reasonable guess that they will point to this as a further example of how the curriculum is used as an instrument of bourgeois cultural imperialism. And they should have a field day. If ever an issue cried out for this sort of analysis it is that of accountability. To hold someone accountable is *prima facie* to deprive him of freedom of choice. It is also evident that the conventional apparatus of testing is likely to bear on students, teachers and schools in discriminatory ways. In terms of reinforcing the indictment of the capitalist system, accountability will have served its turn. It is unclear, however, in what way students, teachers or schools will have been helped.

Writers in the systemic tradition, on the other hand, will be concerned to 'help' by building the technical apparatus of consultation, decision-making and testing by which accountability can be set up. In England, for example, some curriculum experts, working with the national Assessment of Performance Unit, have been pressing the case for 'monitoring of standards' through the use of the Rasch Model of item analysis. This, it is claimed, would provide, at low cost, results which are comparable over different types of curriculum and also over time. Such aspirations have been criticised by other theorists for whom 'The educational reality . . . is altogether different and has to do with a world which is too rich and complex to be reduced, without distortion, to such a simple model' (Goldstein, 1979, p. 217).

I cannot imagine, however, that an issue like accountability will, in itself, provide material for the existential theorist. Such questions lie in the public domain, and the public domain is peripheral to the engagement of the individual consciousness with the curriculum. It will, of course, be a concern in so far as it is part of a complex of matters that affect the quality of a student's encounter with the curriculum of the school.

Those who would advocate a deliberative approach to curriculum problems recognise in the question of accountability a part of the reality with which educators must deal in making curriculum decisions, and therefore something which should be a subject of enquiry. They would not, however, take the *a priori* view that moves for greater accountability are necessarily to be opposed: neither would they see it as their role to accept political and administrative claims at face value and help build accountability systems geared to technical convenience. The fact that accountability enters the arena of public debate is evidence that problems exist which educators should respond to: it is not reliable evidence of exactly what the problems are. The theorist or researcher has to approach the issue in two ways. First, to try to help schools and teachers respond rationally to the specific demands that are being made on them, because that is something that affects the quality of education and that cannot be postponed. Secondly, to work at illuminating the conditions that give rise to demands for accountability and at characterising the connotations of the term itself. The deliberative theorist does not, by seeing his role as helping the school respond to administrative demands, necessarily accept the legitimacy of those demands. Neither, on the other hand, does he accept that the school is always right and the administrator or politician wrong. He recognises here one of those fundamental dilemmas inherent in public educational systems: on the one hand, what schools teach is some kind of public possession contingent on political climates; on the other, the curriculum of the school is also the possession of individuals – those who teach it and those who experience it. The tension between these contrary claims – the national and public, the local and private – admits of no final resolution. Different resolutions have to be found according to place and time. The role of the theorist is to help individuals and institutions to find the resolution that fits their case. It will be unique. Not universal, nor one of a standard set. And though what is decided will represent, ideally, a consensus, it need not be a crude compromise. Deliberation can be inventive. It does not endorse the managerial view that the model for the resolution of competing views must be based on the 'zero-sum' game. And there will be times when no sort of consensus is possible. The moral character of deliberation, which gives it a tendency to consensual decisions, also ensures that there will be occasions when opposition or confrontation is the only rational response. (See, for example, Rand, 1979, pp. 85-6.)

But behind the question of immediate decisions lies that of underlying problems. The causes of curriculum problems are many and varied: political, economic, moral, technological, social, intellectual and personal. Problems do not come with labels neatly tied around their necks, and neither do solutions. They must be elucidated through deliberation and enquiry. What deliberative theory puts forward is not a ready-made diagnosis, nor a ready-made remedy, but the idea of what to attend to and where to place reliance in making the search. What we have to attend to, in the view of the deliberative theorist, is the relationship between institutional decisions about curricular purposes and practices on the one hand, and, on the other, the wishes of publics which have legitimate interests in what is taught and with what result. These are not just economic relationships, involving investment and production; they are, more importantly, moral relationships, involving trust and responsibility. And, as in all such deliberations, practical questions have to be faced: if schools are to respond to publics, how are publics to be defined and how are they to articulate their wishes? If publics are to appraise the work of schools, what kinds of information do they need and how should it be collected and communicated?

In such ways the process can be started of defining the kinds of data and ideas which the work demands. But to get the work done, it is necessary to involve the people who are most directly concerned with the issue in question: to rely on their ability, through deliberation, to search, invent and decide. Through these kinds of approaches, the field of curriculum studies becomes a policy-related endeavour, but one which also respects the concerns and aspirations of groups and of individuals.

Certain difficulties are inevitably raised when ideas such as these are put forward. Which of these are seen as substantial objections by particular critics depends on their individual stance but, for the sake of brevity, I will ignore such distinctions in presenting them.

First objection: is this not just a parade of commonsense? Answer: yes and no. Yes, in the sense that the deliberative theorist does not set out with the idea that the aim of curriculum studies is to evolve a body of theory or a praxiology which is accessible only to initiates who have read the right books, taken the right courses or worked with the right mentors. Everyone can join in. Everyone should join in. But it becomes more than commonsense in that the world within which curriculum decisions have to be made is one among many and we cannot be experienced in all of them. If there is to be profit in writing and talking about something called 'curriculum' it must be because there is something unique to be said about it which is not, by simple transposition, applicable to other activities.

Second objection: but what exactly do I have to do? Answer: if you want to subscribe to a curriculum theory that tells you precisely what to do, you will have to go elsewhere. Deliberative theory does not go in for ready-made solutions or axiomatic forms of reasoning. It suggests that good actions have to be discovered, and that the means for their discovery is the inventive behaviour of people. Thus, while it is clearly possible to specify skills of deliberation in terms of devices, prescriptions and principles, their application is a matter for informed judgement in response to an existing state of affairs, its antecedent state and its possible successors.

Third objection: is this not a very conservative kind of theory? Answer: it depends what you mean by conservative. It does not set out to turn the world upside down. It considers that the world as it is has some good possibilities. On the other hand, it could have quite radical implications in terms of what is taught in schools – which is, after all, what curriculum studies should be about. The main problem with the school curriculum could be, not hegemony, not bourgeois exploitation, not falling standards of literacy and numeracy, but sheer boredom. The boredom that descends when what is taught is insulated from challenging ideas. When the black and white world of the politician and the grey world of the administrator produce an intellectual climate of simple categories of knowledge and minimalist goals. The implication of deliberative theory is that the arena for debate on the curriculum should be a much more open one; that publics, teachers and students should have more influence over what is taught and that fundamental reappraisals of aims and practices should be a continuing social and professional responsibility, not token exercises or reactions to administrative prodding.

Fourth objection: that's all very well, but isn't this all too idealistic? Answer: it's idealistic in the sense that it's based on value commitments – to liberal democratic ideals – and on the belief that, to be effective, policy has to be guided by visions. Not because visions are ultimately attainable, but because morally worthwhile activity depends on their pursuit. It's a truism that if you want people to act responsibly, you have to trust them. That is what deliberative theory, on its practical side, is about. Trusting people to take charge of their destinies, to develop the skills they need to do that, and to exercise them artfully and responsibly. It does not shut them out by demonstrating that they are not 'expert', neither does it tell them that theory has already found the answer to their problem or is on the way to doing so. Of course, what can be done in practice will be constrained: by the life of institutions, by lack of knowledge or time, by sheer cussedness. Deliberative theory recognises the constraints of real decision-making situations and tries to increase appreciation of them. But the fact that constraints exist is not a reason for taking a cynical or defeatist stance. How can it be good for people to act on theories that take a pessimistic view of human nature?

Fifth objection: isn't there a circularity here? 'A society has to *learn to learn* to be able to practice [deliberative] planning; and [deliberative] planning can only be achieved through a process of learning to learn' (Camhis, 1979, p.77).[10] Yes, Deliberative theory has no problems with such apparent paradoxes. I have pointed out a similar one: 'What [Schwab] proposes is a way in which a liberal education can be truly free in that it is not an imposed formula, but the product of its own liberal aims (Reid, 1980, p. 260). Such statements are problematic only within closed systems of reasoning which, implicitly, contain all their conclusions in their premisses. To claim that man contains all his conclusions in his premisses is to advance a proposition of very dubious status.

Deliberation and Dialogue

My account of the deliberative position is perhaps controversial, and it is certainly incomplete. However, the discussion should have served to uncover some basic features of the position and to illuminate some aspects of the central notion of method.

At the outset, I suggested some reasons why I found myself in agreement with the deliberative stance. What further can I add to that in the light of my additional explanations? In 'Rationalism and Humanism' I put forward the idea that 'if choice can be exercised, then the creation of a humane discipline of curriculum studies would seem to be the future that should be sought. The principles underlying such a choice are clear enough to give a coherence to theory and research, but, at the same time, the exact direction which a humane study should take is open (and by its nature has to be so) and gives scope for that debate and discussion between differing positions which, if engaged in a spirit of communal search, seems to me to be fundamental to any enquiry with policy implications' (Reid, 1979c). This sums up my further reason for wishing to develop the deliberative position as one from which to attack curriculum problems. I see it as offering scope for debate and discussion between theorists of different persuasions, without, however, placing all other perspectives in a purely relativist frame of reference. In short, it holds out the possibility of fostering a spirit of critical pluralism by its recognition that the standards of criticism to be applied to curriculum theory and research need not be the unitary standards yielded by styles of thinking based on axiomatic premises.

At this point, we need to pause and consider the question we are addressing. Methods of truth seeking, as I have suggested earlier, tend to develop in fairly closed ways, and to be impervious to criticism from other positions. I may feel that someone with whom I disagree is mistaken, and that his arguments are pure 'Humpty-Dumpty'.[11] The trouble is, that from his point of view, my arguments, too, are Humpty-Dumpty ones. I can only criticise his position from the basis of assumptions that lie within my own logic, and *vice-versa*. If what we are disputing about is a question in natural science, either the issue of whose idea is better can be settled (provisionally, at least) by establishing which one works better (oxygen wins over phlogiston), or, if such a test cannot be made, it probably does not make much practical difference who has the better idea (we could let the question of continuous creation versus 'big bang' be wide open since nothing practical hinges on it – it is truly theoretic). However, if we are disputing about something affecting people's lives and happiness, we can neither be so certain of the meaning of our truth tests, nor so cavalier in the matter of leaving things open for decision. Provisional relativism will not do.

But if relativism will not do, neither will monism. Human affairs are too complex to allow us to back one kind of orthodoxy in the hope that it is a winner. What we have to do is to try to see how curriculum theorising can be an activity that permits the co-existence of a variety of styles of reasoning, which stimulates dialogue between exponents of these various styles and which ensures that the possibility of pluralism is preserved and encouraged. So how can we rationally proceed? The answer, in my view, is to cultivate the idea of method, as opposed to procedure or axiomatic reasoning. Method guides search, but does not predetermine its outcomes. Its logic is not completely closed: if we can feel comfortable with dilemma, paradox and ambiguity, we can pursue a style of reasoning within which the products and processes of various styles of theorising and research can be evaluated and find a place. A precondition of this, of course, is that these other styles have at least some open features. For that reason, I see only restricted possibilities of dialogue between a deliberative position and 'a priorist' radical positions. 'Those "marxists" who claim that it is possible to achieve . . . a science [so secure and well grounded that it provides, once and for all, authoritarian decision procedures for what is to be done] . . . are the true progeny of that great bourgeois thinker, Hobbes. They do not dispute the ideal implicit in Hobbes' project: that it is possible to achieve a scientific understanding of human beings and society which will provide a definite basis for reconstructing or revolutionising society' (Bernstein, 1976, pp. 217-18). The development of more open styles of radical reasoning in curriculum studies is, to my knowledge, a recent development, and one that I am not able to comment on.

But what of the more traditional Hobbesians whose *a priori* assumptions are directed to the preservation rather than the overthrow of existing institutions? In this direction too there are problems about the extent to which dialogue is possible. However, from the point of view of the deliberative theorist, dialogue is necessary. One of the criticisms that has been levelled at the conceptions put forward by writers such as Schwab, and there is some substance in it, is that they tend to have too little regard for the kinds of institutional knowledge that school curriculum decision-making demands. Schwab's category of 'milieu' which, in terms of teaching in higher education, might be thought of largely on the level of the environment of the learning space, becomes, in the case of compulsory schooling, very large indeed. In such a situation, the deliberative process demands, as subject-matter, a rich stock of data, analytical schemes and conceptual frames such as systemic theory can supply. And in this instance it is clearer that many writers and researchers who adopt a broadly systemic stance are not exclusively 'a priorist', but show some eclecticism of outlook.

In the case of both radical and systemic theorists, the possibility of dialogue depends on the extent to which they are content to see what are fundamentally 'a priorist' positions develop towards greater openness. When we turn to the existential position, however, we find less in the way of obvious barriers to dialogue, since it shares with the deliberative stance a concern for people rather than ideas, as the basis for action, and for method rather than procedure. This concern for people is, for the deliberative theorist, more than just a matter of declaring curriculum studies a 'humane discipline'. Schwab points out that 'the initial stage of deliberation . . . is the prime means by which each planner begins to *discover himself*' (my emphases) (Schwab, 1973). And here we can note a substantial overlapping with the central concern of the existential position. On the question of method, it is not possible to give here any close attention to Pinar's 'method of *currere*', but the phrase is suggestive. It is indeed method and not procedure that is at issue. Here too there are chances of fruitful dialogue.[12] Not surprisingly, then, we find especial sympathy for critical pluralism in Pinar's writings, and I cannot do better than conclude with an extended quotation from his 'Reply to my Critics':

> One kind of critical response is born in an interest in assisting the work under scrutiny to become more complete, more sophisticated. This is the criticism of a pedagogue who offers criticism which is usable, which can be integrated into the work, improving it . . .

> There is a second kind of critical response which does not wish the other well, which is not interested in the improvement of his work. It is not born in a pedagogic interest, but in a cathartic one. It is ill-tempered, results not in the development of the Other's work, but in silence . . .
>
> Conversation cannot occur unless the participants are willing to maintain a minimal civility, a pedagogic orientation, and a willingness to be changed by the other. With such conditions present, a vital conversation, indicative of a vital field can occur. (Pinar, 1979)

Only two things need to be added. One is a small commentary on Pinar's plea for conversation. His sentiment is thoroughly in keeping with the ethos of deliberation, and its dependence on trust and responsibility. What additionally should be said is that civility, though necessary, is not sufficient for dialogue to take place. We also have to look to the nature of the intellectual assumptions that undergird theoretical positions. The second is a reiteration of an earlier *caveat*. This paper has, for its own rhetorical purposes, simplified and reified certain positions on curriculum theory and research. If we make the mistake of thinking that these are the only positions, we shall be led to the conclusion that the scope for dialogue is not very great. So it is appropriate to end by reminding readers that reality is more complex than any account that can be given of it, and that there is indeed good hope that a critical pluralism based on methodic approaches to the study of the curriculum can be the occasion of important and varied dialogues with practical as well as theoretical significance.

Acknowledgement

In writing this paper, I am conscious of my indebtedness to a large number of people. To none do I owe a greater debt than to Ian Westbury of the University of Illinois. His knowledge and understanding of curriculum theory, expressed through papers, conversations and correspondence over several years, have been a major factor in the shaping of my own ideas. I am also grateful to the editors of this volume, Len Barton and Martin Lawn, for their encouragement and helpful suggestions.

Notes

1. Comparisons could be made between the categories and dimensions I have used and those suggested in other analyses of intellectual or political positions. For example, Eysenck's constructs of radical/conservative and tough-minded/tender-minded, or the fox versus hedgehog distinction used by Isaiah Berlin in his essay on Tolstoy: 'The fox knows many things [exploratory?], but the hedgehog knows one big thing ['a priorist'?]'.

2. Hunters of my own assumptions will note here the correspondence between the chosen themes and Aristotle's four types of cause.

3. All of these authors except Grumet are represented in *Curriculum Theorizing* (Pinar, 1975), which presents a very wide collection of writings and hinders rather than helps understanding of the uniqueness of the existential position. In particular, it is something of an historical accident that it makes it appear as though existential and radical writers share a common platform. They were united more by what they opposed than by what they stood for. See also Pinar and Grumet (1976).

4. In retrospect, I can see that good curriculum writing was being produced, but that it did not always advertise itself under that name. I think, for example of *Culture Against Man* (Henry, 1963), which I found impressive.

5. Dewey was a writer of remarkable range of whom my knowledge is very imperfect and who seems to be regarded with a strange mixture of respect and bafflement by many curriculum writers. (Many others just ignore him.) It seems clear, however, that most of his central ideas are within what I define as the deliberative tradition. His intellectual connections with Schwab and others are discussed by Westbury and Wilkof (1978), in their introduction.

6. I am tempted to add Karl Popper, who is distinctly 'deliberative' in some of his conclusions, if not in his intellectual origins.

7. The words of Samuel Johnson, eighteenth-century president of King's College (later Columbia University), quoted by McKeon (1967, pp. 182-3).

8. Strictly speaking, his conclusions were wrong as judged by a method that started from different premisses. 'Galileo could describe mathematically how a stone would fall under ideal conditions . . . Aristotle's physics . . . could not measure its motion . . . Aristotle could do more important things. He could explain why a stone fell' (Gillispie, 1960, p. 11).

9. Callahan traces connections in America at the turn of the century between curriculum and 'scientific management'. The 'scientific' influence goes back much further. Spencer, another nineteenth-century proponent of the application of scientific laws to human affairs, had much to say about education and his writings were very popular in the United States (Callahan, 1962).

10. The original has 'transactive', not 'deliberative', but the sense is clearly similar, if not identical.

11. 'When I use a word . . . it means what I choose it to mean – neither more nor less' (Carroll, 1872).

12. I suspect that one of the problems about communicating the nature of deliberative method is that its focus is on curriculum tasks that are also the subject of procedural and axiomatic theorising. As a result, deliberative theory tends to be seen simply as a branch of systemic theory. Familiarity with method in more foreign contexts (such as *currere* or Zen) could be a way into an understanding of deliberative method that starts from more compatible grounds.

Bibliography

(Note: in addition to works referred to in the text, the following bibliography includes a number of books and articles dealing with or related to a deliberative curriculum theory. I have not, however, attempted to provide a comprehensive list in this area.)

Anderson, Digby C. (1981) *Evaluating Curriculum Proposals: a Practical Guide*, Croom Helm, London

Apple, Michael W. (1979) *Ideology and Curriculum*, Routledge and Kegan Paul, London

Barnes, Douglas (1976) *From Communication to Curriculum*, Penguin Books, Harmondsworth

Beauchamp, George (1975) *Curriculum Theory*, 3rd edn, Kagg Press, Wilmette, Illinois

Bernstein, Richard J. (1976) *The Restructuring of Social and Political Theory*, Harcourt, Brace, New York

Bloom, B. S. (1976) *Human Characteristics and School Learning*, McGraw-Hill, New York

Booth, Wayne C. (ed.) (1967) *The Knowledge Most Worth Having*, Univ. of Chicago Press, Chicago

Booth, Wayne C. (1974) *Modern Dogma and the Rhetoric of Assent*, Univ. of Chicago Press, Chicago

Booth, Wayne C. (1979) *Critical Understanding: the Powers and Limits of Pluralism*, Univ. of Chicago Press, Chicago

Bourdieu, Pierre and Passeron, Jean-Claude (1970) *La Réproduction: Eléments pour une Théorie du Système d'Enseignement*, Editions de Minuit, Paris

Bowles, S. and Gintis, H. (1976) *Schooling in Capitalist America*, Routledge and Kegan Paul, London

Brown, Harold I. (1979) *Perception, Theory and Commitment: the New Philosophy of Science*, Phoenix edn., Univ. of Chicago Press, Chicago

Callahan, R. E. (1962) *Education and the Cult of Efficiency*, Univ. of Chicago Press, Chicago

Camhis, Marios (1979) *Planning Theory and Philosophy*, Tavistock Publications, London

Carroll, Lewis (pseud.) (1872) *Through the Looking-Glass*, London

Chamboredon, J-C. and Prévot, J. (1973) 'Le "Métier d'Enfant"', *Revue Française de Sociologie*, 14, pp. 295-335

Connelly, M.F. (1972) 'The Functions of Curriculum Development',

Interchange, 3, pp. 161-77
Connelly, M.F. and Ben-Peretz, M. (1980) 'Teachers' Roles in the Using and Doing of Research and Curriculum Development', *Journal of Curriculum Studies*, 12, 2, pp. 95-107
Crane, R. S. (1967) *The Idea of the Humanities and Other Essays Critical and Historical*, Univ. of Chicago Press, Chicago
Eisner, Elliot W. (1979) *The Educational Imagination: on the Design and Evaluation of School Programs*, Macmillan, New York
Gillispie, C.G. (1960) *The Edge of Objectivity: an Essay in the History of Scientific Ideas*, Princeton Univ. Press
Goldstein, Hervey (1979) 'Consequences of Using the Rasch Model for Educational Assessment', *British Educational Research Journal*, 5, 2, pp. 211-20
Henry, Jules (1963) *Culture Against Man*, Random House, New York
House, Ernest R. (1974) *The Politics of Educational Innovation*, McCutchan, Berkeley
House, Ernest R. (work forthcoming) *Evaluating with Validity*, Sage Publications, London
Kallós, D. and Lundgren, U.P. (1976) 'An Enquiry Concerning Curriculum: Foundations for Curriculum Change', mimeograph, Pedag. Inst., Univ. of Gothenburg
Kerlinger, F. N. (1964) *Foundations of Behavioral Research*, Holt, Rinehart, New York
McKeon, Richard (1952) 'Philosophy and Action', *Ethics*, 62, pp. 79-100
McKeon, Richard (1967) 'The Battle of the Books' in Booth (1967), pp. 173-202
McKeon, Richard (1977) 'Person and Community: Metaphysical and Political', *Ethics*, 88, pp. 207-17
Pinar, William F. (ed.) (1975) *Curriculum Theorizing: the Reconceptualists*, McCutchan, Berkeley
Pinar, William F. (1979) 'A Reply to my Critics', unpublished paper, Univ. of Rochester, New York
Pinar, William F. and Grumet, M. (1976) *Toward a Poor Curriculum*, Kendall-Hunt, Dubuque, Iowa
Pratt, David (1980) *Curriculum Design and Development*, Harcourt, Brace, New York
Rand, Per (1979) 'Accountability and Resistance: the Norwegian Teaching Profession Under the Occupation', *Educational Analysis*, 1, pp. 85-6
Reid, William A. (1978) *Thinking About the Curriculum: the Nature*

and Treatment of Curriculum Problems, Routledge and Kegan Paul, London
Reid, William A. (1979a) 'Making the Problem Fit the Method: a Review of the "Banbury Enquiry" ', *Journal of Curriculum Studies,* 11, pp. 167-73
Reid, William A. (1979b) 'Practical Reasoning and Curriculum Theory: in Search of a New Paradigm', *Curriculum Inquiry*, 9, pp. 187-207
Reid, William A. (1979c) 'Rationalism or Humanism? The Future of Curriculum Studies', *Journal of Curriculum Theorizing*, 2, pp. 93-108
Reid, William A. (1979d) 'Schools, Teachers and Curriculum Change: Moral Dimension of Theory-Building', *Educational Theory*, 29, 4, pp. 325-36
Reid, William A. (1980) 'Democracy, Perfectability, and the Battle of the Books: Thoughts on the Conception of Liberal Education in the Writings of J.J. Schwab', *Curriculum Inquiry*, 10, 3, pp. 249-63
Reid, William A. and Walker, Decker F. (eds.) (1975) *Case Studies in Curriculum Change: Great Britain and the United States*, Routledge and Kegan Paul, London
Schwab, J. J. (1969a) *College Curriculum and Student Protest*, Univ. of Chicago Press, Chicago
Schwab, J. J. (1969b) 'The Practical: a Language for Curriculum', *School Review*, 78, pp. 1-24
Schwab, J. J. (1973) 'The Practical 3: Translation into Curriculum', *School Review*, 81, pp. 501-22
Sharp, R. and Green, A. (1975) *Education and Social Control: a Study in Progressive Education*, Routledge and Kegan Paul, London
Stenhouse, Lawrence (1975) *An Introduction to Curriculum Research and Development*, Heinemann, London
Tylor, E. B. (1871) *Primitive Culture: Researches into the Derivation of Mythology, Philosophy, Language, Art and Custom*, 2 vols., John Murray, London
Vickers, Geoffrey (1965) *The Art of Judgement*, Chapman and Hall, London
Vickers, Geoffrey (1968) *Value Systems and Social Press*, Tavistock Publications, London
Walker, Decker F. (1975) 'Curriculum Development in an Art Project' in Reid and Walker (1975)
Westbury, Ian (1972a) 'The Aristotelian "Art" of Rhetoric and the "Art" of Curriculum', *Philosophy of Education*, 28, pp. 126-36

Westbury, Ian (1972b) 'The Character of a Curriculum for a "Practical" Curriculum', *Curriculum Theory Network*, Fall, pp. 25-37

Westbury, Ian (1977) 'Educational Policy-Making in New Contexts: the Contribution of Curriculum Studies', *Curriculum Inquiry*, 7, pp. 3-18

Westbury, Ian (1979a) 'The Curriculum: What is It and How Should we Think about It?' in Bloomer, M. and Shaw, K. E. (eds.), *The Challenge of Educational Change*, Pergamon, Oxford

Westbury, Ian (1979b) 'Schooling as an Agency of Education: Some Implications for Curriculum Theory' in Dockrell, W. B. and Hamilton, D. (eds.) *Rethinking Educational Research*, Hodder and Stoughton, London

Westbury, Ian and Steiner, William (1971) 'Curriculum: a Discipline in Search of its Problems', *School Review*, 79, pp. 243-68

Westbury, Ian and Wilkof, Neil J. (eds.) (1978) *Science, Curriculum and Liberal Education*, Univ. of Chicago Press, Chicago

Wheeler, D. K. (1967) *Curriculum Process*, Univ. of London Press, London

Willis, George (ed.) (1978) *Qualitative Evaluation: Concepts and Cases in Curriculum Criticism*, McCutchan, Berkeley

Willis, Paul (1977) *Learning to Labour: How Working Class Kids Get Working Class Jobs*, Saxon House, Farnborough

Wise, Arthur E. (1977) 'Why Educational Policies Often Fail: the Hyperrationalization Hypothesis', *Journal of Curriculum Studies*, 9, pp. 43-57

Part Four

CURRICULUM PRACTICE

INTRODUCTION

The relationship between curriculum theory and curriculum practice is unclear. Curriculum theorists have not helped this relationship by producing theoretical models of curriculum practice nor by their pragmatic excursions for data. Even the eclectic approach, devised solely to produce a more relevant method of informing practice, is unable to explain clearly the basis on which theory is abstracted and used.

Both writers in this section are concerned with the practitioner's lore; its operation, meanings and dilemmas. This concern for understanding practice has led them to be wary of the attempts by theorists to explain the phenomenological world of the teacher.

Rob Walker explains the practical research emphasis that he has developed in order to observe and record the lives and work of teachers. The emphasis on a practical approach led him to devise a kind of educational research that was committed to its subject, the teacher, although the tensions with the pure research enterprise continue to exist. The accurate collection of subjective data, the need to protect the rights of subjects in a confidential relationship, and the vital concern to write the research *for* a particular readership, the teachers themselves, have been the over-riding aims of this approach. Interestingly, the search for a new relationship with the observed has a strong historical link with a British tradition of social observation in literature, documentary films and historical research. The question, rightly raised by Walker, of the degree of critical theoretical development that may be lost in this type of research is important to the issues raised in this book, though our answers may differ.

The question of a practitioner's world that theory cannot grasp or analyse is central to Mike Golby's paper. In a partly autobiographical account, Golby develops a critique of the field of curriculum studies from the point of view of a student and a teacher within it. He argues that curriculum studies is largely produced for, but not by, teachers – a situation he finds unacceptable if the concern of curriculum studies is *really* the improvement of teacher practices. In order to create a properly dialectical relationship, teachers need to reflect upon, and articulate, their ideas concerning their work; moreover, because curriculum studies is not the exclusive domain of teachers, there is a need to relate their work to a view of curriculum activity that is acceptable to a wider audience. Obviously, this is a particular articulation of the problems relating to self and structure.

A concern for solutions to the problem of theory and practice in curriculum studies would have to recognise the separate, private nature of school practice and, at the same time, the social context in which all research takes place, where the distribution of power is of key importance.

7 GETTING INVOLVED IN CURRICULUM RESEARCH: A PERSONAL HISTORY

Rob Walker

I came to curriculum research in the late 1960s with some training in applied science and sociology and some experience as a teacher. The curriculum problem I was given to work on was one that had arisen within the Nuffield Science Teaching Project. The background to the problem was that the project was at that time moving into its second and third generation of curriculum development projects ('A' levels, secondary science and primary science) and was planning pre-service training courses for graduate scientists, master's degree courses and other university award-bearing courses. The importance of these courses was that they permitted the development of a permanent institutional base (the Centre for Science Education at Chelsea College) for the work. University requiements and regulations also involved the recruitment of people with social science backgrounds to teach the 'education' components of courses and, thus, the gradual development of an educational (as opposed to a curricular) research base.

Nuffield Science Teaching Project

The problem I was presented with concerned changes in the teachers' classroom role that seemed to be linked to the kinds of curricular changes involved in the adoption or implementation of Nuffield Science. The NSTP had been partly conceived as an updating of school science curricula, and had spread to cover a range of areas and levels, but one continuous theme that emerged more or less clearly from the different projects was the encouragement of forms of discovery learning. (The following quotations are taken from a SAFARI booklet, issued by the Centre for Applied Research in Education (CARE, n.d.). The ILEA booklet was distributed to all London parents in 1975.):

> Nuffield Science: Ten different science courses for children of all ages from 5-18 have been produced during the last ten years by groups of teachers working with the financial support of the Nuffield Foundation. In these courses there is much more emphasis

than in traditional science on understanding what to do with scientific facts and much less emphasis on remembering facts. Also individual practical work plays a more important part and is more closely integrated with the overall development of such courses. (ILEA, 1975)

Pupils must approach their studies through experiments designed to awaken their spirit of investigation. They must be given opportunities to observe and explore so that they develop disciplined imaginative thinking. (Nuffield, 1966)

Chemistry is an experimental science and it can only be taught in a laboratory. (Nuffield, 1967)

Obviously the effect on classroom techniques will, in many cases, be revolutionary. (Nuffield, 1966)

The curriculum projects identified a number of teachers who were seen to exemplify this conception of teaching, and some of whom were recorded on film for training purposes, but, on the whole, the implications of the changes required in the classroom role of the teacher were not thought through in terms of social science concepts, nor were they observed or recorded systematically. (An exception to this was Dorothy Alexander's evaluation of Nuffield Secondary Science (1974)). Seen from the social science point of view, although there were a number of concepts available that seemed appropriate for such an analysis, there had at that time in Britain been very few attempts to apply them to classroom interaction. Most of the available empirical studies were either studies of the school, or studies of the system. One of the main difficulties I faced was that of finding a starting point from which to collect the kind of information that would meet the questions implicit in the problem. Major problems were: What to look at? How to record? Very few of the techniques immediately available provided access to what went on in classrooms, or related what teachers did to what (and how) pupils learnt. Those techniques that were available (classroom interaction analysis, for example) were reviewed and scrutinised with some care (Walker, 1971, 1972b) but were found too inappropriate, mainly on the grounds that they embodied a view of conventional classroom behaviour that was narrower than the range of behaviours conceived by the curriculum developers (Walker, 1972a; Walker and Adelman, 1975b).

I first began observing in classrooms in order to test out the feasibility and appropriateness of some of these (almost entirely American) instruments. I chose to visit classes selected for me by curriculum developers in the NSTP which they felt in some way were exemplary or extraordinary. Sometimes I found myself in teaching laboratories with unusual designs, sometimes in classes doing most ambitious and exciting projects. One teacher I returned to frequently was identified for me by someone who said: 'He is an amazing teacher. I used to teach with him and I don't really understand what makes him so exceptional, but he does something that works. If you can find out what the secret is we would all be grateful.'

This marks a dilemma which I feel is still unresolved. Needless to say, I never did discover this teacher's 'secret', though watching him teach and talking to him I think I learnt things about his teaching which were communicable to others. The dilemma arises from a commitment to *applied* research, to attempting to find forms for helping one teacher to learn from another, with a simultaneous commitment to the research enterprise itself, to valuing the process of research, wanting to understand for myself and for other researchers. Stated like this the dilemma does not seem impossible to resolve; after all teachers, too, can be researchers, and researchers teachers: the overlap between the two concerns must be considerable. But in practice it is a dilemma that returns and recurs; the interests and concerns of practice and of theory are different: the overlap is at best partial.

Having begun to observe teaching and classrooms one tradition of social science research that did seem appropriate to us (Clem Adelman joined the research at about this point) was the tradition of participant observation, particularly as recast in the form of 'grounded theory' (Glaser and Strauss, 1967). From this starting point developed a line of useful theorising which was to include Garfinkel's ethnomethodology, sociolinguistics and ethnosemantics, all of which provided ways of looking at interactional data of various kinds. In the context of the problem of teacher role changes, such theories took us close up to the details of teacher-pupil interaction, to fine-grained differences between group, class and individual instruction.

Following the precepts of 'grounded theory' as we understood them, we attempted to lay out sets of data that we could begin mapping conceptually. One of the first conceptual maps we produced is shown in Figure 7.1.

This map was produced from descriptive accounts and from some audio-taped lessons, and attempted to lay out a set of alternative

Figure 7.1: Categories for the Description of Social Context

FORMAL ACTIVITIES	Teacher Control HIGH	LECTURE low pupil participation
		INSTRUCTION high pupil participation
	Teacher Control LOW	READINESS low pupil participation
		DISCUSSION high pupil participation
INFORMAL ACTIVITIES Task identical	Teacher-directed	division of labour LOW
		division of labour HIGH
	Pupil-directed	division of labour LOW
		division of labour HIGH
INFORMAL ACTIVITIES Task differentiated	Teacher-directed	division of labour LOW
		division of labour HIGH
	Pupil-directed	division of labour LOW
		division of labour HIGH

Note: These terms are for the analytic description of classroom events. They are exhaustive in that any activity should fit into at least one of them but at any given moment should fit into only one: therefore sequences of change can be described. They are not intended as universal categories of the type used (for example) by Flanders. At any given moment in the classroom it may be difficult to decide whether an activity is, say, readiness or discussion, discussion or lecture; however, in looking at the overall form of a lesson, these terms can be used. In this sense they are terms at an intermediate level.

Source: 'The Social Setting of the Classroom' (Walker, 1971).

communication structures which provided varying contexts within which teacher and pupils interacted. In other words, instead of assuming a constant social structuring of communication (as we felt interaction analysis tended to do), we attempted to put together a set of conceptually related labels that did rather more than simply list alternative contexts.

A major problem at this stage of the research arose from the lack of a precise descriptive language with which to talk about different kinds of classroom activity. To some degree this first map helped, but it quickly got swept aside by the range and quantity of the data we were collecting. This was especially true once Clem Adelman was able to perfect a film recording system (Adelman and Walker, 1972, 1974) that allowed us to collect 'archives' of classroom material. Having direct audio-visual recordings vastly increased the capacity of human memory, especially in that it allowed the replay of selected incidents almost indefinitely.

Figure 7.2 outlines the 'map' that emerged from working with audio-visual records. It was about this time we first saw early drafts of Basil Bernstein's paper on the classification of educational knowledge (Bernstein, 1971) and we both attended a regular seminar run by Bernstein at the University of London Institute of Education. The paper was important to us because it provided a link between the increasingly fine-grained studies we were beginning to carry out in classrooms and the 'higher' levels of curriculum and sociological theory.

While this 'pure' research development had accelerated rapidly, the applied aspect had run along parallel lines, mainly in connection with the pre-service, postgraduate certificate courses where we attempted to get students observing their own teaching, partly with the help of recordings we made in their teaching practice classes (Walker and Adelman, 1975a). However, at this point we faced a dramatic change in the development of ideas which was not due to any intellectual crisis but to the sudden termination of grant support and the need to find alternative employment. In the event, both Clem Adelman and I found our separate ways to the Centre for Applied Research in Education in the University of East Anglia, though to work on projects with different emphases and concerns. Clem worked with John Elliott on the Ford Teaching Project (see, for example, Adams, 1980) where they developed the idea of 'teachers as researchers', using a series of methods to help teachers begin to research their own teaching and providing a continuing network which would act as a critical audience

Figure 7.2: Classrooms: A Researcher's Typology

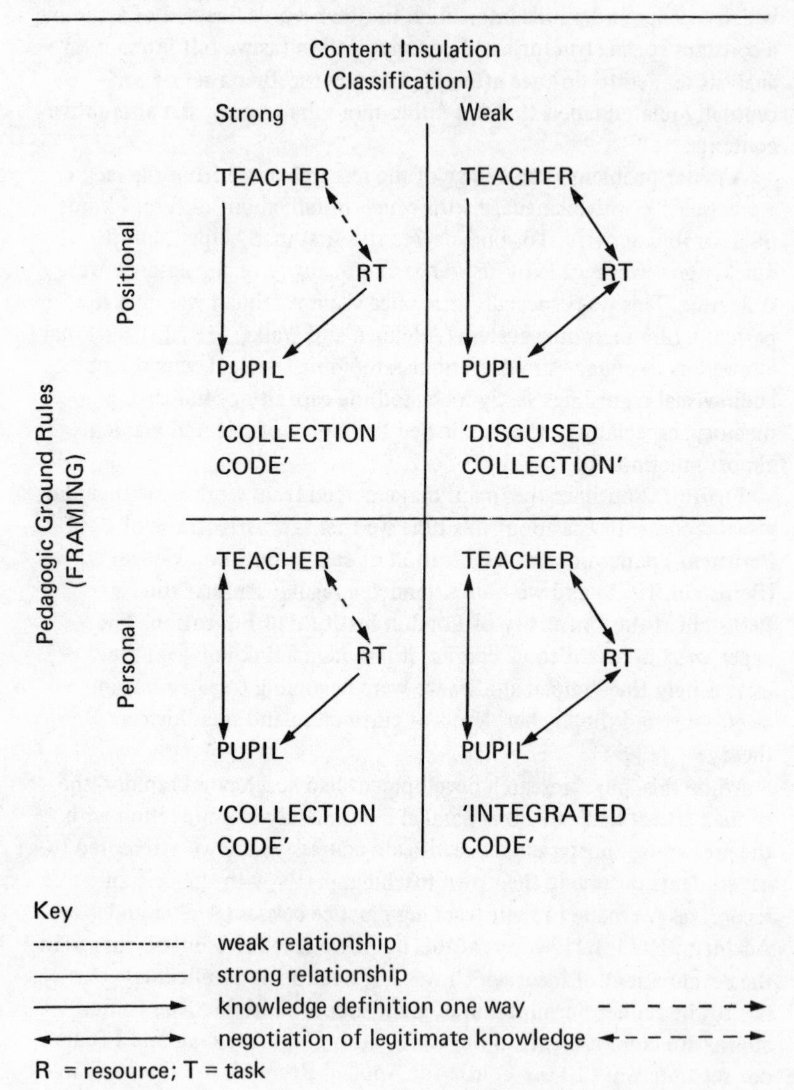

Note: Pacing maybe weak or strong in each 'type' – e.g. weak pacing of strong content insulation/positional pedagogic ground rules is superficially similar to strong content insulation/personal pedagogic ground rules.

Source: *The Use of Objects in the Education of Children Aged 3-5* (Adelman, 1976).

for such work. Interestingly, the Ford Teaching Project also began with the idea of looking at 'enquiry-discovery' teaching, though this focus diminished as the project concentrated more on encouraging the 'self-monitoring teacher', irrespective of the pedagogy espoused. Later, though, Clem returned to some of the themes we had begun to look at earlier, in a study which used film to look at the use made of objects in nursery classes (Adelman, 1976).

The SAFARI Project

Meanwhile, I found myself working with Barry MacDonald, also in CARE, on a project intended to complement the Ford Teaching Project, and called SAFARI ('Success and Failure and Recent Innovation'). This project was designed to operate at the levels of management and policy-formation in education and while the focus, again, was on curriculum innovation, the concern was not so much on the individual teacher and classroom as on the system as a whole. The main reports of the project (for example, MacDonald and Walker, 1976, 1978) reflect this concern directly, looking in some detail at the processes of innovation and dissemination in Britain and America. Again, though, as it seems with any project that begins with a problem that is conceived essentially as a problem of practice, we faced a number of methodological and theoretical issues. What kind of information to collect? How to record it? How to present it? It took the best part of a year to arrive at a resolution to work with what we called 'case study' methods (MacDonald and Walker, 1974; Norris, 1977). The development of these methods was not seen in simply technical terms, but to involve issues of audience, of the rights of subjects in research and of the ethics of conventional research practice. SAFARI aspired to conduct studies in what MacDonald termed the 'democratic' mode; these were studies addressed directly to educational practitioners (whether teachers or administrators) and designed to provide a means whereby practitioners could speak one to another through the medium of the research report. We tried to side-step some of the theoretical debates that were current at the time by pursuing, fairly singlemindedly, other issues, particularly those of audience and the rights of subjects in the process of research.

One of the key features of SAFARI case studies was the attempt to make the perceptions of the subjects one of the main constituents of the study – to 'build the world of the teacher and the administrator into the study'. In many conventional studies the researcher's analysis constitutes the main narrative line in the study, providing a key to selected quotations from the subjects, which are used mainly as devices to illustrate the text. SAFARI attempted to make the words of the subjects constitute the main narrative and to reduce the dependence of the reader on the interpretations of the writer. Barry MacDonald had, prior to SAFARI, already developed this style in the evaluation of the Humanities Curriculum Project. (See, for example, MacDonald, 1979a.) In this case the school studies formed only one part of an evaluation plan, and so, although the studies were dominated by the teachers' views and did not provide any means of getting behind these to what was happening in the classroom, the reader of the evaluation did have other means for 'triangulating' on the teachers' viewpoint. The evaluation provided video tapes of classroom discussion and measurement data on pupils which told the story of the project in other ways. SAFARI did not have the resources to mount a large-scale, multi-method study and had to depend much more on the case studies themselves; therefore it was necessary to find ways of relating teachers' accounts to their practice within the case study.

Given a commitment to using research methods that were available to practitioners we chose to rely heavily on observation and description. We devised an outline plan for conducting school case studies (MacDonald and Walker, 1975) which involved, initially, interviewing of teachers, followed by a feedback phase, followed by observation of lessons before compiling a final draft for comment. The feedback, or negotiation, phases in the study were seen as crucially important, partly for the ethical reasons mentioned previously, but also because they provided some escape from criticisms directed at the reliability of descriptive observation. We attempted to overcome these criticisms, at a technical level, by setting the studies within a design which required the circulation of draft copies of the case study to participants for comment, addition and checking at several stages before reaching a final draft.

The approach SAFARI developed laid particular emphasis on the rights of subjects to alter the research record. The intention was to develop methods which would more accurately capture 'subjective' data. There seems, for example, no point in keeping interview data sacroscanct if people feel on reflection, and on reading the transcript, that they could make the point better. More than this, we wanted to give people the chance to reconsider the effect of publicising something they might have said about those with whom they worked. On the grounds of fairness it seemed right to allow people to edit the record if they felt it might have repercussions for them, once others saw it. This position has been criticised by a number of researchers who see it as a weakening of the research position. Giving the subject the right to alter the record is seen as overprotecting him. 'What do you do,' we have been asked, 'when the subject admits to illegal, immoral or corrupt behaviour, and then wants to delete the admission from the record?' Such critics argue that the researcher/evaluator has to respect the public right to know as well as the subjects' right to privacy. Other critics (for example, Jenkins, 1977) have argued that the SAFARI position is a rather subtle sleight of hand. Protection of subjects' rights is seen as a device for breaking down their resistance and, while presenting a rhetoric of subjects controlling the uses made of data, this is used to disguise a range of social and informal pressures that are brought to bear in order to secure their agreement to the release of sensitive data. Far from being a position of weakness, it is argued, the SAFARI position is, in fact, a position of disguised strength.

It is true that the SAFARI position was deliberately set out as a controversial one. Given the trend for government bureaucracies to take over research funding from private foundations, and, in doing so, often exerting much more direct control on the researcher/evaluator, we felt it important to emphasise issues of freedom and control, both for the subject and for the researcher. Having read Garfinkel we knew the value of disrupting taken-for-granted assumptions as a means of learning. SAFARI initially took an extreme position of offering virtually total editorial new forms of case study research in contexts which had heavy evaluative overtones. In looking at case studies of curriculum innovation we were continually conscious of the way in which the study entered the scene being observed. Case studies in such contexts readily become political resources for people: they have consequences for their lives even before the studies are complete. Conventional research procedures for ensuring distance and objectivity often did not seem adequate in such situations; for instance offering anonymity has limited use in situations (which are very common in evaluation studies) where everyone knows everyone else. The SAFARI stance was designed to meet some of these conditions and, in particular, to create a more honest position from which the research/evaluator might operate, given the growing intervention of sponsors in the research process. It demanded a high degree of self-denial on the part of the researcher/

evaluator, for it required them to relinquish some of their conventionally held rights to control the interpretations made of data, and required them also to strive for neutrality as well as objectivity (denying, for example, the possibility of a solely Marxist – or any other – interpretation).

Working through the model in practice led to a number of quite serious practical problems many of which are considered in more detail by Norris (1977). The model assumes, for instance, that each participant has equal rights in relation to the study. Yet it is in the nature of the situations typically studied that the participants have unequal rights in relation to each other in almost every other respect. In practice it is often very difficult to offer equal rights to people at different points in the same hierarchy. To offer a head teacher, assistant teachers and pupils 'equal rights' in relation to a study that involves them all is not easy, and may be impossible. To give one example: in one of the SAFARI school case studies I gave copies of tape-recorded interviews to each of the teachers involved so that they could check back to the tapes if they had any queries about how I had edited and transcribed what they had said. I explained that I wanted them to keep the tape confidential but was offering them the copy so that they could use it if they felt I had misquoted, or quoted them out of context. On a later visit to the school I found that the headmaster had asked the teachers to hand over the tapes so that he could listen to them. When I asked the Headmaster about this he explained that he had become concerned at some of the questions I had asked and since the reputation of the school was his responsibility he had wanted to make sure that none of the teachers had said anything 'they shouldn't have said'. In a situation like this it is difficult to argue. Clearly the Headmaster had broken the research contract, but had done so in order to protect the interests of the school, an interest he clearly felt over-rode any agreements reached with me.

To give another example: while it is possible to apply the principles and procedures to statements made by individuals about their own beliefs and practices, things quickly get involved once they begin talking about each other. If a teacher makes deprecating remarks about a colleague, and insists on their remaining in a draft which that person will read, then what are the colleague's rights? Are they simply restricted to the right of reply? Similarly, when people disagree about the balance of a study, a resolution is not always possible. One person may insist that data on the private lives of the teachers remains a prominent part of the study, another may insist it should be reduced in significance.

In more recent studies we have tended to soften the SAFARI position somewhat, in part because, knowing some of the difficulties that arise, it is difficult to hold to the SAFARI position and to promise a report at the end of the project. The SAFARI Project itself found that its reports tended to be either methodological and directed to other researchers, or broad analytic and programmatic statements directed to practitioners; the empirical studies often tended to remain in the files, held up in the negotiating process. A more recent study of the work of Local Authority advisers and inspectors met a similar fate (Walker, n.d.). The softening of the SAFARI position has been especially marked in evaluation studies, which, more than research studies, often involve a commitment to reports within quite strict deadlines. So, for example, the National Science Foundation Case Studies in Science Education Project which was an eleven-site national study of the state of pre-college science education in the USA (Stake and Easley, 1977), though it drew heavily on SAFARI experience, tended to rely on each fieldworker to negotiate his own studies within the framework of 'rights of subjects' conditions required by the universities and federal agencies involved. Another recent study, designed by Barry MacDonald, of bilingual education in America (MacDonald, 1979b) drew a distinction between public and private information, giving subjects the right to edit 'personal' information, but not information which was publicly available.

This kind of shift in the position offers some concession to the criticism made both by structuralists and by bureaucrats commissioning the reports, for it allows the researcher a stronger hand in interpreting public statements, and, to some degree, makes it possible for the researcher to argue for the public right to know what individual subjects may prefer to suppress. Certainly it marks a shift from the earlier SAFARI position, which was once challenged by Howard Becker with the problem: 'How would you study a corrupt police department?' (To which the rather glib reply was: 'By including the victims of corruption as subjects of the study, and therefore entering a commitment to ensuring representation of their view.') What was valuable about this kind of discussion was that it forced careful consideration of the boundaries of the study, of who was to be included and who excluded. Conventionally social scientists approaching a case study have tended to take for granted the boundaries of an institution, often accepting uncritically lines of demarcation drawn by the institution itself. The SAFARI position on the other hand tends to encourage the researcher/evaluator to design studies which cross accepted social and institutional levels and boundaries, and try to hold within one study people with very different value and power positions. For example, the bilingual study mentioned above attempts to take a cross-section of one city, including empirical material relating to the state legislature, the city educational administrative system and a particular school and its classrooms. One of the main studies of innovation conducted by SAFARI attempted to case-study four secondary schools, the work of the advisers and the role of the senior administrators in the LEA, *within one* study. This is quite a different focus from conventional participant observation studies, which tend to take one institution, or one level in the system and to study that as a coherent whole.

One of the dangers inherent in taking a single issue and studying a cross-sectional slice of the system is that it exposes the researchers' lack of detailed understanding of the system and tends to push them towards a heavy reliance on technical skills. Rather as in a television current affairs debate or documentary programme of the 'Man Alive' variety, the researcher can become the professional broker between conflicting and differing interest groups. Our experience is, though, that in practice this rarely happens. Usually the study is visible only locally and the people involved tend to respond more as individuals than as advocates of a position or a policy. Perhaps surprisingly, this is particularly true of the people occupying relatively high positions in the hierarchy.

Historically it seems that conventional approaches to participant observation derive from approaches adopted to study autonomous and self-contained pre-literate village communities, and, in contemporary society, to the study of deviant sub-cultures. Participant observation has been slow to adapt to the study of mainstream institutions in large-scale contemporary societies except where settings can be treated as if they were autonomous and self-contained. What I think has happened is that the initiative for the development of a documentary tradition in this area has been largely taken up by the arts and by jounalism. Certainly documentary film makers, photo-journalists and writers have moved in on what in the 1920s and 1930s looked to be part of sociology – largely, I believe, because they were able to develop and use new techniques that became available faster and more effectively than in social science (Barton and Lawn, 1979). Though there have been some notable attempts to reintegrate the documentary tradition (particularly 'mass observation'), these have mostly failed in terms of the development of social science, which has for the most part opted for the development of abstract theory or for the collection of statistical data.

In a small way SAFARI attempted to bring the documentary tradition into educational research. It saw its research roots going back to the work of Willard Waller (1932) and attempting to revive the traditions of Chicago School sociology, using techniques derived from the arts and from journalism. For example, one SAFARI study involved the collection of professional life histories from a group of twenty teachers who had been involved in science curriculum development programmes but, rather than attempt a conventional analysis, the 'raw data' was handed over to a radio producer who had a professional script writer edit the material in the form of a radio play (Pick and Walker, 1976). In a more recent study we have attempted to help a school look at itself using photographs taken in a series of classrooms. Whereas photographs have been used in other studies as illustration, or occasionally as a parallel but separate commentary to the text, the aim was to use them as a primary source of data. We used them particularly as a way of collecting interview responses from teachers and children, later assembling a 'case study' in the form of an exhibition of photographs with an accompanying text drawn from the comments of the subjects (Walker and Weidel, 1979).

The ways in which conventional research has dominated the use of new techniques is clearly seen if we consider the uses we have made of video-tape. For the most part we have tended to use video-tape as though it were a passive, non-interpretive and mechanical recording system. Aware of some of its selective and intrusive effects we have tried to minimise these wherever possible. If we had been more imaginative we might have attempted to use these qualities in the medium rather than try to ignore them. We accept that the questionnaire and the interview are intrusive and interventive and that people are likely to think more deeply, perhaps even to change their minds, as the result of being subjected to such research instruments, but in very few studies have we been able to use the interactive power of video-tape. As we have moved away from the experimental tradition in social science we have come to adopt the notion that to intervene is not to be scientific, which on reflection reveals a somewhat curious view of science. Surely what is important is not to reduce our intrusiveness, but to learn to 'control' it – to be able to intervene but to be able to see what effects we are having. Part of the logic of the SAFARI rhetoric was precisely this, for we found ourselves in situations where to study at all was to intervene. It was clear that to adopt the conventional research stance would have been a pretence. By offering our subjects the right to intervene in the process of research, even ultimately to terminate the study, we were attempting to find ways of controlling our intrusion.

Of course it is much harder to establish the credibility of such a stance than we might at first have thought. People would become irritated when we insisted on rehearsing their rights at the start of the study: 'You don't need to worry about all that. I have nothing to hide. I wouldn't tell you anything I wouldn't tell anyone else.' But of course they would. It was sometimes difficult to insist, to say in reply: 'This might seem tedious now but we think it is essential. We are not accusing you of having anything to hide, but only we know what we could do with the words you have spoken. By rearranging them, by putting them alongside another statement from another source, short of misquoting you we could even inadvertently put you in an embarrassing or difficult position. We're not prepared to let you give us the freedom to do that without your having some comeback on us.' And in every study we have conducted we have reached a point where we have been glad we had insisted.

Those who have criticised the SAFARI rhetoric for adopting too soft a position, for conceding too much to the rights of the subject, have sometimes failed to see the power that the rhetoric can give the researcher once the principles and procedures are established. In effect you can say to people 'Feel free to tell me whatever you want. Our conversation is confidential. If you want it to go no further we can edit it from the record.' As Jenkins has pointed out in his critique (Jenkins, 1977) it is often much more difficult for people to edit the record than we tend to assume. The authority of the researcher cannot be ignored as a factor in the situation, nor can the fact that everyone involved has suspicions as to what others might have said to you. Confidentiality may be intended to protect the individual, but its effect is often to divide people and to engender mistrust.

Further Comments on the SAFARI Approach

I have discussed the 'SAFARI approach' here as though it were a discrete and coherent methodology but this is misleading. What is distinctive about the approach is its concern to evolve a set of different formal relationships between researchers/evaluators, subjects/participants and audiences. It is less a methodology than a set of ethical principles translated as procedures for the design and conduct of research/evaluation projects. Looked at another way, the aspiration is to develop an alternative educational professional role for educational research.

The clearest, though brief, definition of the approach is probably that given by MacDonald (1974) in terms of a 'democratic mode' for evaluation studies. Once discussion of the democratic mode gets beyond bare outlines and principles, of course, it is the case that methodological issues rapidly enter the debate, so that when we tried to write a programmatic statement to help frame the approach we found ourselves often confusing methodological concerns and issues of an ethical kind (Walker, 1980). It is also true that many people looking at the approach have tended to look for a distinctive methodolgy and have been somewhat surprised to find that the methods advocated are in fact rather simple versions of participant observation and unstructured interviewing that seem borrowed more or less directly from the Chicago sociologists of the 1920s. This situation has been compounded by the fact that very few empirical studies have appeared which illustrate or exemplify the approach. The SAFARI Project itself designed an ambitious case study of curriculum innovation in one Local Authority, mentioned earlier, which included four case studies of schools carried out by a team of five case study workers (John Elliott, Helen Simons, Lawrence Stenhouse, Richard Pring and Rob Walker). Each of these studies were carried out within the guidelines advocated by SAFARI, but adapted to the circumstances of the individual case. But this study has still not been published as a whole; one case study, particularly, ran into severe problems at the negotiation stage, and all of them took far longer to complete than the original design specified.

A distinctive feature of SAFARI's LEA study was the simultaneous commitment to the 'approach' already outlined and to a shortened version of 'ethnographic' study which we termed 'condensed fieldwork' (Walker, 1980). Ray Rist has recently argued strongly (Rist, 1980) against abbreviated studies as well as against 'ethnographic' studies carried out by people without professional credentials in anthropology. We argued in SAFARI, however, that while the style of ethnographic reporting was well-suited to the needs of policy-determining bodies, the problem with orthodox ethnographic approaches was the time they took to complete (Walker, 1977). Typically a 'pure' ethnographic study involves a year spent in the field and perhaps two or three years spent writing up and publishing. Not only is this extremely costly, but the kind of problems faced by evaluators and applied researchers can rarely wait this long. The need is usually for a more descriptive, transient and ephemeral report which is produced within the time scale of decisions.

A major impetus in deriving the SAFARI approach arose from trying to find suitable forms for the application of ethnographic techniques within the time scales required by decisions. We were prepared to accept reports with a short, useful life if they were in fact of use. Our concern with protecting the rights of subjects came from a point well expressed by Wolcott at the 1978 AERA Meeting in San Francisco, where in responding to some papers concerned with the use of ethnographic methods in educational evaluation he said that few ethnographers would be happy to work in the kind of context faced by evaluators, where their reports might be used to judge whether or not the culture under study should be extended, cut back or terminated.

Although I said earlier that the approach was distinctive in terms of its attempts to recast the formal relationship between researchers, subjects and audiences, there have been studies that additionally involved methodological innovation. Adelman made extensive use of tape-slide recordings of classroom interaction between teachers and children in the Ford Teaching Project. (See, for example, unit 27 of Open University, 1976.) Fox used a remarkable range of methods in his evaluation of Teacher Corps Training Programs, including statistical time series analysis and the use of a poet, a photographer and a musician as well as narrative accounts and interview studies (Fox *et al.*, 1976a and b). Recently Smith has set up a study to search for alternative methods that can be tested and developed within the context of educational evaluations (Smith, 'Research on Evaluation Program'). Eisner and Jenkins have both long advocated the use of literary criticism as a source for evaluation methods (see, for example, Hamilton *et al.*, 1977) and Walker (work forthcoming) has suggested that writing fiction provides a solution to some practical evaluation problems.

Although there are no exemplary studies that fully reveal the approach in practice, there are a number of studies that have been influenced by aspects of the approach, and which have led to some reformulation and mutation of the original plans. Norris's book, mentioned earlier, revealed some early qualms by those who originated the approach, studies by MacDonald *et al.* (1980), H. Simons (PhD thesis, forthcoming) and Walker (1980) follow some of the precepts into practice, as do a range of student dissertations at CARE, at the University of Cambridge Institute of Education, at the University of London (Curriculum Studies) and at the Centre for Instructional Research and Curriculum Evaluation at the University of Illinois. Interestingly, it has often been teachers studying part-time and attempting to carry out research studies in their own schools who have had most success in completing studies using aspects of the approach. This is some consolation to those of us who outlined the approach because, while many of the difficulties that have emerged were ones we did not foresee, an early aspiration was to create forms of educational research that practitioners could themselves adopt and adapt. The heavy reliance of descriptive observations and unstructured interviews advocated by SAFARI puzzled some researchers who felt it foolish to neglect more sophisticated methods when they were available. SAFARI's aspiration, though, was to take research skills already implict in teaching and administrative roles and to create conditions and procedures which encourage and improve their use. The aspiration was to *avoid* deskilling the practitioner and creating yet another specialised professional role. A rhetorical phrase we used several times when formulating the approach was that: 'the most important thing a research or evaluation study can leave behind is the ability and inclination of the subjects to pick up where we finish and to continue the study themselves'. Paraphrasing Auden, we often said: 'Case studies are never finished, only left.'

It is appropriate therefore that quite a lot of the energy of those who originated the approach has gone into building it into in-service courses of various kinds and supporting students who continue to work in the situations they are researching. Interestingly, these students, collectively, probably hold the greatest experience of the research in field-work terms, a fact capitalised on by the Classroom Action Research Network, which attempts to provide a forum for the exchange and collection of this experience. (A *Classroom Action Research Newsletter* is available from the University of Cambridge Institute of Education, Shaftesbury Road, Cambridge.) The difficulty is made acute by the fact that part-time research degrees typically involve a number of years' work, and so many of the most interesting studies are not available on the shelf, so that the field is restricted to what has tended to become a rather close professional network.

One of the incidental effects of much of this emergent research has been to side-step many of the disciplinary debates current in education. Those working on case studies within the framework of a set of principles and procedures of the kind advocated by SAFARI tend not to start from particular debates within sociology, history, psychology, philosophy or even curriculum theory but to begin from immediate professional concerns. Some studies find themselves breaking through into theory, but many keep such issues in the background or on the periphery. The weakness of this approach is that it tends to lead to studies that are of narrow interest, particular concern and often transient and ephemeral in nature. Their strength is that they are often professionally usable. This has sometimes led to the criticism that such studies represent a cul-de-sac, and that until they can work within a theoretical framework it will be impossible to accumulate knowledge and push into new areas. On the other hand, others see applied research and evaluation as fields in their own right and are prepared to admit a loss of some analytic insight or critical theoretical development in attempting to develop research forms which connect directly with problems of professional practice.

This view involves accepting a role for research that is more conservative than the one normally adopted, for it implies acceptance of the status quo and of certain basic assumptions built into the system. We have always argued that we see this as a form of research that is more appropriate to situations where things are likely to get dramatically worse than in situations that are more open to radical change. Events, in education and outside, in the past five years have led us to feel that this is an increasingly necessary stance for some educational researchers to take.

Summary

I have tried to summarise some of the research studies I have worked on in the last twelve years in terms of some connecting themes. One important line of continuity concerns an interest in problems of innovation in education, and particularly with curriculum development. The first studies I described here began with the problem of understanding changes in teachers' classroom roles as they took up science curricula requiring 'discovery' rather than 'rote' learning in the pupils; later studies were more detailed and fine-grained observations of classroom teaching though they also revealed a dissonance between research as 'pure' inquiry and research as an 'applied' activity intended to improve education directly.

Just what 'applied research in education' might involve was a theme picked up in later projects – the Ford Teaching Project, which I have mentioned only briefly here, and the Ford SAFARI project, which I have described in rather more detail. The important thing about SAFARI was not that it attempted to introduce phenomenological styles of research in education, but that it attempted to test the feasibility of a model of applied research which involved a shift in the balance of power to control the progress of research. SAFARI attempted to give teachers and administrators a form of research that they could conceive in service terms. It attempted to reduce the power of the researcher in determining the focus of the research and the kinds of interpretations made. In practice, the testing of this idea created a number of interesting paradoxes and revealed the complexity of the original issue.

In terms of the continuity of the theme of understanding the process of educational innovation SAFARI marked for me a point where I realised the importance of the wider administrative system and of the political context within which changes were made possible. As well as looking at the details of classroom practice I found myself trying to understand the role of the head teacher, the work of LEA advisers and the workings of the DES and the Schools Council.

Bibliography

Adams, Betty (1980) 'The Ford Teaching Project' in Stenhouse, L. (ed.), *Curriculum Research and Development in Action*, Heinemann

Adelman, C.L. (1976) 'The Use of Objects in the Education of Children Aged 3-5', report to the SSRC: grant nos. HR 3234/1, HR 3661/1

Adelman, C.L. and Walker, R. (1972) 'An Alternative to Television', *Times Educational Supplement*, 19 May

Adelman, C.L. and Walker, R. (1974) 'Stop-Frame Cinematography with Synchronised Sound: a Technique for Recording in School Classrooms', *Journal of Motion-Picture and Television Engineers*, vol. 83, no. 3, pp. 189-91

Alexander, D. (1974) *Evaluation of Nuffield Secondary Science*, Schools Council Research Studies, Macmillan, London

Barton, L. and Lawn, M. (1979) 'Back Inside the Whale: a Curriculum Case Study', unpublished paper, Westhill College, Birmingham; revised version to be published in *Interchange*, Ontario Institute for Studies in Education, Ontario, 1981

Bernstein, B.B. (1971) 'On the Classification and Framing of Educational Knowledge' in Young, M.F.D. (ed.) *Knowledge and Control: New Directions for the Sociology of Education*, Collier-Macmillan

Centre for Applied Research in Education (CARE) (n.d.) 'The Nuffield Approach', mimeographed SAFARI booklet, Univ. of East Anglia, Norwich

Fox, G.T. *et al.* (1976a) *1975 CMTI Impact Study*, Office of Education contact no. 300-75-0100, Univ. of Wisconsin, Madison

Fox, G.T. et al. (1976b) *Residual Impact of the 1975 CMTI*, Office of Education contact no. 300-77-0500, Univ. of Wisconsin, Madison

Glaser, B.G. and Strauss, A. (1967) *The Discovery of Grounded Theory*, Weidenfeld and Nicholson, London

Hamilton, D. *et al.* (eds.) (1977) *Beyond the Numbers Game*, Macmillan, London

Inner London Education Authority (ILEA) (1975) *In Other Words: a Layman's Guide to Educational Terms*, London

Jenkins, D. (1977) 'The Knight's Move' in Norris (1977)

MacDonald, B. (1974) 'Evaluation and the Control of Education' in MacDonald and Walker (1974)

MacDonald, B. (1979a) *Towards Judgement*, vol. 2, CARE, Univ. of East Anglia, Norwich

MacDonald, B. (1979b) 'Bilingual Education in the USA: a Proposal to the Ford Foundation', CARE, Univ. of East Anglia, Norwich

MacDonald, B. and Walker, R. (eds.) (1974) *Innovation, Evaluation-Research and the Problem of Control*, SAFARI Interim Paper 1, CARE, Univ. of East Anglia, Norwich

MacDonald, B. and Walker, R. (1975) 'A Design for Studying Curriculum Innovation within a Local Education Authority', paper read to a BERA meeting, Stirling

MacDonald, B. and Walker, R. (eds.) (1976) *Changing the Curriculum*, Open Books, London

MacDonald, B. and Walker, R. (1978) 'The Intransigent Curriculum and the Technocratic Error', *Zeitschrift fur Padagogik*, 24, pp. 581-99 (German text)

MacDonald, B. *et al.* (1980) *Understanding Computer Assisted Learning*, CARE, Univ. of East Anglia, Norwich

Norris, N. (ed.) (1977) *Theory into Practice*, SAFARI Interim Paper 2, CARE, Univ. of East Anglia, Norwich

(1966) *Nuffield Chemistry: Introduction and Guide*, Longman/ Penguin, London

(1967) *Nuffield Chemistry: Handbook for Teachers*, Longman/ Penguin, London

Open University (1976) *Curriculum Design and Development*, course E203, Open Univ. Press, Milton Keynes

Pick, C. and Walker, R. (eds.) (1976) *Other Rooms, Other Voices*, CARE, Univ. of East Anglia, Norwich

Rist, R. (1980) 'Blitzkrieg Ethnography: on the Transformation of a

Method into a Movement', *Educational Researcher*, February, pp. 8-10
Smith, N.L. (n.d.) 'Research on Evaluation Program', North West Regional Educational Laboratory, Portland, Oregon
Stake, R.E. and Easley, J. (1977) *Case Studies in Science Education*, 15 vols., Centre for Instructional Research and Curriculum Evaluation (CIRCE), Univ.of Illinois College of Education, Urbana, Illinois
Walker, R. (1971) 'The Social Setting of the Classroom: a Review of Observational Studies and Research', unpublished MPhil. thesis, Univ. of London
Walker, R. (1972a) 'Some Problems that Arise when Interaction Analysis is Used to Assess the Impact of Educational Innovation', *Classroom Interaction Newsletter: Research for Better Schools*, Philadelphia
Walker, R. (1972b) 'The Sociology of Education and Life in School Classrooms', *International Review of Education*, XVIII, pp. 32-43
Walker, R. (1977) 'Descriptive Methodologies and Utilitarian Objectives: is a Happy Marriage Possible?' in Norris (1977)
Walker, R. (1980) 'The Conduct of Educational Case Studies' in Dockerell, B. and Hamilton, D. (eds.) *Rethinking Educational Research*, Hodder and Stoughton, London
Walker, R. (n.d.) 'Classroom Practice: the Observations and Perceptions of LEA Advisers and Others', final report to the SSRC: grant no. HR 4247/1
Walker, R. (work forthcoming) 'On the Uses of Fiction in Educational Research' in Smetherham, D. (ed.) *Inside Evaluation*, Nafferton Books, Driffield
Walker, R. and Adelman, C.L. (1975a) *A Guide to Classroom Observation*, Methuen, London
Walker, R. and Adelman, C.L. (1975b) 'Interaction Analysis in Informal Classrooms: a Critical Comment on the Flanders System', *British Journal of Educational Psychology*, 45, pp. 73-6
Walker, R. and Weidel, J. (1979) 'Using Photographs in a Discipline of Words', mimeograph, CARE, Univ. of East Anglia, Norwich
Waller, W. (1932) *The Sociology of Teaching,* Wiley, New York

8 PRACTICE AND THEORY

Mike Golby

In this chapter I shall offer some comments upon the work of the curriculum theorists from the standpoint of one who teaches curriculum studies in a university to seconded teachers. I shall attempt to relate some of the themes in previous chapters to the decisions that confront a teacher of curriculum who has for some years been most particularly concerned with the development of the theory/practice relationship. I shall take the liberty of indulging in an autobiographical description of the evolution of a personal strategy for curriculum studies, and to discern in it its assumptions, its weaknesses and strengths and the promise it may have for future development. My focus will be on curriculum studies as a professional pursuit for mid-career teachers, though I am sure that much of relevance to them will also apply to younger, and indeed older, teachers. Though curriculum may clearly be addressed from non-professional standpoints my focus is a professional one, acknowledging the need to seek common languages with a wider constituency.

In the hope that my account will not be unduly psychologistic I shall also attempt to criticise current institutional structures for curriculum studies, and INSET in general, and suggest some ways in which curriculum theory might be more adequately brought into relationship with practice through revised structures and procedures. My account will contain reflections of my own concerns, which are professional and philosophical.

Theorising and Practising

As one who gravitated to curriculum studies in pursuit of the relevance of theory to practice in education, I think something must be said at the outset about the nature of the theory/practice relationship. I find myself in agreement with Bill Reid's observation that resolution of the problem of practicality comes about through the realisation of the fact 'that "the practical" and "the theoretic" are essentially different and cannot be assimilated to one another' (p. 169, above). I think it worth trying to explain how I got to this conclusion for it was by a route that others may have taken, and others, still, may be looking for signposts.

The awareness that theory and practice are identifiable and separate things people do in and around education may not seem a stunning insight. There are, after all, real people labelled theorists and tangible institutions called colleges and universities whose trade is indisputably in the theory of education. There are, likewise, people and real tangible institutions called teachers and schools whose trade is in the practice of teaching pupils. The real problem is in articulating the relationship between these people and institutions and between the activities of each. I say this without wishing to suggest that the present activities of either should be taken for granted. The problem is not simply a bridge-building one between firm ground on either side but rather to produce a concept of theory and practice which, as well as relating them together in ways which are productive, will also enable each to be carried out in the illumination afforded by the other. Articulating the relationship between theory and practice, in other words, should leave room for alteration in the conduct of both. Nor, in trying to explain the significance of my personal realisation of the discreteness of theory and practice, do I wish to suggest that theorists cannot be, or become, practitioners and *vice versa*. In fact, for reasons I shall try to explain, I think it highly desirable that something of the kind should come about. There may be limitations in this direction, however, and I shall shortly discuss what these might be.

My personal entry into teacher education came just at the initiation of the BEd. degree. At that time the three-year course initiated in 1961 had run through a couple of generations of students and in the pursuit of academic rigour and status the theoretical element of the course was becoming differentiated into the emergent 'disciplines of education'; this process is landmarked by Tibble (1966). The advent of the BEd. degree gave an enormous impetus to this academicising of the education courses into constituent disciplines. My own appointment was to teach philosophy of education to primary-school teachers. I remember well at interview being informed that the panel were looking for a successful primary-school teacher, which I believed I was, who was also a philosopher, which I certainly believed I was not. My first degree, taken eight years earlier, did not seem to qualify me for that title and my impulse was to apologise to the panel for wasting their time. However, appointed I was and launched upon the quest for fulfilment in a new milieu. There was, of course, plenty of literature around as grist to the academic mill and, indeed, it was intellectually very refreshing and timely for me to engage in philosophical analysis with well-motivated and intelligent students. I have no doubt of the philosophical value of addressing epistemological and ethical questions in the concrete context of education. What I did doubt at the time, and still do, is the practical value accruing from such studies. That is to say, it seemed to me, then as now, that the decisions facing teachers were many-sided. Philosophy, to be sure, attends to many fundamental aspects of such decisions but it does not provide a mechanism to move towards solutions. Indeed, when a solution to a problem is found it ceases to be of philosophical interest and passes to the world of other disciplines or to the world of the practical. Philosophy, then, it seemed to me, propelled me in the direction of finding new questions, reformulating old ones etc. and it did not concern itself with the arts of decision-taking in professional contexts.

Now, I am not at all sure that the prospectus under which I worked required that *qua* philosopher I should work in those professional directions. I remember only being distressed to see students who were capable and committed at the conclusion of the three-year course reduced on occasion at the end of the fourth year, following an intensive elective course in philosophy of education, to indecision and fundamental personal uncertainty. I do not deny that they had been educated, and not only the visibly transformed individuals who were, anyway, in a minority, but I do doubt the professional value, at that time in their career, of a course which had sundered its conception of professional preparation into four separate elements – elements whose origins were not in the study of the professional lives to be led by teachers but, rather, in what took the attention of academics working in the disciplines deemed relevant to education at a particular point in time. Over this situation there stood for me two open-ended questions. How were these disciplines to relate together? What other forms of experience, enquiry and practice were available to supplement this theoretical diet? (Golby, 1976)

The first of these questions came home strikingly to me when dealing with a spate of enquiring students following a psychology seminar a few doors along the corridor. My psychological colleague had referred those interested in the moral side of punishment to me, as a philosopher, since he felt incompetent to answer their questions in this direction. As a psychologist, he had to operate within his own positivistic frame of reference. This appeared an absurd situation to me. That experienced teachers, albeit with respectable degrees in the disciplines of education, should be so bewitched by their own propaganda as to operate this kind of division of labour when labelled lecturers in education seemed to me both laughable and deplorable. This episode is, I believe, only an illumination of what was the continuing and general state of affairs in educational theory, and remains so in many courses. Attempts to intervene in this situation by suggesting a topic-centred approach met with little success. Structuring a course around themes like learning, teaching, punishment, knowledge etc. was not popular with those who wished, above all, to maintain their subject identity. The rhetoric paraded rigour and standards at this point. All of this is not unfamiliar to teachers seeking various forms of integration in school. Likewise, attempts to group students and tutors together for continuous periods of time in the teaching practice arrangement were to little avail. It was even difficult to achieve a continuing relationship as a supervising tutor with particular schools. I do not believe that the college I was working in was atypical in these matters; in fact, I have good reasons to believe that we coped as well as most colleges at the end of the 1960s with these matters. The root problem seemed to me to be in the unexamined assumption that theory, in the forms then evolved, could exist independently from other aspects of our students' experience. In particular, could it exist separately within the disciplines, which themselves existed independently of teaching practice and independently of subject study which was the big brother of the teacher education curriculum? While I have now come to believe that theory is *separate from* practice I emphatically reject the idea that it is *autonomous of* practice. Theory in an important sense succeeds rather than precedes practice.

Towards the end of the 1960s, then, in the teacher education curriculum there existed subject study, in terms of which it was assumed the students would acquire a personal education and a major teaching subject for school; secondly, there was education theory, generally subdivided into constituent or foundation disciplines; thirdly, there were various practical elements, encompassing professional studies or curriculum studies of a pedagogical nature, and, finally, work in schools of which teaching practice, the periodic ordeal by children, was the major set piece. These elements were taught by very largely separate groups of lecturers, though teaching practice tended to include more people than the other elements, for simple logistical reasons. (See Browne and Skilbeck, 1975.)

It was into this scene that curriculum theory made its entrance onto the teacher education stage. The cue was the upgrading of the three-year course into a degree course, for some students extending over four years. The backdrop was provided by the emergence of the first wave of results and publications from the curriculum development movement. There was, thus, the beginning of a literature of curriculum development and a visible importation of curriculum theory textbooks from the US – no doubt the result of astute publishing initiatives. Curriculum was born as the study of practice, but it was schizoid from birth, riven by the tension between, on the one hand, the desire to carve out and legitimate a genuine academic area and, on the other hand, to provide real professional relevance in a theoretical study. The conflict between relevance and respectability is still very much with us and probably the major task of those of us working in the field today is to pursue the possibility of a full academic recognition for practical study. Respectability beckons us towards the use of established disciplines, an 'off the peg' dignity, relevance towards direct utility. The search is on, and well exemplified in this book, for what Jenkins and Shipman (1976) call a practitioners' theory about practice. Early orthodoxies left much to be desired. Slavish following of American textbooks tended to cast courses into what Reid calls the managerial-technical paradigm. Bloom (*et al*., 1971), Tyler (1949), Kerr (1968) and Wheeler (1967) were heavily used in the early 1970s. At about the same time the first Open University curriculum course emerged (Open Univ. 1972). This was a significant event, for the Open University materials in this, as in many other fields, were to have an extraordinary influence upon teaching in other institutions, and not just as a resource for what was already being taught. For the Open University has had a quite disproportionate power to define what is legitimate for other institutions, particularly in teacher education across the binary line. The reasons for this may not be far beyond the mystificatory power of well produced printed materials and the enormous psychic power of the BBC to make events and opinions official. (During the war my mother told me, as countless other mothers must have told their children, not to believe anything in the papers 'until it's on the BBC'.) The first Open University course contained the seeds of the tension then developing between the systems approach, found in the units on planning by objectives, and the sociological perspective that wanted to see curriculum as ideology in action related to wider societal groups and their debates. This particular approach was celebrated in the Open University's successor course, *Curriculum Design and Development*, first offered in 1976. By then the managerial paradigm had waned in some quarters to be succeeded by a sociological and, later, radical approach. It is one of the ironies of life that the managerial approach, which, whatever else it did, at least claimed to offer techniques to manage, was supplanted in the Open University course by the elusive idea of ideology, a cornerstone of that radical sociology that was to cause criticism and perhaps some loss of respectability when developed in another Open University course, *Schooling and Society* (1978). The *Curriculum Design and Development* course, however, did find room for accounts of innovation of a relatively grassroots kind – for example, of the Ford Teaching Project. It was symptomatic of the state of play at the time, however, that such studies were quite detached from the theoretical frameworks the course offered. Those remained within the sociological tradition.

My own pursuit of relevance in education theory took me from the philosophy of education into curriculum theory at BEd. level and on to the Open University to participate in making *Curriculum Design and Development*. From there I moved to a conventional university as lecturer in education with responsiblity for curriculum. It was in considering my strategy for teaching a degree course to seconded teachers that I was able to reconceive my view of what was possible, to seek to come to terms with the separation of theory from practice by working out a relationship between the theoretical and practical aspects of the syllabus I inherited. The paradox with which I entered this new situation was that what seemed most interesting in the field was apparently of least practical value and what seemed most trivial seemed to attract considerable allegiance among practitioners. Intellectual interest and practical relevance seemed at odds with one another. Curriculum conceived as a form of social and cultural action attracted me, but many of the teachers I interviewed and their employers, who, after all, were paying the bill, expected planning by objectives. In addition, I had a formidable predecessor to follow. Jack Walton had been recruited by Robin Pedley as a successful and innovative headmaster. In his work at the Exeter University Institute of Education Jack Walton had obviously attracted a large following in the schools. Jack is an activist. In some contrast, I had no vision I was prepared to see as my mission. I wanted to promote a reflective professionalism, to develop the capacity to make informed autonomous judgements in school colleagues. I had no wish to be seen as a catalyst of specific curriculum innovations in schools in the region. This is not to say I am without convictions on curriculum matters. That is far from the case but, temperamentally and ideologically, I believed in the autonomy of professional judgement.

How to provide, for mid-career teachers on a one-year full-time course in curriculum, an experience of intellectual challenge and interest – an experience that would at the same time sharpen their individual abilities to make informed judgements on professional issues? I had long since abandoned the idea of preformed theory, if indeed I ever did believe in a body of *a priori* knowledge relevant in some clear way to practice. I believed that there were numerous perspectives available on most issues of curriculum design and development and conceived my task as displaying those open issues with the maximum intellectual honesty. I was by then school-oriented, probably change-oriented but not avowedly so (certainly, anyway, not conservative in intent) and assuredly a 'non-apriorist', in Reid's terms. In the course of a four-year period teaching this course at BPhil. and MEd. levels I have developed what was a series of visits to noteworthy schools into a systematic investigative exercise. I shall describe this strategy presently but, first, I shall summarise the view of theory I have found myself operating. That teachers are detached from their working environments and sent to a centre such as a university in the expectation that they will return refreshed and more sensitive and able practitioners is a brute fact. It is a datum of the curriculum development process for those working at such centres. We can muse how much more sensible it might be to receive a number of teachers from single schools, since the school is the arena for curricular action, and we can yearn for the sort of extended contact with individual schools that might facilitate deeper knowledge and a better relationship of our theory to their practice. But these *desiderata* are not to be. Theory, then, is for the moment institutionally separate from practice. It is also temporally separated in the sense that, in the dispensation I am describing, theory is pursued sequentially between half-lifetimes of practice. These are contingent, but formidable, facts. There may eventually be ways around them but for the moment they are data for the development of the in-service course I am teaching.

But is there a sense in which theory is not only contingently but also logically apart from practice? In one irreducible, logical sense the answer to that question is 'yes'; and there is a sliver of emotional comfort in the observation for one whose abiding motive has been to cross the theory/practice barrier.

Theory is distinguishable from practice. It is distinguishable in the sense that doing theory is not at the same time to be doing the relevant practice. To clarify this point I wish to make a distinction between activities and the practices of activities. Both to theorise and to practise is to engage in an activity. An activity is a pursuit defined in a necessarily social and cultural context by its characteristic ends and the distinctive means to those ends (Langford, 1971). Activities are purposive in a way that routines, rituals and habits are not, though there may well be routines, rituals and habits contained within the pattern of an activity. Teaching is an activity but it contains within itself all manner of automatic performances. Some of these will be defensible on analysis as constituents of the most efficient route to desired ends; for example, in organising the environment of learning within a classroom there are certainly desirable and standard performances on the part of the teacher making for maximum efficiency. Ways of addressing groups of pupils, techniques for control and the like can be analysed, perhaps even on a behaviouristic basis. These routines, habits, etc. may be learned, it seems to me, in an indeterminate range of ways. They may be learned from first principles, so to speak, by attending to relevant aspects of a theoretical overview, for example, behaviouristic psychology, and they may be learned more through initiation into practices on the classroom floor. In practice, I suppose, these performances are picked up through an elusive blend of the two, for the classroom is an environment where events are not entirely mute. Teachers talk to one another and to the student and this talk contains its own 'common sense' on these matters.

Teaching as an activity, then, contains a wide range of elements. There is an interesting philosophical debate as to which elements, however the elements constituting teaching may be defined, may be essential to the 'concept' of teaching (elements without which it would be impossible to deem that teaching, as such, was intended or taking place – in contrast with, say, indoctrination or training). This debate is at its most interesting between the rationalists, such as Scheffler (1965), who maintain that in some important sense teaching must be an attempt to display the logic of a subject and respect the rationality or point of view of the learner, and the behaviorists, who would claim that change in observable behaviour is all that a public process such as teaching can intelligibly be said to aim at. These questions in the philosophy of mind I shall have to beg while acknowledging their complexity. I shall assume that teaching must, by definition, make public to a learner or group of learners some manifestation of the structure of the subject being taught. Teaching as an activity, I postulate, is the intentional passing on of some subject-matter (and I use the term 'subject-matter' without wishing at this point to be tied to any particular conception as to what a 'subject' is). Anything that can be taught, from the tying of shoelaces to mathematical calculus, from pushpin to poetry, may be called a 'subject' without offence. I also acknowledge that there are cases where we want to say that teaching has occurred without any intention on the part of the 'teacher'; here I shall use the device of saying that such uses are 'parasitic' upon the standard usages where intentionality is required. We would not be able to employ non-intentional formulations without the paradigm cases of intentionality. This point would hold for similar cases in the use of other concepts where the outcomes of a process or interaction are labelled in a courtesy way for their similarity to standard results obtained in a context of intentionality. We could be indoctrinated or trained without someone having intended that result. There are interesting and deep puzzles here. For present purposes, however, I shall say that teaching is an activity having as its intended end the learning of pupils. Intentionality and learning are the keywords then and this formulation remains neutral on the *value* of the learning and the particular *subject-matter* of the learning involved. It also admits that teaching may be unsuccessful and that on occasion learning may occur without the intentionality of a teacher.

What this analysis is intended to do is to pave the way for the educational application of the distinction I now wish to make between the nature of an activity and the nature of specific and individual practices of the activity. Practice, I wish to say, is the performance of an activity. An activity is defined by its characteristic ends and the means appropriate to those ends. Practice is defined as practice of a given activity. Practice is specific, local and individual. When we practise we are always practising something, and what we are practising is an activity. Activities may be defined in a highly general way, e.g., the activity of teaching, or in a highly specific way, e.g., the activity of teaching maths. The degrees of specificity, right down to something like 'the activity of teaching these children in this classroom the calculus today' seems to me not to alter my main point that an analysis of the nature of an activity will always be distinguishable from any specific and individual performances of the activity. Describing an activity provides a search for principles governing its conduct in terms of ends and means. Practices, by contrast to activities, are always individual and unique performances situated in a concrete context. Theory is the articulation of specific and individual performances, which are always themselves and not another thing, with concepts addressing the ends and means of the activity engaged upon.

It should be noted here that I am not suggesting that an activity lays down some kind of perfect script for the performances of individual actors. I would want to leave room for the idea that our knowledge of the nature of an activity is deepened through the pragmatism of practice; unrealistic ends become modified, new strategies or procedures develop. What is rather suggested is that clarification of the ends and means of particular practices is only possible through a process of comparison (to use a rather gross term for the relationship as I have it in mind) between an individual performance and the public meaning of an activity. I said earlier that activities are socially defined and the force of this is that activities and hence the practices thereof are only discriminable in respect of a common language; a language provides the possibility of seeing pursuits as identifiable and, as such, makes pursuits possible in a culture. There is, then, a meaning to the concept of teaching provided in our language and to which practices of teaching must conform if they are indeed to be teaching practices rather than another thing. And this point holds however specifically we might define activities.

Theory, then, is the articulation of specific and individual practices with concepts of the ends and means defining the activities as social pursuits. Here, a second most important point arises which will take us further into a consideration of the personnel and institutions involved in this process of relating theory and practice.

To engage in theorising is to engage in the practice of an activity. To be a theorist is to be no less of a practitioner than to be a teacher, in that theorising has its own ends and means, and that particular and individual practices of theorising may be held up to concepts of the nature of the activity and thereby criticised. This view opposes conceptions of theory which render it as free-floating principles, or knowledge, and seeks to focus on the things people do, and their accompanying intentions when they practise the activity of theory. What are the definitive intentions involved in the activity of theorising and against which particular and individual practices may be scrutinised?

Here there is the complication that theorising encompasses a range of importantly differing activities under the same heading. I shall mention only two in the awareness that in doing so there is a great danger of over-simplification. There is, however, a distinction to be made between those theoretical activities whose end is to provide true accounts of the world and those whose end is in some way interventionist in seeking to propose and effect change. Theory in the positivistic sense, certainly, seeks to give a general description of things as they are; so, too, does metaphysics. Curriculum theory in this genre would seek to give a true account of what is going on in the curriculum. Clearly, such accounts are possible from a very wide range of standpoints and perspectives. No such account would be non-theoretical in itself in the sense that it would not be criticisable in terms of its own procedures and ends; this reveals that the practice of theorising will itself permit of being brought into relationship with concepts of the nature of the task, such that there will be a theory of theoretical practices. This infinite regress need not trouble us here though it is of great philosophical interest.

Another and different conception of theory refers to the aspiration to produce change. Such theory refers to the ends and means involved in activities which seek to intervene in and not only to describe the world. The curriculum can be studied as an activity concerned to find the truth, from any of a wide range of perspectives, about its functioning, results etc. Equally, the curriculum can be studied under a professional aspect as something over which to gain control within a particular capacity. The practitioner's (i.e., teacher's) study of the curriculum is only one of such interventionists' studies, for, clearly, other parties to the curriculum have their own interests, rights and duties to pursue in relation to intervention. For example, local and central government, managers and governors, parents and of course pupils, all have their own studies to make of the curriculum. That there exists little, if any, well-focused curriculum work concerned with their perspectives is a merely sociological or political point, of considerable interest but one that does not affect my point here.

In distinguishing two broadly different conceptions of curriculum study, the one concerned with truth, the other with change, I am not of course denying the subtle inter-relationships between them. Change, after all, will be the more effective the better founded on knowledge it is. I only wish to emphasise that the quarter from which the study is pursued, its characteristic ends and means, are of its essence. Curriculum theory in its present state of development is very largely a theory produced under the aspect of intervention (Reid's managerial-technical and radical traditions), produced in the main for professional teachers but not, interestingly enough, *by* professional teachers. One might say that teachers' practices of the activities of curriculum planning, teaching and evaluation have been articulated with the conceptions of those activities held by others, mainly by academics whose interests have often lain elsewhere than in the school. Lines between the truth- and change-orientation have been crossed. This presents an important dilemma. I would argue that, while no one conception of curriculum study has a prima facie priority over others, in so far as we do wish to improve teachers' practices, considerable energies will have to be directed toward the end of helping teachers explicate their own conceptions of their work (Reid's deliberative tradition). At the same time, however, since the curriculum cannot be deemed exclusively professional territory, energy will also have to be directed toward the end of articulating teachers' conceptions of ends and means with those of the other parties I have identified. We shall have to seek a democratic theory of the curriculum which will in effect be a language for the analysis of curriculum practices against a concept of curriculum activity acceptable in the wider society. The project I shall shortly describe had some interesting, perhaps ominous, results in this connection.

Thus far, then, I have said that the activities of theory and the activities of practice are discriminable in that the practitioners of each are aiming at different goals through distinct means. Doing theory will always be a different thing from practising where the theory in question is the theory of the practices in question. I mean by this to reiterate that doing theory *is* practising; it is practising the activity of theory. Theorists are practitioners of theory.

Studies of the truth about the curriculum and studies about how to gain professional or other control or skill in the curriculum will always be different pursuits from the first order pursuits of planning, teaching and evaluating which may be said to constitute curriculum activity. This point needs to be treated with considerable caution for it is not claiming that the pursuits of theorising and practising curriculum activity are autonomous of each other. This is so in two directions. No kind of study would be possible without the brute existence of the phenomena of the curriculum in the first place. In that sense, theory is parasitical upon practice. Conversely, no kind of curricular practice in the brute world would be possible without the intentionality and means to ends taken, however crudely, into their practice by practitioners by virtue of acting at all. Practice in that sense requires theory, a given practice being defined, as I say, by its relationship to the means and ends of its corresponding activity. There is, then, a two-way relationship here. Equally, the division of labour between theorists and practitioners in institutions is at best only pragmatically justifiable. There is no *a priori* reason why a theorist of an activity could not be also a practitioner for, in at least a weak sense, this is already conceded by saying that practice requires theory in order to be identified as such. There may be practical reasons why theory cannot be fully developed in particular contexts because of the pressures and stresses they impose, because of lack of time etc. In that case, if we wished more closely to identify the practices of theory with the practices of curriculum we would have to consider making schools more hospitable environments for reflection and research. School-based INSET is a step, albeit a short one, in this direction. I believe that at this juncture I have probably said as much as I need and am able to say in explaining a personal concept of the theory/practice relationship. I hope it is not too easily regarded as a middle-aged apologia of a thoroughly socialised theorist, who has now perhaps gone beyond the point of no return to schools. I hope also that the philosophical points I have made do not seem either hopelessly obscure and obscurantist or totally naïve convolutions of the obvious. This is the route, however it seems, by which I have arrived at the stance towards curriculum studies which now underlies my work. I shall go on now to describe a strategy within an advanced course in a university which represents some of this thinking in action.

My predecessor, Jack Walton, had bequeathed me a diploma course, recently uprated into a BPhil. (Ed.) course, in which a theory course was complemented by visits to schools where innovative and interesting work was going on. The flavour of the course was dynamic; a review of modern approaches in primary and secondary education was offered in a clear recommendatory spirit; the rationale of planning by objectives was taken seriously as a planning device; schools were selected for the course visits for their reputation as forward-looking institutions. The course appeared then to be professionally prescriptive and committed to a definable battery of principles for curriculum development. The experience of students was structured around the idea of giving them inspiration, imagination and insight from their reading and observation so that they would go away refreshed and with new impetus in progressive directions.

Coming from the making of the Open University course E203, *Curriculum Design and Development* (1976), I found I had a cooler feeling towards the business of commitment than had Jack Walton. There was added to this as a reinforcer the clear realisation that nobody could follow Jack Walton by doing his thing. Socially, it was necessary to forge another identity. To attempt to follow Jack by acting out his catalysing role in local schools would not only be temperamentally difficult for me, it would also invite comparisons and I knew I could not compare with Jack's extraverted dynamism. In addition, of course, times were changing anyway. By 1976 the steam had very visibly gone out of the utopianism of the early movement for curriculum development; a more sobre and reflective mood was abroad, the Schools Council was initiating its Impact and Take-Up Project, in October James Callaghan made his Ruskin College speech which initiated the Great Debate on education.

This general and personal situation indicated the need for a rethink on the aims and methods of the Exeter BPhil. (Ed.) course in curriculum. I shall not pretend that this was achieved at a stroke. I recognise, instead, that in the first year of my responsibility for the course I followed the existing syllabus very closely, deviating mainly by introducing readings from the OU course, in particular the fundamental concept of that course that curriculum is best seen as ideology in action. So the three ideologies provided by Malcolm Skilbeck in unit 3 were pushed to the fore and this approach has been a graft to have stuck in the development since. The series of visits to schools I retained. I did not know the local possibilities so I used Jack's contacts. It was in regard to the visits that my disquiet with the hidden agenda of the course became apparent to me. For it seemed that the visits presented themselves as a kind of Cook's tour of educational sights. There seemed to be two things wrong with this. First, the impressions available to a group of visitors to a school after a day's experience, however deeply organised and well spent, seemed altogether too fragile a basis for any conclusion substantial enough to sustain a theory course, with its aspirations towards objectivity and generalisability. Secondly, the visits were disconnected from one another, in different parts of the world, and so there was no possibility of seeing how the curricula exemplified related together locally, though of course there are even less tangible relationships at an ideological level. In practice, too, the tone of these visits tended to the celebration of the hero innovator. Staff members and head teachers talking to the university course members naturally felt they had been selected for achievement and there was a good deal of righteous breast-beating about the obstacles to reform. In short, the visits tended to the rhetorical and presented a very slanted slice of school life to the course members. This is, of course, perfectly acceptable given the aim of inspiring the recipients. My feeling however was that inspiration was not really lacking, but real intelligent sensitivity on the cultural and ideological roots of the existing common or garden curriculum was.

In developing the course, therefore, I turned my attention to the idea of addressing the extraordinariness of the ordinary. In particular, since I wanted to explore the concept of curriculum as a selection from the culture, I hoped to relate the everyday curriculum not only to its history but also to its current social context. Part of this context resides in the idea of localism. To what extent is curriculum a selection from the culture surrounding the individual school as well as a selection from a much wider cosmopolitan culture? Aspects of Midwinterism were at work here, but also I had been involved with the Open University's course *Education and the Urban Environment* (1978b) as a consultant and had been much impressed by Stuart Hall's depiction of the school as a 'beached institution', the subject of both vertical forces, in the shape of the examination boards and universalistic values and horizontal forces in the shape of the demands of the local culture (Hall, 1977). These considerations propelled me in the direction of organising visits to schools in one geographical area in the hope of seeing how they related together as institutions within the education system and how they related as individual schools and as a group to their surrounding culture.

Education Map of Tiverton Project

Following up what Michael Apple calls 'concreta' in everyday rather than 'innovative' situations, I was looking for a milieu in which one might hope to find the sort of issues I had dimly in mind exemplified. Tiverton in mid-Devon offered promise. It had been recently reorganised into a three-tier system with first schools (ages 5-9), middle schools (ages 9-13) and a comprehensive school (ages 13-18). The secondary school was an amalgamation of the former grammar school and two secondary modern schools, one in the town of Tiverton, the other eight miles away in the small town of Bampton. Additionally, the East Devon College of Further Education was on the same campus as the new comprehensive school and there was the background presence of the public school, Blundell's. This area contained just a sufficient number of institutions for a group of seventeen course members to get to know at a level sufficiently above superficiality in the course of a university term. The aims of the Education Map of Tiverton project were explained to participating schools and course members as follows:

(1) To provide course members with a shared experience with which to relate the theoretical aspects of their courses to educational practice.
(2) To introduce course members to educational practice and thinking in schools dealing with age ranges with which they are unfamiliar.
(3) to give course members an understanding of the aims and organisation of representative schools from infant to secondary.
(4) To examine the relationships between the curriculum of

different schools in the same locality.

(5) To set schools in their social and cultural context.

(6) To consider in a local context the issues and problems of curriculum development.

(7) To provide those interested with a report on the observations made and issues discovered.

The final aim expresses the desire to take schools seriously into participation by offering them a report for their consideration. As far as the course was concerned the investigative work would issue in an assessable essay. The essays were to be used as the basis for a shared effort in producing the Report. The agenda for the essays was set as follows:

First Assessed Essay

Curriculum may be conceived as 'selection from the culture' (Lawton). Further, we may propose that the curriculum should provide a 'map of the culture' (Reynolds and Skilbeck) to the young. Individually and as a group we have considerable experience, relative to any other observers, of the patterns of curriculum and varieties of thinking about the curriculum to be found in the Tiverton area. You are invited: (1) to discuss the approach to curriculum studies summarised in the terms given above and in the practical work we have been doing: (2) to make a series of judgements on the curriculum scene in Tiverton with reference *both* to the general picture so far as it can be discerned *and* to one specific area of the curriculum or theme of importance to curriculum development: and (3) to make suggestions for ways forward in curriculum development in Tiverton.

The results of this work in the first year of its operation appear to me to deserve and repay analysis. There are, it seems to me, two major aspects to an evaluation of the work. How coherent as a theory of the relationship between practitioners and those acting as theorists is the account I have given *when translated into a practice itself*? What are the impediments to the development of this conception of the theory/practice relationship *in practice*?

It is clear in the first place that the first attempt at this sort of dialectic in Tiverton was highly successful so far as the theorists were concerned, but very much less successful so far as the practitioners were concerned. The key idea of criticism and commentary as a tentative, exploratory and invitational activity was rapidly accepted by the in-service teacher-critics themselves. This is perhaps not surprising in that they had the benefit of relevant reading in the shape, for instance, of Popper, whose work had been discussed with the group by Richard

Pring; they had also read the theory of evaluation, particularly in the non-positivistic traditions (Parlett, 1975). Moreover, I like to believe that they had the benefit of a course which constantly entertained and took seriously their own criticism. It is also the case that, in a naïve sense, it is easier, that is, less threatening, to be a critic than to be the subject of criticism. I think it is naïve to believe this because the degree of agonising that goes into responsible, argued and informed criticism belies the idea of destructive bashing which is the popular view. Nevertheless, it may have been easier to get started for this sort of reason in the university context; and once started this sort of work is quite wonderfully self-sustaining. The sort of sensitivity to the issues current in the course group can be gauged, I believe, from this extract from the foreword to the Report. Although the foreword was written by me it was debated and agreed by the course group and in fact it is the only part of the Report presented in the words of the course tutor.

> In presenting the Report, as part of a professional bargain between the schools and the university, a number of important points need to be made. Firstly, although the knowledge of Tiverton education gathered by the group is considerable – and vastly more than can be assembled in the Report – we are acutely aware of how tentative and partial it remains. No outsider can ever aspire to "insider" knowledge, whether of a school, family or town, without prolonged and deep immersion in its life. We have compiled a large number of snapshots but we cannot know the schools and the town as they are known to those working and living there. This observation, incidentally, has provided us with much food for thought concerning the knowledge of individual schools available to other outsiders such as local authority advisers, HMIs, parents, governors and politicians.
>
> Secondly, and following from our awareness of the limited nature of our knowledge, we are extremely cautious in making judgements and recommendations for consideration in Tiverton. We believe, however, that there is value in presenting in an honest fashion the perceptions of a group of experienced teachers engaged in systematic and theoretical study. We offer in the Report many observations, some judgements and recommendations and a large number of questions. All of these are founded in our experience but none of them is unarguable. Indeed, we hope that the substance of this Report will be well argued in the months to come and will provide starting points for further curriculum development in Tiverton. In this regard, it is worth saying that all of the issues raised

in the Report have been thoroughly debated in the course group. It is not the case, however, that we ourselves have arrived at total consensus on every question.

Thirdly, and in the light of these points, we must say a word about our view of criticism. There would be little point in cataloguing in these pages all those aspects of education in Tiverton we found positive and encouraging. There were many such. What the professional teacher requires, however, is a sense of what is problematic, difficult or inconsistent in his practice. Only by considering such areas can all practice be brought into line with the best. It is important, therefore, that readers of this Report appreciate our intentions. There is emphasis here on what is debatable rather than secure. We hope that this emphasis will not lead to a conclusion that we are negatively critical. We are critical, but critical as sympathetic colleagues rather than as adversaries. We must also say that in presenting our Report we also acknowledge the numerous strides made by all in Tiverton following re-organsiation and the continuing efforts being made to sustain curriculum development there. We hope that this acknowledgement will be seen as the proper context for the consideration of what follows.

The Report falls into distinct sections. While first, middle and secondary schooling have a section apiece, we have also looked at the general cultural background, the relationship between the school system in general and life outside. We have also identified some particular themes which have interested course members and appear in all phases of education. Our Introduction offers a perspective on the theoretical ideas informing the project as a whole. (Exeter Univ. School of Education, 1980)

Course members, then, were well briefed, thorough and humble in their posture towards the schools. I believe it is also true that the report itself is generally non-extravagant and provisional in tone. It is exploratory rather than dogmatic, though, of course, some of the implied opinions and beliefs are unargued. The conversation from one side, then, as I see it, is cultured and open-ended. Unfortunately, however, the response was mixed. The report was personally taken to each head teacher by a course member who had some relationship with him during the work. The accounts of the reception were indicative of the kind of responses that were to develop. Many heads were glad to receive the document and looked forward to discussion of it. They also accepted invitations to come to the university to formulate further ideas for the development of the work. Others, however, by the very act of turning at once to the section specific to their own school and announcing scepticism (to put one or two responses mildly) confirmed an impression that a head teacher solidarity was forming in one area of the education service of the town. It should be noted that no remarks were made in the Report on specific schools but it was sectionalised under the phases of education. I do not wish to speculate here on the reasons for this development. For one thing, I am not perhaps in a position to know enough to appraise the situation fully, for another, to attempt to portray the local situation would inevitably involve coming close to identifying colleagues in the schools and I have no wish to embarrass them. It can be said, however, that personalities as much as principles come into play when dealing with pre-existing institutions. A course group in a university has a relatively short-lived and intense existence. Although it inherits a course tutor's experience and understanding, and responds to outside expectations of it, a course group is a relatively malleable entity. Schools are by contrast inheritors of deep traditions making up the 'common sense' of the institution; they are also characteristically more hierarchical social groups than the more mobile squad of the course group.

This consideration opens up the question of the institutional structures within which my conception of the dialogue between theory and practice is to be best conducted. Most interesting issues of differential power distributions among conversationalists arise. Status, for example, may ensure attention but it can also condition a hostile response to suggestions. I believe that local authority advisers find it difficult to give advice that is received in the spirit it is offered for this sort of reason. In the context of our work in Tiverton, I was struck how quickly the report was called the 'university report' and expressions such as 'the university says' started creeping into conversations. We ourselves were insufficiently sensitive to this throughout the exercise. We were happy to find so many doors opened for us as 'the university' but unhappy to attract the suspicion attaching to our views, which seem to have been seen as in some special way authoritative and prescriptive. Maybe the most potent critic is he who comes from a lowly position, provided he can get a hearing. I believe that pupils are cogent and authoritative critics, but I am not sure this view is popular in schools or likely to gain ascendancy under any readily perceivable future scenario! As a concrete instance of our naïveté on this essential point let me refer to the glossy and well-produced form in which the report was presented. The print unit in our Curriculum and Resources Centre makes a highly professional job of pamphlets, brochures and teaching materials for schools. Likewise, our Report came with a line drawing of Tiverton town hall on the front, entitled 'Curriculum Studies: a Report to Schools, University of Exeter School of Education'. The print inside was well reproduced on good paper and stapled securely. It is twenty-seven pages in all and ends with a brief bibliography. All of this may have added to the intimidating and socially distancing nature of the inherent relationship between the institution of the university as home of the critic and the school as home of the practitioner. All of our hopes that our practice as commentators might be itself criticised by school teachers to help us in developing the work may have been little to set against the massive cultural forces involved in the relationship of institutions having vastly different social power to define meanings, to enforce their points of view. A conversation, which was an abiding metaphor for our work, is characteristically something conducted among those who consider themselves equally worth listening to. What we as university-based workers in education experienced was an aspect of the backlash against authority, exacerbated by the particularly poor record of university research in the eyes of teachers.

At another level, however, we found that Gramscian hegemony was thriving in Tiverton. Hegemony is characterised, as I understand it, by a deference so complete as to be unquestionable in the structured consciousness of an individual or group. In our work in the town, the presence of Blundell's public school did appear to invite inevitable comparisons with other educational endeavours there and was remarked upon in that context by numerous teachers, parents and even pupils. The best example in my own experience was to hear a headmistress of a highly successful school congratulate herself on acquiring a Blundell's teacher as a manager. I would suggest that she was working in a totally alien tradition educationally, but one that she saw as in some way only a postulant to the ideal. This is of course interpretation and reflects my own ideological stance perhaps more than anything else. I will squarely admit to this since I do not believe a non-ideological view possible. Blundell's school was not on our list of visited institutions and in the early days of the work course members challenged me on this. My honest answer was: first, I have no connection with Blundell's and, indeed, I am more than a little shy of the contact (I am sure that this is unjustified and one would be well received) and, secondly, that I prefer for the present to keep my prejudices intact! I am of course hopeful of further personal education in this matter in the future.

At subsequent meetings connected with this project the Director of the University of Exeter School of Education, Professor Ted Wragg, has said that co-operative and investigative work of this nature runs risks that purely theoretical activity does not. I agree that university work must be investigative; if it is in education it ought to be concerned with schools but if it is to be co-operative in a genuine sense some quite large realignments of institutions is going to be necessary. I do not believe that reliance on personal relations is enough to sustain the sort of work I personally want to do. Good working relationships will be a necessary but not sufficient condition for any progress to be really significant. After all, many of my colleagues do excellent work with school teachers and they all say that a major initial task is breaking down the barriers erected by status and false ideas about the power of theory.

Conclusions

I conclude that the problem facing the development of the relationship between theory and practice is as much institutional as conceptual. Until Stenhouse's vision of the teacher as researcher (Stenhouse, 1980, ch. 17) comes to be there will remain the conundrum of how to intervene in school in the interests of professional self-development without producing counter-productive results. In the case of the project I have described, the head teachers of three of our dozen or so schools were quite adamant in wishing to have nothing further to do with follow-up work. This must be seen as a failure in our practice of the idea of theory as commentary but it is also a reflection on a status quo which so structures the perception of teachers that they are unable to respond to an innovation which is at least a genuine attempt to address professional curriculum problems from a standpoint of informed collegiality.

How are such teachers going to be able to handle accountability to a laity who may well not share the professional socialisation of teachers? Can teachers long continue to work with world views which seem to consist only of a panorama of right and wrong solutions to educational questions (and, I have observed, other questions too)? How can such teachers be educated into a conception of theory in education as the dialogue of the practitioner with the ways and means of his art? My suggestions in this regard are that school-focused in-service education and training must be taken seriously and the complex institutional forces moulding practices in individual schools urgently researched.

This research is, I believe, of necessity individual to every school but, fortunately, there is a growing consciousness of the need to redefine educational research in the universities and colleges. There may thus be manpower available of the right disposition at least in the near future. Moreover, given only the financial backing (a big 'if') the manpower might be quite plentiful with the run-down of initial teacher training.

The other priority alongside this reconceptualisation is to see if the individualised model of course provision in universities and colleges might be amended somewhat. If departments or whole schools could be enrolled on courses, relevant courses would become more possible. Such courses would also have to be flexible in terms of time and the big science of the one-year full-time MPhil. or MEd. yield some of its resources perhaps to more modest grassroots exercises. All of these *desiderata*, however, are dependent for their success, it seems to me, on an adequate and pragmatic theory of the study of the curriculum. It has been to the end of searching out something of the kind that this chapter has been addressed.

Bibliography

Bloom, B. *et al.* (1971) *Handbook on Formative and Summative Evaluation*, McGraw-Hill, New York

Browne, J.B. and Skilbeck, M. (1975) 'The Balance of Studies in Colleges of Education' in Golby, M., Greenwald, J. and West, R. *Curriculum Design*, Croom Helm, London

Exeter University School of Education (1980) 'Curriculum Studies: a Report to Schools', unpublished, limited circulation report, Exeter Univ.

Golby, M. (1976) 'Curriculum Studies and Education for Teaching', *Education for Teaching*, National Association of Teachers in Further and Higher Education, no. 100, Summer

Hall, S. (1977) 'Education and the Crisis of the Urban School' in Raynor, J. and Harris, E. *Schooling in the City*, Ward Lock, London

Jenkins, D. and Shipman, M. (1976) *Curriculum: an Introduction*, Open Books, London

Kerr, J.F. (1968) *Changing the Curriculum*, Univ. of London Press, London

Langford, G. (1971) *Human Action*, Doubleday, New York

Open University (1972) *Curriculum: Context, Design and Develop-*

ment, course E 283, Open Univ. Press, Milton Keynes

Open University (1976) *Curriculum Design and Development*, course E203, Open Univ. Press, Milton Keynes

Open University (1978a) *Schooling and Society*, course E202, Open Univ. Press, Milton Keynes

Open University (1978b) *Education and the Urban Environment*, course E361, Open Univ. Press, Milton Keynes

Parlett, M. (1975) 'Evaluating Innovations in Teaching' in Golby, M., Greenwald, J. and West, R. *Curriculum Design*, Croom Helm, London

Scheffler, I. (1965) *Conditions of Knowledge*, Scott, Forseman

Stenhouse, L.A. (1980) *Curriculum Research and Development in Action*, Heinemann, London

Tibble, J.W. (1966) *The Study of Education*, Routledge and Kegan Paul, London

Tyler, R.W. (1949) *Basic Principles of Curriculum and Instruction*, Univ. of Chicago Press, Chicago

Wheeler, D.K. (1967) *Curriculum Process*, Univ. of London Press, London

9 CURRICULUM POLITICS AND EMANCIPATION

Martin Lawn and Len Barton

In late 1978, we began an intensive discussion on the problems we found with curriculum studies; this discussion was heightened by a weekend course with our students. These problems were eventually grouped into three or four main areas: the relationship between the field and the contributing disciplines, the nature and creation of theory within curriculum studies, the relationship between theory and practice, and the creation of a research methodology. In our readings at the time, a question which provoked a lot of discussion for us came from an article by Michael Apple (1975), which asked: 'What *should* be the relationship between curriculum thought and other disciplines upon which it may draw for support, insight and guidance?'

Michael Apple also introduced us to questions of the reproduction of ideology and culture in schooling and the curriculum, an area of research which was seriously underdeveloped in this country. At the same time, we came across an important statement by William Pinar (1978) on the new directions in curriculum thought that he was developing and encouraging in the USA. He asked that: 'a fundamental reconceptualization of what curriculum is, and how it functions, and how it might function in emancipatory ways' should be undertaken.

Not only were these two writers concerned with the past, present and future nature of the field, but they introduced two areas of thought which were underdeveloped – Apple's emphasis on the structural, ideological and political nature of schooling and the curriculum, from an increasingly Marxist standpoint, and Pinar's emphasis on personal reflexivity and exploration as a prerequisite for radical change, from an existentialist and phenomenological viewpoint. In raising these questions and approaches, they provided us with means to introduce our own concerns and interests which other forms of literature did not. We continued our work in these areas, culminating in a research trip to the USA and Canada which included conversations with Pinar, Apple and Grumet.

In this country, our work on curriculum theory and the problems we have outlined above led us to recognise the uniqueness of the work undertaken at the Centre for Applied Research in Education at East Anglia. Further discussion and visits to CARE helped us to recognise a research perspective which we called 'naturalistic', and which, on further investigation, we tentatively connected to a largely forgotten social science tradition – the social observation or documentary movement (see Barton and Lawn, 1979). We also found that a tradition of humanistic research or deliberation, discussed by Bill Reid in a recent book (1978) helped us in our own enterprise.

Our increasing interest in two areas of curriculum study, the individual and the social context, and the relationship and tension between these two areas, have produced this book. Our problem, and that of our students, was with the connections between the polar opposites of self and structure. It seemed to us unsatisfactory to leave the interesting questions and investigations of these two different areas to their mutually isolated research traditions. We are not naïve enough to believe that by merely bringing together a number of issues a relationship has been established. That is up to the reader and to further research.

The writers in this book are united by their opposition to strongly deterministic modes of analysis, in which the individual has few options, if any, and many directives, and an ahistorical, asocial idealism which depicts man as the rational master of his situation. They are united by their concern for a more dynamic interaction between the individual and society, which comes from their need for change; this is realised at different levels and in different ways in their work – for instance, in a concern for a just society or an individual reflexivity. These writers are engaged in the pursuit of an explanation or portrayal of social reality. This involves them in the use of various styles of presentation and methodological analyses in their endeavour to present their argument in as effective a way as possible. They are also interested in change, but change for human betterment, both personal improvement and structural transformation. A particular interest is shown in their own roles as teachers and researchers which involves them in moral and political contradictions. Every writer describes his or her own intellectual affiliations and, while they do not all express an interest for a dialogue with alternative perspectives to their own, we believe that they imply the necessary establishment of a dialogue. This is a task for us all.

In his discussion of the nature of curriculum deliberation Reid has expressed his own view about this question of dialogue; he maintains that: 'I see it as offering scope for debate and discussion between theorists of different persuasion, without, however, placing all other perspectives in a purely relativist form of reference' (p. 179 above). What would be the features of this enterprise? We will now try to outline some of them.

If this is to be a *serious* dialogue then those involved must guard against misrepresentations and oversimplifications of other people's ideas. This point has been raised by Whitty in his analysis of Lawton's contributions to curriculum studies, where he suggests that:

> If Lawton and others working along similar lines are genuinely committed to the realisation of social justice, it is to be hoped that they will in future engage in serious dialogue with those on the left who disagree with them, rather than reducing their arguments to caricature. (page 62, above)

Obviously participation in this kind of dialogue will entail knowledge of other perspectives, read from primary, not from secondary sources!

The manner in which this dialogue is conducted is vital. As the dialogue will involve a consideration of the 'intellectual assumptions undergirding' the different perspectives, then those involved will need to develop an openness, humility and willingness to acknowledge mistakes or the limitations of their own position. Because of the complexity of the issues involved and the mutually challenging nature of the dialogue, contradictions will become apparent. Such experiences and the lack of quick or forseeable solutions will have to be coped with, particularly when one appreciates that a perspective

> . . . designed to reveal the broad panorama of historical developments and institutional systems conceals the minutiae of the social life of individuals, and a perspective suited for penetrating deeply into human relations and face-to-face interaction loses sight of the larger historical and institutional context. (Blau, 1976, p. 4)

Certainly, the writers in this book bear witness to the difficulties involved in the development of understanding and explanation of issues at the micro- or macro-level of society and, more importantly, of the possible links between the two and how we are to attempt to conceptualise, investigate or explain such relationships.

We do not wish to minimise the problems involved in creating and sustaining a dialogue of this nature. As a result of the institutionalisation of knowledge and the tendency towards dogmatism and exclusiveness, certain forms of 'dialogue' will inevitably lead to deadlock or unsatisfactory conclusions. There could be 'a "dialogue of the deaf" (those who persist in old concepts and are incapable of hearing new voices) and . . . a "dialogue of beautiful souls" (those who indulge in mutual idealisations and cheap accommodation)' (Lochman, 1970, p. 185). Both of these must be avoided and, if suspicion and ignorance are to be overcome, the critical reflection demanded will be exciting and disturbing. What is essential to note is that the type of dialogue we are advocating for curriculum studies can begin only if the participants are willing to acknowledge that they do not possess all the answers, are aware of the complexities of social reality and are confused or uncertain about many significant issues.

The contributions to this volume are also concerned with the relationship between theory and practice. Teachers are viewed not merely as the subject of powerful constraints and ideas, but are themselves creators of theories and are involved in acting upon the world about them. We believe that this is not to be a dialogue between 'academics' alone, but must include teachers, given the dignity and respect that they deserve. Thus, as Golby notes:

> The problem is not simply a bridge-building one between firm ground on either side but rather to produce a concept of theory and practice which, as well as relating them together in ways which are productive, will also enable each to be carried out in the illumination afforded by the other. (page 215, above)

One of the difficult but essential tasks will be that of developing a language that has a wider constituency, or at least, learning to write and talk with a sense of audience. We must try to overcome some of the alienation and isolationism that is being experienced by participants at different levels of the educational system. What we need to learn is the ability to talk *to one another* and not *at each other!* By advocating a serious dialogue between the parties involved in curriculum studies we are not denying or suggesting that tensions or differences between perspectives are to be overlooked. Quite the reverse, because the challenge involved in this process will lead to these differences being more clearly defined. Secondly, we do not believe such a dialogue involves an approach that maintains that each perspective is of equal value and thus cannot be distinguished qualitatively. We are mindful of the warning of Reid, in his book, where he argues that: 'To opt for eclecticism is to deny the central business of the field, and of any field or discipline, which is to clarify the nature of its core problems, however hard an enterprise that may be' (Reid, 1978, p. 105).

Lastly, the call for a dialogue is not derived from a belief that, through a synthesis of the perspectives involved in this field, we can produce a single, uniform, unique approach within curriculum studies.

Biography and Life Histories

Working with some of the ideas that we have expressed above we have chosen a specific contradiction that we wish to explore – that is, the connection between the teacher as an individual and the social environment. This is an area that is underdeveloped in curriculum studies. We know very little of the personal experiences and struggles of teachers, nor is there a clear understanding of the relationship between the state and the school curriculum: how does the State mediate its control of teachers and the curriculum and could it do so, paradoxically, by promoting professionalism and autonomy?

We could never accept a theoretical analysis which saw the teacher as being the passive reproductive agent of the state, nor could we accept analyses which depicted the teacher as the autonomous creator of educational ideas and practices, free from serious constraints. One aspect of the ideas in this book that we will take up here is that of the exploration of the relationship between teachers and the curriculum as determined and determining, passive and resisting.

It is not surprising that curriculum studies cannot connect with teachers – they are often an unknown quantity to themselves. We mean by that, they are often isolated from each other at work, by the pressures of school life, the timetable and subject divisions. They have this isolation in common with most workers but, unlike other workers, they are part of an industry which is constantly supervised, publicised and discussed. Yet teachers are still an unknown quantity. A recognition of this fact, coupled with arguments raised in this book and constant discussions with teachers and students, has led us to reconsider means of researching that start from a different point in relation to the teachers than is common in curriculum research, and that incorporate a collective approach and self-exploration. We mean by this that the teacher's dilemmas are our dilemmas and that teachers work with researchers jointly on the research enterprise.

C. Wright Mills, in an absorbing discussion on the uses of history, shows how history may overcome the polarity in the study of self and structure with which this book is concerned. He begins this essay: 'Social Science deals with problems of biography, of history, and of their intersections within social structures' (Mills, 1970, p. 159). We would insert 'curriculum studies' for 'social science' and still take this statement as our leading aim. Wright Mills goes on to argue that biography needs to be understood within a reference to the societal institutions in which it takes place and with a concern for the growth of consciousness and self-image in the individual. A study of man without a concern either for his self-awareness or societal structure leads to a distorted picture.

The emphasis on biography is not just a useful tool for the researcher endeavouring to produce a more complete picture of reality; it is also a means to self-awareness on the part of the teacher. Teachers, underneath the role-play necessary for survival in schools, are often uncertain about themselves, their aims and achievements, and, as we have noted, are isolated from each other. Biography or autobiography, within a supportive or collaborative system, can help to release teachers from this isolation. Alvin Gouldner describes this loss of contact with self as due to the power of cultural prescription; in this case, for teachers, it means their constant socialisation and experience of managerial imposition: 'men must accept their own unique talents and varying ambitions as authentic . . . they must consider the possibility that their personal impulses and special talents have as much right to be heard as the cultural norms' (Gouldner, 1975, p. 320). This is a goal that researchers and writers in other disciplines have considered. Our search for an illuminative approach to the notion of conjunctural space, bound by our concern for self and structure, led us to similar research issues in other disciplines. A most fruitful approach is that developed within oral history.

The reconstruction of the daily lives, work and society of working people in the last hundred years is a fairly recent but rapidly growing area of historical study, often as part of a people's history, combining with wider sources. In an interesting discussion of the variety of work in oral history, Paul Thompson describes three such ways – first, the single life story (life history) narrative which may be presented as one biography or with others to reproduce the past history of a community or, in our case, a class of teachers. Secondly, a collection of stories, extracts or partial accounts of lives, which can be grouped around common themes – a family or community history. Thirdly, a more analytical version of oral history may use either of these approaches but expose them to a cross-questioning in order to derive a general argument, previously hidden in the detail and anecdote (Thompson, 1979).

In each of these ways, teachers may be studied. There are few life histories of teachers in state schools; there are published fragments, some novels or anecdotes based on public school or progressive teacher reminiscences. While we do recognise that there is important ethnographic research in the sociology of education being established, we, nevertheless, maintain that teachers are the 'great unknowns' of education. If we take what Paul Thompson calls a 'collection of stories' we could try to understand issues like the reconciliation of idealism and function in teachers' everyday work, or (a difficult task) explore the concept of proletarianisation through teacher's reflexive accounts interrogated by pertinent questions. In the same way as that in which writers like George Ewart Evans have reconstructed a past rural life with customs, language and workskills now extinct, educational researchers need to reconstruct the working lives of teachers today, especially in the light of the resurgence of managerial intervention and the arrival of the computerised classroom.

The research process would have to be collaborative – the researcher sharing the work with the researched. Indeed, these very roles would be merging. The difficulty (or the advantage) of naturalistic research is that it leaves the researcher 'unhorsed' – that is, techniques and skills and the sole right to interpretation, are exchanged for deeper insights and an empathetic relationship. Thompson mentioned a category in oral history research that emphasises analysis and argument, and we have discussed 'interrogation' with questions. This should be undertaken within a collaborative relationship, the researcher(s) taking responsibility to interpret wider movements – of historical period or of written memoirs etc – back into the process of reconstruction: this is necessary in order to check personal recollection and the construction of theory from theory. This has to be an open and clear process, otherwise it is abused.

A very successful example of a working-class oral history project is the one based at Centreprise on a Worker's Educational Association Course. This was founded in partial response to the enthusiasm of the socialist History Workshop annual conferences. It started with the idea that –

> Working people's own ideas about their lives are not much heard except in private conversations. The People's Autobiography of Hackney, a WEA Group, aims to record and publish some local people's ideas about their lives. It offers people the opportunity to shape the way aspects of their lives appear in print, and share them with a wider audience than the pub or living room. (*People's Auto-*

biography of Hackney, 1976, p. 6)

The past was to be resurrected in print and connected to the present as an aid to the maintenance of a local class consciousness. Photographs were used, deliberately taken to identify the work of the writers.

One particular project, 'Working Lives', was made up of a number of accounts which 'took people's experience of their work in Hackney from the beginning of the century up until today, and linked them as continuous and dominating experiences in working class life' (Worpole, 1977, p. 11).

The accounts included that of a teacher, a Thames lighterman, a demolition worker and a tailor. In a preface to the second volume, dealing with the period 1945 to 1975, the production team mentioned two aspects of work, for the people who had written, that united them all – a general argument. People valued the service they gave in their work to others and, in turn, the help they received; service, regardless of the job, was valued. Yet this service was given in spite of a contradictory force, the arbitrariness of the employer's demands, which were paramount in the job.

In describing the project on 'Working Lives', it was mentioned that the group which acted as recorders and transcribers were themselves not specialists or academics but fellow workers. Particularly, editing was not an individual but a group act: 'for example, in a given meeting a postman and a teacher might find themselves leading a group discussion with an ex-demolition worker about his account of his work' (Worpole, 1977, p. 11).

Autobiographies, an approach suggested by Thompson, have also been produced at Centreprise. Local people recounted, and reflected upon, aspects of their lives – childhood, searching for jobs, economic conditions, craft skills and family life. The criteria used eventually to decide on publication is of interest:

> We felt it important to weigh the quality of expression against the extent to which a particular individual's experiences could clarify, express with precision, stand for and carry the weight of the typical and common experiences of a much larger group of people who could find and recognise large parts of their own lives within a particular autobiography. (Worpole, 1977, p. 6)

This is a development of another oral research tradition which leaves 'commonality' up to the reader; Studs Terkel, a prominent American recorder of life histories in the reconstruction of American society, mentioned: 'Each of the subjects is, I feel, uniquely himself. Whether he is an archetypal American figure, reflecting thought and condition over and beyond himself, is for the reader to judge, calling upon his own experience, observations, and an occasional look in the mirror' (Terkel, 1968, p. 19). It is of interest to note the difference in approach between 'look in the mirror' and 'typical and common experiences'; this tension between an individual perception and construction of shared meanings is important to us.

The work at Centreprise, while strong and established, is not now unique in Britain and has influenced the style of oral history, reinforcing a concern with life histories and the collection of accounts. There are differences between the approaches reviewed in Thompson's book. There is a very strong emphasis on collaboration at Centreprise and workers with professional roles (that is academic backgrounds) have had them eroded. Oral history still lays claim to be a part of the discipline of history, and it is within this discipline that an oral historian works – using its ideas and following its academic path. Value and meanings may be allotted on the basis of the historical perspective of the researcher, not the personal world of the researched.

From this brief and general discussion of biography and life history as a research method, we have been attempting to make tentative proposals on the nature of collaborative research in curriculum studies but yet we recognise that pressures will act to divorce the researcher from the teacher, especially in the education climate of today. There is a danger that this kind of research could be co-opted by dominant forces in educational management and used as a new database in curriculum decision-making.

The approach we envisage here must bear in mind this penetrating observation of John Berger's on his writing about peasant communites:

> Everyone from schoolchildren to grandparents know more than we did about certain aspects of life here. Everyone was in a position, if she or he so chose, to be our teacher, to offer us information, and, protection. And many did. This relationship between teacher and pupil is complex. Those who teach us are aware that our local ignorance is related to the fact that we have access to another body of knowledge, a knowledge of the surrounding but distant world. It is assumed that . . . there is an area of which our knowledge must be as intimate as is theirs of life here . . . thus, *through our ignorance we were like novices and through our assured experiences, we are*

independent witnesses. (our emphasis) (Berger, 1979)

Conclusion

This book is the result of personal struggles and debates within curriculum studies. We hope that it will make a serious and exciting contribution to the effectiveness of the subject. The focus of the book, self and structure, should be an area of vital concern to curriculum studies, and so should our emphasis on the tense relationship between these two extremes, expressed in terms of conjunctural space, contestation, resistance or reflexivity.

We have also emphasised that, for us, a perspective approach to curriculum learning and research is essential. It helps to use perspectives to organise the individual contributions into coherent frameworks, to provide theoretical clarity and to increase effectiveness of problem-solving. We are opposed to the ideology of eclecticism which, for us, is neither practically nor theoretically tenable. Instead, we advocate an open dialogue between perspectives, leading to a frankness of approach and a more adequate understanding of the practical.

We are presenting this book in awareness of the present social and political climate, which is one of crisis and conflict. For curriculum studies to be both a defender of and a promoter of change within the curriculum, it needs to be concerned with the ideas and directions that are proposed within this book. The days of acting as a handmaiden to consensus curriculum policy-making are gone: the choice is between a more effective defence of curriculum – with clarity of argument and problem-solving – or acting as the unwitting agents of the state. A personal and a political reflexivity are necessary to revitalise curriculum studies.

Bibliography

Apple, M. (1975) 'Commonsense Categories and Curriculum Thought' in Macdonald, J. and Zoret, E. (eds.) *Schools in Search of Meaning: ASCD Yearbook*, Association for Supervision and Curriculum Development, Washington, DC

Barton, L. and Lawn, M. (1979) 'Back Inside the Whale: a Curriculum Case Study', unpublished paper, Westhill College, Birmingham; revised version to be published in *Interchange*, Ontario Institute for

Studies in Education, Ontario, 1981
Berger, J. (1979) *Pig Earth*, Writers' and Readers' Publishing Co-operative
Blau, P. (ed.) (1976) *Approaches to the Study of Social Structure*, Open Books
Gouldner, A. (1975) *For Sociology: Renewal and Critique in Sociology Today*, Penguin Books, Harmondsworth
Lochman, J. (1970) *Church in a Marxist Society*, SCM Press, London
Mills, C.W. (1970) *Sociological Imagination*, Penguin Books
People's Autobiography of Hackney (1976) *Working Lives*, vol. 1, *1905/1945*, Centreprise
Pinar, W. (1978) 'The Reconceptualisation of Curriculum Studies', *Journal of Curriculum Studies*, vol. 10, no. 3
Reid, W. (1978) *Thinking About the Curriculum*, Routledge and Kegan Paul, London
Terkel, S. (1968) *Division Street: America*, Penguin Books
Thompson, P. *The Voice of the Past: Oral History*, Opus Books
Worpole, K. (1977) *Local Publishing and Local Culture: an Account of the Work of the Centreprise Publishing Project, 1972-77*, Centreprise

CONTRIBUTORS

Michael Apple Professor, Department of Curriculum and Instruction, University of Wisconsin, Madison, USA.

Len Barton Senior Lecturer, Education Department, Westhill College, Selly Oak, Birmingham, UK.

Maureen Clark Teacher, Helenswood School, Hastings, UK.

David Davies Staff Tutor, Faculty of Educational Studies, Open University, Milton Keynes, UK.

Madeleine Grumet Associate Professor, Education Department, Hobart and William Smith Colleges, Geneva, New York, USA.

Mike Golby Lecturer, School of Education, University of Exeter, Exeter, UK.

Martin Lawn Senior Lecturer, Education Department, Westhill College, Selly Oak, Birmingham, UK.

William Pinar Professor, Graduate School of Education, University of Rochester, Rochester, USA.

William Reid Lecturer, Faculty of Education, University of Birmingham, Birmingham, UK.

Rob Walker Lecturer, Centre for Applied Research in Education (CARE), University of East Anglia, Norwich, UK.

Geoff Whitty Lecturer, School of Education, King's College, University of London, UK.

AUTHOR INDEX

Adelman, C. 195, 197
Althusser, L. 131, 140
Anyon, J. 30, 153
Apple, M. 16, 66, 113, 165, 228, 237
Auld, R. 17

Bartholomew, J. 63
Barton, L. 63, 64, 204
Becker, H. 203
Benton, T. 91
Berger, J. 245
Bernstein, B. 8, 141
Bernstein, R. 180
Blau, P. 239
Bloch, E. 127
Bloom, B. 218
Bobbitt, F. 22
Bourdieu, P. 58, 60, 140
Bowles, S. 84, 140, 165
Braverman, H. 133, 150
Browne, S. 217

Chamboredon, J. 45
Chessum, R. 14
Clarke, J. 66, 75, 153
Collins, R. 133, 136
Comis, M. 179
Corrigan, P. 91
Crane, R. 173
Cremin, L. 20, 27

Dale, R. 59
Dewey, J. 29, 119, 121, 122
Didion, J. 117, 118, 119

Easley, J. 203
Edwards, R. 150
Eisner, E. 208
Elliott, J. 63, 64, 199, 207
Everhart, R. 154

Finn, D. 56, 63, 72, 73
Freire, P. 35

Garfinkel, H. 201
Gintis, H. 84, 140, 165
Giroux, H. 15, 17, 66
Glaser, B. 195
Golby, M. 216, 240
Goldstein, H. 175
Gouldner, A. 242
Grace, G. 11, 13, 14, 155
Gramsci, A. 73, 84, 107, 108, 137, 138
Grant, N. 72, 73
Green, A. 74, 165
Green, M. 37, 113
Grumet, M. 37, 113

Habermas, J. 37
Hall, S. 73, 77, 86, 135, 137, 138, 228
Hallowell, A. 117
Halsey, A. 73, 75
Hamilton, D. 208
Hammletts, P. 18
Hargreaves, A. 66
Hebdige, D. 76
Holly, D. 104
Holt, J. 35
Hopkins, A. 12
Hirst, P. 58
Huebner, D. 30

Jacoby, R. 120
Jameson, F. 127, 150
Jenkins, D. 201, 206
Jenks, C. 131
Johnson, R. 61, 91, 136

Karabel, J. 73, 75
Keddie, N. 74
Kerr, J. 218
Kleibard, H. 37, 133
Kohl, H. 35
Kozol, J. 35

Langford, G. 221
Lasch, C. 118
Lawn, M. 63, 64, 204
Lawton, D. 45, 46, 47, 48, 51, 52, 229
Lobkowicz, N. 23, 24, 25, 26

Lochman, J. 240

McCutcheon, G. 39
MacDonald, B. 64, 200, 207
MacDonald, J. 36, 39
McKeon, R. 169, 173
Maggio, D. 134
Mann, J. 28
Marcuse, H. 121, 122, 123, 124, 126
Mead, G. 117
Mead, M. 117
Mills, C.W. 241
Mouffe, C. 137

Noble, D. 142
Norris, N. 199, 202

Ozga, J. 18
Ozolins, U. 55, 56

Parlett, M. 230
Passeron, J. 60
Peters, R. 58
Pick, C. 11
Pinar, W. 30, 37, 113, 115, 167, 181, 237
Ponty, M. 33
Prescott, W. 65
Prevot, J. 165
Pring, R. 207

Rand, P. 176
Reid, B. 114, 214, 224, 238, 240
Richards, C. 115
Ricoeurs, R. 123, 125
Rist, R. 207

Sartre, J. 39, 41, 126
Scheffer, I. 221
Schwab, J. 30, 170, 181
Searle, C. 106
Selden, S. 133
Sharp, R. 74, 165
Shipman, M. 218
Simons, H. 207
Skilbeck, M. 47, 65, 217, 229
Sockett, H. 51
Stake, R. 203
Stenhouse, L. 207, 234
Strasser, S. 34
Strauss, A. 195

Taylor, P. 72
Terkel, S. 245
Thompson, P. 242
Tibble, J. 215
Tyler, R. 22, 218

Walker, R. 11
Waller, W. 205
Walton, J. 226
Walton, P. 72
Wheeler, D. 218
Whitty, G. 45, 46, 63, 74, 239
Williams, R. 108, 109
Willis, P. 42, 84, 91, 154, 165
Worpole, K. 244
Wright, E. O. 132, 144, 145

Young, J. 72
Young, M. 59, 88, 141

Zaretsky, E. 118

SUBJECT INDEX

Accountability 174-6, 234
A priorism 162, 175, 181, 220
Autobiography 33, 37, 113, 115, 214, 242, 243-4; appropriation 123-4, 125, 126, 129; critical remembrance 126; distanciation 123-4, 126, 128; method (currere) 113, 115, 116, 122-4

Base-Superstructure 134, 137, 144, 147
Biography 241, 242, 245

Cambridge, University of, Institute of Education 208
Capitalism 79, 100, 118
Case studies 200-3, 209
Centre for Applied Research in Education (CARE) 48, 62, 63-4, 67n, 193, 197, 208, 237; *see also* SAFARI, Ford Teaching Project
Centreprise 243-5
Chicago School of Sociology 205
Christianity 24-6, 34-5
Classroom interaction: tape-slide recording 195-7, 208
Contradictions 37-8, 85-6, 114, 135-7, 139, 143-4, 147, 170, 238; *see also* Reproduction
Critical pluralism 179
Culture 100; cultural capital 140; selection from 53, 227, 229
Currere *see under* Autobiographical method
Curriculum: common culture 52-4, 55-6, 58-9; consensus 246; *Continental Op* and the – 17; control of 11-12; field 13, 20-3, 27, 28, 29, 49-50, change 224-5, truth 224-5; hidden 141, 145, 147, 148, 149; ideologies: managerial-technical 20-3, 45-6, 133, 140, 141, 218, 242, neutral 59, 133, 134, 140-1, social-democratic 44, 45, 71, 72, 74, 89-90, 94, socialist 76-7, 78, 79; projects 193-5, 200; romantic critics of 35

Department of Education and Science 12, 82, 95
Deliberation 113, 160, 166-73, 238; procedure and method 171, 180; problems 176, 179
De-skilling 80, 150-2, 154-5, 157n, 209
Dialogue 179, 181-2; bridge building 179, 215, 240; conditions for 238-41; difficulties 233, 239-41
Domination, education as 131, 134, 137

Eclecticism 145, 169, 191
Ethnographies 147, 148; marxist 148, 149
Evaluation 206-9; teacher corps 208
Existentialism 33, 113, 165-6, 237
Exploitation 131

Faith, bad 39n
Ford Teaching Project 199, 208, 210, 219

Greeks 23, 25, 26, 33-5; Aristotle 23, 172-3, 187n; *see also* Theorising

Hegemony, ideological 136, 137-9, 146, 233; bourgeois 52, 73, 85; discourse 50; reconstruction of 54, 57
Hermeneutics 30, 33, 36
History, oral 242-3, 244-5; uses of 241
History, working class 153
History Workshop 243

Individualism 118-19, 121, 140, 166, 238, 239
Intellectuals, role of 137, 141

Justice, social 48, 53-4, 55-7, 60, 62, 66

Knowledge, useful 61; classification

of educational 197; transmission 81

Labour Party 55-6, 71-3, 75, 76
Labour process *see under* Teachers
Legitimation 134, 136; *see also* Reproduction
Life histories 241, 245

Marxism 30, 76, 84, 87, 91, 113, 120, 161, 180, 237; and curriculum theory 66; naive 51, 62; neo-Marxists 37, 46, 132, 137; *see also* Ethnography, Hegemony, Reproduction
Mental/Manual 148, 150

National Union of Teachers 80, 81, 89, 95, 96, 97, 98, 101
Naturalistic, fallacy of 32, 33; research 243; *see also* CARE
Nuffield Science Teaching Project 193, 194, 195

Open University: Curriculum: Context, Design and Development (E283) 15, 218, 236; Curriculum Design and Development (E203) 45, 47, 48, 64, 218, 219, 226, 227, 236; Curriculum, new course 65; Education and the Urban Environment (E361) 228, 236; Schooling and Society (E202) 219, 236

Pedagogy 59, 77, 83, 94, 199; pedagogical subtext 77, 86; socialist 102; transitional 102
Phenomenology 33, 74, 123-4, 191, 210, 237
Pluralism 52, 180; critical 179
Possibilitarianism 74, 107
Practice and Theory 16, 23, 169, 191, 192, 214-15, 217, 220, 222, 223-4, 225, 240
Pragmatism 15, 45, 168
Progressivism 76, 90, 92-3, 101, 104
Proletarianisation 243; *see also* De-skilling and Labour process
Psychoanalysis 120, 123
Psychology: function of 166, introspective 166; half truths 54
Pupils 76, 78-9, 81, 84, 86, 90-1, 92-5, 99, 100-1, 102-4, 106

Racism 92, 97, 99; anti 94, 103; ideas 102
Radical Education 76, 78-9, 87, 92, 94, 95, 96, 98, 100
Rational curriculum planning 174; *see also* Curriculum ideologies, managerial-technical
Reconceptualism 31, 33-4, 68, 237; and novelists 33
Reflexivity 238, 246; critical 113; personal 237
Relativism 180, 238
Reproduction, cultural 60-1, 113, 131-2, 135, 137, 139, 141, 142, 147, 237; conjunctural 73, 84-5, 91, 108, 242, 246; contestation/resistance 135, 139, 144, 145, 147, 149, 154-6, 246; problems 84; *see also* Contradictions and Schools
Reproduction, economic 11, 84, 142; *see also* Theory, correspondence
Research Methodology 237; applied research 210; classroom observations 194-5; collaborative research 243; ethical issues 200-6; ethnography 147, 148, 207, 208; participant observation 195, 204, 207; problems of procedure 199

SAFARI 193, 199-210; *see also* CARE
Schools: as places of work 150; as sites of ideological production 113, 147, 148, 150; *see also* Teachers
Science and theory 24, 25, 163-4, 171, 173
Self 14, 16, 119, 120, 126, 192, 238, 242
Sexism 92, 94, 102; non-sexist 97
Social 246; social hierarchy 74; social mobility 11
Socialist Teacher 76, 81, 89-90, 101
Sociology of education 55, 65, 66, 71
State 12, 13, 46, 72, 78, 99, 137, 145, 241; state apparatus 87
Structure 16, 74
Subjectivity 116, 119, 121, 128, 147, 200, 201
Subtext 71, 77
System 162
Systemic 163

Teacher Journals: *Teachers' Action* 76, 79-81, 86, 87, 88, 98-9, 100; *Teaching London Kids* 76, 77, 82, 83, 88, 103, 104, 105-7; *see also* *Socialist Teacher* and *Radical Education*
Teachers 11, 13, 74, 80, 141, 143-4, 191, 221-2; accountability of teachers 174-5; class situation of teachers 79, 80, 83; ideology of teacher autonomy 15, 45, 73, 108, 241; professional skills 95; professionalism of teachers 46, 78, 95, 96, 97, 219, 241; socialist teachers 75, 79, 82, 87, 91, 96, 99, 104, 108; teacher as researcher 195, 199, 234-5; teacher training courses 174, 193-4, 217-20; teachers and the labour process 145-6, 149, 150; teachers' consciousness 97; teachers' isolationism 241; *see also* Deskilling, Labour process, Proletarianisation
Teachers Against the Nazis 102-3
Technical determinism 113; technical exercise 50
Theorising 165; styles of theorising 23, 161-2, 164-5, 169; political theorising 173; theoretic 169; *see also* Christianity, Science and Greeks
Theory: correspondence 84, 138, 144, 145; grounded 195; psychological 33; *see also under* Practice and Theory

Working class 75, 89-90, 105